Diverging Space for Deviants

Diverging Space for Deviants

THE POLITICS OF ATLANTA'S PUBLIC HOUSING

Akira Drake Rodriguez

The University of Georgia Press

ATHENS

Library of Congress Cataloging-in-Publication Data

Names: Rodriguez, Akira Drake, author.
Title: Diverging space for deviants : the politics of Atlanta's public housing /
    Akira Drake Rodriguez.
Description: Athens : The University of Georgia Press, [2021] | Includes
    bibliographical references and index.
Identifiers: LCCN 2020051371 | ISBN 9780820359519 (hardback) | ISBN
    9780820359526 (paperback) | ISBN 9780820359502 (ebook)
Subjects: LCSH: Public housing—Georgia—Atlanta. | Housing policy—
    Georgia—Atlanta. | African Americans—Housing—Georgia—Atlanta.
Classification: LCC HD7288.78.U52 A85 2021 | DDC 363.5/8509758231—dc23
LC record available at https://lccn.loc.gov/2020051371

Contents

Illustrations

MAPS

TABLES

Acknowledgments

I write entirely too much, don't edit well enough, and thus am over my word limit. So, these acknowledgments will not be flowy gratitudes but a definitive list of my Day Ones. Thank you to everyone, but in particular:

My family: Deborah M. Drake, Stephen S. Drake, Afi Drake Scope, Malik Drake, Imani Scope—thank you for your food, money and support. To my in-laws, Miriam Chico, Julia and Nefertiti El-Amin, Jeremiah, Louis, and Barbara Rivera, thank you for your unending support. Much love to my extended family, cousins, etc.

My friends: Leslie Henriquez, Alanna Williams, Ashon Crawley, Kendra Hardy, Erika Kitzmiller, Ben Teresa, Seth Klempner, Paul Kim, Andrew Zitcer, Lee Polonsky, Ryan Good, Devin Michelle Bunten, Regina Baker, Sophie Hochhäusl, and Davy Knittle. Thank you all for continuing to have lunches, ask me about the book, and generally not abandon me after I would disappear to not write.

My committee: James DeFilippis, Kathe Newman, Bob Lake, Deirdre Oakley, and my adopted committee of Michael Leo Owens, Laura Wolf-Powers, Mara Sidney, David Imbroscio, Timothy Weaver, Carolina Reid, Richardson Dilworth, Elaine Simon, Ed Goetz, Larry Vale, Jason Hackworth, Megan Hatch, J. Rosie Tighe, Domingo Morel, Henry Taylor, and Barbara Ferman. Thank you for your care, collaboration, support, lunches, feedback, and intellectual trailblazing.

Extremely cool Black academics who've been supportive: Kelechi Uzochukwu, Prentiss Dantzler, Tony Reames, Nathaniel Wright, Cameron T. Herman, LaToya Eaves, Camilla Hawthorne, Willie Wright, Adam Bledsoe, Jovan Lewis, Brandi Summers, Ashanté Reese, Brandi Blessett, Tia Gaynor, Andrew Greenlee, Jocelyn Taliaferro, Lisa Bates, Elsie Harper-Anderson, Mark Joseph, Mike Lens, Harley Etienne, Jeffrey Lowe, Stacey Sutton, Fallon S. Aidoo, Andrea Roberts, April Jackson, Tisha Holmes, Jamila Michener, Aaron Mallory, Deshonay Dozier, Aretina Hamilton, and Mia White. Thank you all!

My department(s): the University of Pennsylvania Weitzman School of Design, Department of City & Regional Planning—Lisa Servon, Francesca Russello Ammon, Domenic Vitiello, Tom Daniels, Eugénie Birch, Randy Mason, Ken Steif, Megan Ryerson, Erick Guerra, Vincent Reina, Matthew J. Miller, Jamaal Green, Zhongjie Lin, John Landis, Dana Tomlin, Bob Yaro, Fritz Steiner, Kate Daniel, and Roslynne Carter. Thank you for the job and postdoctoral support.

Temple University's Department of Planning—Lynn Mandarano and Jeff Doshna, along with VCU Wilder School's Department of Planning, and Rutgers University Newark's Department of Political Science. Thank you for employing me and supporting my research endeavors. It is truly not easy to write a book without a salary.

My students! Thank you for listening to me talk through this book for the last five years. Now you can listen to me talk about schools!

To the Antipod Sound Collective: Brian Williams, Alex Moulton, dp, Allison Guess, KT Bender, and Priscilla Vaz. Thank you for creating space for future sound collectives in the academy.

My associations and funders: Urban Affairs, Atlanta Studies, American Association of Geographers, Metropolitics, Antipode, Hedgebrook, Spencer Foundation, University of Pennsylvania's Office of the Vice Provost of Research.

My coauthors, past, present, and future: Rand Quinn, Robert Brown, Chandra Ward-Stefanik, Majeedah Rashid, Nakeefa Garay, Adam Straub, Kenton Card, and Annette Koh.

The wonderful archivists, librarians, and civil servants who provided the data for this manuscript: Meredith Mitchem, Taqiyyah Yasin, Beata Kaczcowka, Joe Hurley, Tiffany Atwater Lee, Derek Mosley, Kathy Shoemaker, Jena Jones, Katherine Fisher, Michelle V. Asci, Aletha Moore, Kayla Bartlett, Peter Roberts, Andrea R. Jackson, Caryn Ficklin, Courtney Chartier and the wonderful staffs at the Emory Stuart Rose Manuscript Archives and Rare Books, Atlanta University Center Robert Woodruff Library and Archives Research Center, Auburn Avenue Research Library, James G. Kenan Research Center at the Atlanta History Center, Georgia State University Special Collections libraries and archives. Thank you to the city of Atlanta for such wonderful hospitality and investment in this collective spirit of history. Special shout out to the cafeteria staff at the AUC.

My interviewees: Larry Keating, Leon Eplan, Maxwell Creighton, Shirley Hightower, Sister Elaine, Lindsay Jones, William Allison, Eric Pickney, Hope Bolden, Noel Khalil, Egbert Perry. Thank you for giving me your time and energy, recounting these somewhat difficult stories many years later.

My editors: Tamara Nopper, Mick Gusinde-Duffy—two people who really saw potential in a not-great dissertation, and some very rough rewrites. Thank you for your faith. Special thanks to copyeditor Jane Curran, the two anonymous readers who provided generous and generative feedback, and the staff of the University of Georgia Press.

My husband, Rubén Dario Rodríguez Jr., and my son, Jackson Jordan Rodríguez. Finally glad to be functioning at 100 percent again. Thank you, my loves, for your patience.

Abbreviations

AAVE	African American Vernacular English
ACC	Atlanta Charter Commission
ACM	Atlanta Child Murders
ACOG	Atlanta Committee for the Olympic Games
ACPH	Citywide Advisory Council on Public Housing
ADW	*Atlanta Daily World*
AFSCME	American Federation of State, County, and Municipal Employees
AHA	Atlanta Housing Authority
ANDP	Atlanta Neighborhood Development Partnership
ANUFF	Atlanta Neighborhoods United for Fairness
ANVL	Atlanta Negro Voters League
APD	Atlanta Police Department
APS	Atlanta Public Schools
AUC	Atlanta University Center Consortium
BoP	Bureau of Planning
BPP	Black Panther Party
CACUD	Citizens Advisory Community for Urban Development
CACUR	Citizens Advisory Council for Urban Renewal
CAU	Clark Atlanta University
CBD	Central Business District
CCP	Community Connection Program
CGP	Comprehensive Grant Program
CIAP	Comprehensive Improvement Assistance Program
CIC	Commission on Interracial Cooperation
CNH	Corporation for Improvement of Negro Housing
CNO	Council of Neighborhood Organizations
CRA	Civil Rights Act
CRC	Community Relations Committee
DCD	Department of Community Development
DEP	drug elimination program
EDC	Economic Development Corporation
EOA	Economic Opportunity Atlanta
FHA	Federal Housing Administration
FHLB	Federal Home Loan Bank

GBI	Georgia Bureau of Investigation
HBCUs	historically Black colleges and universities
HOPE	Housing Opportunities for People Everywhere
HUD	Department of Housing and Urban Development
IAC	Interagency Council
IPS	Interstate Protective Services
LIHTC	Low-Income Housing Tax Credit
MARTA	Metropolitan Atlanta Regional Transit Authority
MPC	Metropolitan Planning Commission
NAACP	National Association for the Advancement of Colored People
NABOM	National Association of Building Owners and Managers
NACD	National Association of Community Development
NAREB	National Association of Real Estate Boards
NPU	Neighborhood Planning Unit
OBRA	Omnibus Budget and Reconciliation Act
PHA	public housing authorities
PHDEP	Public Housing Drug Elimination Program
PHMAP	Public Housing Management Assessment Program
PRWORA	Personal Responsibility and Work Opportunity Reconciliation Act
PWA	Public Works Administration
REDDOG	Run Every Drug Dealer Out of Georgia
RMC	resident management corporation
RP	revitalization plan
RRP	revised revitalization plan
RSED	Resident Services and Economic Development
STOP	Committee to Stop Children's Murders
TCCH	Temporary Coordinating Committee on Housing
T/CH	Techwood and Clark Howell Homes Tenant Association
TUFF	Tenants United for Fairness
UCDC	University Community Development Corporation
UJH	University/John Hope Homes Resident Management Corporation
UTC	United Tenants Council, Inc.
WSMDC	West Side Mutual Development Corporation

Timeline for Atlanta's Public Housing Political History

1892   White Democratic primaries are established in Georgia, privatizing the Democratic Party and permitting the organization to racially discriminate in statewide elections

1906   Racial terror strikes Atlanta, resulting in at least thirty deaths and the destruction of several in-town Black communities by white residents; Black residents cluster together in contingent communities as a defense mechanism

1915   *Carey v. Atlanta* decision strikes down Atlanta's first racial zoning ordinance

1922   Atlanta Planning Commission introduces racial zoning plan prohibiting the purchase of property by one race when the properties on that street are owned by the majority of another race

1929   Great Depression begins; unemployment rates reach 25 percent

1933   President Franklin Delano Roosevelt signs initial New Deal legislation—the National Industrial Recovery Acts—which includes Federal Emergency Administration of the Public Works

1934   Demolition of first home in Beaver Slide community in Atlanta by Secretary of the Interior Harold Ickes for the University Homes development

1935   Dedication of Techwood Homes by President Roosevelt

1936   Opening of Techwood Homes (August 15)

1937   President Roosevelt signs the Wagner-Steagall Housing Act that creates the United States Housing Authority (renamed the National Housing Agency in 1942), authorizing the demolition of slum housing and construction of low-cost housing by local housing authorities; opening of University Homes (April 15)

1938   Atlanta City Council creates the Atlanta Housing Authority (May 18)

1939   Atlanta Housing Authority begins construction of six housing developments—two for white families (Clark Howell and Capitol Homes) and four for Black families (Herndon, Eagan, Grady, and John Hope Homes)

1940   Atlanta Housing Authority signs forty-year lease for Techwood and University Homes with the federal government (officially take over ownership in 1954); Grady Homes opens

1943   Construction on public housing developments "at a standstill" as labor shortages from World War II slow down housing production across the United States

1946   *King v. Chapman* decision from the Georgia Supreme Court rules the all-white Democratic primary is unconstitutional, kicking off a number of voter registration drives in Black communities

1948   Mayor William B. Hartsfield hires eight Black police officers, the first in Atlanta history

1949   Reelection of Mayor William B. Hartsfield, largely through support of growing Black electorate; Congress enacts the 1949 Housing Act in response to wartime housing shortages, subsidizing the demolition of slums for large-scale Urban Redevelopment projects

1951   Atlanta City Council and Georgia State Legislature approve the Plan of Improvement, annexing an additional eighty-one square miles and over one hundred thousand people into Atlanta's city limits

1954   *Brown v. Board of Education* Supreme Court decision declares the provision of separate but equal educational facilities for Black and white children as unconstitutional; the "flight" of white residents from urban to suburban areas increases after this decision is implemented locally; Congress enacts the 1954 Housing Act, which combines slum clearance powers of the 1949 Housing Act with additional funding for redevelopment and preservation of residential and commercial properties; authorizes the construction of eight hundred thousand public housing units across the country; decouples the one-for-one rule mandating that each home cleared in a slum must be replaced with a new housing unit during renewal/redevelopment

1955   Perry Homes opens

1961   The Housing Act of 1961 includes funding for multisite private rental housing, a step out of public housing for low-income families unable to afford homeownership

1964   Civil Rights Act passes; Jesse Blayton appointed as first Black commissioner on AHA Board

1966   Rebellion in Atlanta's Summerhill neighborhood highlights growing tensions between and within Atlanta's Black community

1968   Department of Housing and Urban Development created by President Johnson during the War on Poverty, issues a Tenant Selection and Assignment Policy that admits all applicants on a first-come, first-served basis, eliminating local admission policies. Atlanta Housing Authority is forced to close its segregated admission offices and create a centralized (nonrace-based) admissions process

1970	First meeting of the Citywide Advisory Council on Public Housing (ACPH), a centralized decision-making body for public housing tenant associations
1974	Election of Maynard Jackson, the first Black mayor of a major city in the South; moratorium on constructing public housing enacted by President Nixon; Congress enacts 1974 Housing and Community Development Act which authorizes Section 8, a housing voucher policy designed to revamp the traditional public housing program
1979	Initial disappearances of Black young adults and children soon known as the Atlanta Child Murders; nearly one-third of the victims are from public housing communities
1981	Election of Andrew Young as mayor of Atlanta
1990	Reelection of Mayor Maynard Jackson; announcement that Atlanta would host the 1996 Olympic Games; beginning of Resident Management Corporations
1993	Atlanta Housing Authority hires Renee Glover as executive director (later renamed chief executive officer); HOPE VI program is piloted in Atlanta
1996	HOPE VI becomes a national program
1998	University and John Hope Homes RMC dissolved; John Hope Homes slated for demolition and redevelopment
2000	Demolition is completed for Perry Homes
2002	Election of Shirley Franklin, first Black woman mayor of Atlanta
2009	Demolition begins for University and Bowen Homes
2011	Demolition begins for Hollywood Courts and Bankhead Homes, ending the traditional public housing program in Atlanta

Diverging Space for Deviants

Introduction

In 1980, Techwood Homes and Clark Howell Homes, two adjacent public housing developments just north of downtown Atlanta, were in desperate need of renovation and repair. In response to the ten thousand housing code violations found during a long-overdue inspection of the two developments, Atlanta's Bureau of Building's director Catherine Malicki threatened to file a lawsuit against the Atlanta Housing Authority (AHA) for its role as "the worst slumlord in the city."[1] Built in 1936 and 1940, respectively, Techwood and Clark Howell Homes were sparsely maintained over their forty-year existence when federal, state, and local funding all significantly decreased in response to shifting national priorities that increased the political disposability of the local public housing population.

The transformation of the public housing program's residential population from white, working-class men and their families to Black, working-poor women and their families reduced the political support and actual funding for the program. This disinvestment in both the program's tenant population and physical developments reflects the nation's long history of spatially marginalizing populations and their political interests within the governance of the city. Yet within this spatial marginalization resides a host of political opportunities for these residents that are explored in this text.

Despite the weakened political support, the residents of Atlanta's public housing developments worked steadily to center themselves, and others like them living outside of the developments, in urban planning and policymaking. The primary institution of tenant organization and mobilization was the public housing tenant association. Local and national community-based organizations also supported tenant needs when tenant associations were not fully representative of constituent interests.

For decades, tenant associations worked with and against local public housing authorities (PHAs) to transform the physical spaces of the housing developments to reflect the political development of participating and nonparticipating tenants.

When the Department of Housing and Urban Development (HUD) made modernization funds available to PHAs through the Comprehensive Improvement Assistance Program (CIAP) in 1980, the joint tenant association for Techwood and Clark Howell Homes used its capacity for tenant activism and participation in local planning decisions to support the AHA's application for modernization funds. Using federal funding both to improve the physical space and to create political capital for grant recipients is one of several means of structuring political opportunities for public housing tenants through the organizing mechanism of tenant associations.

The full statement issued by the Techwood and Clark Howell Homes Tenant Association (T/CH), then led by U.S. Postal Service worker Israel Green, demonstrates the potential for both spatial production and political inclusion in public housing politics:

> The Tenant Association (T/CH) goals for modernization and improvements:
>
> I.
>
>   1) The uniqueness of this area, and its location and value within the Central Area of Atlanta, must be acknowledged: this justifies intensive and innovative modernization techniques, and programs of improvements.
>   2) The resulting community should be safe to all occupants and visitors at all times as well as satisfying aesthetically and functionally. However, modernization and improvement should aim to inspire pride and satisfaction in the living environment and a feeling that someone cares, rather than to reinforce and perpetuate hostilities and antagonism.
>
> II. The following objectives are expressed in order to recognize and achieve the above goals.
>
>   1) Parking: Emphasizing public transit should reduce requirements for off-street parking vehicles.
>   2) Recreation facilities should be designed for all age groups, population characteristics. Indoor as well as outdoor recreation facilities are needed. Girls as well as boys, elderly as well as young should be served.
>   3) Disposals: Systems for the collection and removal of garbage, trash, and other refuse from the area should be re-designed in order to function properly in this high-density setting. Present city pick-up systems should be avoided or substantially improved.
>
> Further, the Tenant Association insists on commitments to an adequate child development program for all children in the area, full economic development, and participation by the whole community (business and job opportunities).
>
> Finally, the Tenant Association demands guaranteed full participation in the review process.[2]

Tenant associations are useful for politicizing apolitical programs. The Techwood/Clark Howell modernization statement underscores the foreseeable political opportunities of modernization funds. In this case, the modernization of public housing developments was used as an opportunity for tenant associations to direct federal funding into cash-strapped cities. Urban disinvestment that began in the post–World War II era was disproportionately borne by low-income, nonwhite neighborhoods. Modernization funds were an opportunity to address this disinvestment at the neighborhood scale, as evidenced by the focus on transit, recreation, sanitation, and childcare.

In the 1980s, Atlanta's population was stagnating, violent crime was on the rise, and there was little outside investment in the city. These conditions were fairly common for large, majority-Black cities in the United States at the time. The modernization statement explicitly addresses what residents considered to be the problem: an un(der)developed community planned by everyone but its residents. While politicians were increasing police budgets and using the logics of defensible space to transform cities into bifurcated spaces of privatized affluent leisure and marginalized public surveillance, public housing residents were advocating for improved infrastructure, economic development, and a built environment that was both safe and welcoming to outsiders.[3]

This book presents a history of Atlanta's public housing tenant associations that challenges the mischaracterized trope of the politically deviant public housing tenant and the declension narratives that suggest public housing developments were built to fail and mismanaged into decline. Public housing tenants are considered politically deviant because of the long history of situating nonwhite, non-elite, nonvoting, and nonhomeowning people in the developments. Further, the public housing program, frequently characterized as a problem, has suffered from decades of managerial scandals, residential crime, and blight-inducing disinvestment in the built environment, to the point where the demolition and disposition of all units feels inevitable.

At their best, tenant associations work not so much to conform the tenants and developments to the hegemonic political and spatial norms of the ruling elite (such as normalizing voting as political participation and normalizing single-family home ownership as land use) but instead to bend those norms to the political practices and spatial logics of public housing tenancy. At their worst, they are inactive or intentionally subvert the interests of the tenant population for the individual gains of their often-powerful leadership. This book contributes to the tenant activist literature by illuminating some of the conditions that create progressive and regressive tenant politics.

At the time of the Techwood/Clark Howell modernization statement, over 10 percent of Atlanta's population—nearly fifty thousand residents—lived in public housing developments. The political power of public housing tenants grew with the citywide poverty rate in the 1960s and 1970s as middle-class residents left the city to purchase homes in the federally subsidized suburbs. Since their origins, public housing tenant associations provided political education, forums, and campaigns for and by populations that were spatially marginalized and, thus, more likely to be disenfranchised from the political system.

Public housing tenant associations also created innovative uses for spaces and places that were similarly abandoned by urban governments favoring market-rate real estate development to shore up declining urban tax bases due to suburbanization. During the 1980s, proposals to sell Techwood and Clark Howell and redevelop it into commercial and private residential properties were overwhelmingly rejected by tenants. As Marion Green, a former Techwood/Clark Howell tenant association president and wife of Israel Green, noted, "Techwood can be a beautiful place . . . and it's the most convenient neighborhood that there is."[4] During her tenure, Green led the successful initiative to get Techwood listed on the National Register of Historic Places—yet another tenant association effort to leverage federal resources to counteract local disinvestment and neglect.

However, within twenty years, Techwood and Clark Howell were both demolished to make way for athlete housing at the 1996 Centennial Olympics in Atlanta. Later, the site would be redeveloped into mixed-income housing through the new HOPE VI program. It is renamed Centennial Place, removing virtually all traces of the Techwood and Clark Howell "homes" and the marginalized residents who once lived there. Although tenant resistance would cede greater concessions than what were originally planned, in the end, the tenant association favorably endorsed the plans for a publicly funded demolition and redevelopment that would benefit a private developer and housing management company.

The resident plans of inclusive redevelopment, ranging from modernized multifamily public rental housing for some and private single-family homeownership for others, all but evaporated after drawn-out negotiations that split tenants into factions that were co-opted and exploited by private and public interests.[5] The construction jobs that were begrudgingly set aside for tenants were temporary, and over half of the tenant population was permanently displaced, never to return. All that remains of Techwood and Clark Howell Homes is the original community center—a historically preserved monument to the first public housing development in the country, a plaque commemorating the modernization of these developments, and boxes and boxes in the archives.

Using these archives and other data sources, I reconstruct a history of Atlanta's public housing through the politics that produced the developments and the politics that were subsequently produced by the tenants. Building off the research of critical public housing scholars such as Rhonda Y. Williams, Amy L. Howard, Lawrence Vale, Edward G. Goetz, Michael Leo Owens, and others, *Diverging Space for Deviants* examines how politically deviant public housing tenants reappropriate, or diverge, the marginalized spaces of public housing communities to reflect the political interests of those intentionally excluded from urban planning and other political processes.

From the first Black, middle-class, married, heterosexual tenants who were legally excluded from voting in Georgia's white Democratic primaries to the last Black, working-poor, women-headed households that risked eviction for failing to notify surveilling housing managers of their newborn children, this work traces the political development of "deviant" public housing residents through the spatial transformation of their surrounding communities. These spatial divergences include the construction of the first public auditorium for Black Atlantans to safely assemble in the "slums" of the 1930s, and the transformation of vacant public housing units in the "projects" to use as temporary foster care for children of substance abusers in the 1980s. These divergences provide a new means of conceptualizing political participation, spatial production, and urban planning throughout urban history.

Race, Planning, and Atlanta's Public Housing

The United States public housing program begins in Atlanta, with Secretary of the Interior Harold Ickes pushing down a plunger to demolish the first "slum" house in an event widely covered by the national press in September 1934. The public housing program in Atlanta was shaped—through separate initiatives—by John Hope, the first Black president of Morehouse College and head of the University Homes advisory committee until his death, and Charles Forrest Palmer, a real estate developer. Hope's and Palmer's disparate approaches to slum clearance and public housing construction mimic the precarious political coalition that converged to push the first public housing policies through Congress.

The downtown property owner Charles Palmer was more interested, as his autobiography *Adventures of a Slum Fighter* suggests, in clearing the slums that threatened the value of his holdings.[6] Hope, on the other hand, was driven by a more urgent material need—the growing housing crisis in the Black community that had not yet recovered from the white supremacist-induced property destruction and murder spree known as the 1906 Atlanta Race Riot. In spite of these differing approaches to poverty, property, and land use, the two men worked together to support a new federal initiative addressing their converging interests.

The 1906 race riot predates the first planning body in Atlanta by three years, and many of the causes of this riot would structure the planning of the twentieth-century city. The 1906 gubernatorial campaign between two white supremacists, Hoke Smith and Clark Howell, used their influence as former and current newspaper owners to sell papers and garner votes over false allegations against Black men: for raping white women, taking the jobs of white men, and otherwise desecrating white space in the years following Emancipation. A frequent target in these accusations were the spaces and places that provided cover for these deviant acts: the bars of the unregulated slums and the "disorganized" Black community-based political institutions, such as the Mason Hall, were all roundly condemned by the elite press.[7]

Yellow journalism on increasing Black literacy, decreasing Black farm tenancy rates, and Black-perpetuated sexual violence fueled the four-day spree of white violence on Black persons and communities in September 1906. In an effort to put Black Atlantans *in their place*, white Atlantans of all class backgrounds participated in the murder of at least ten Black citizens, the destruction of hundreds of homes and several businesses, churches, and schools.[8] These attacks on Black spaces were not uncommon in cities faced with increasing Black populations and tightening labor and housing markets.

Since these riots, race has functioned as a central organizing logic in the planning and spatial production of Atlanta.[9] Atlanta officially adopted a racialized zoning code with its first comprehensive plan in 1922, distinguishing itself early on from other southern cities that preferred only the threat of extralegal violence to confine Black residents into certain areas of the city. Class also motivated desires to contain Black integration into white communities. It was not, after all, white *renters* who protested Black residency through the formation of all-white civic homeowner associations.

Efforts to institutionalize legal residential segregation were headed by these white homeowner civic associations. These groups continued to have significant power in planning and shaping the city, particularly in the beginning when urban planning was done in fits and starts by voluntary civic committees. As scholar LeeAnn Lands writes, "when localized action failed to stall black movement and rental housing incursions, demands for racial segregation quickly made their way into dominant, Progressive Era rhetoric, and such ordinances and land use controls became 'necessities' for 'proper' growth and development."[10]

Another lesson that emerged from the riot, in the words of John Hope's wife and Neighborhood Union founder, Lugenia Burns Hope, was that "the white man learned . . . that there must be cooperation." Hope was referring specifically to an incident when Black professors and college administrators mounted an armed defense to protect Atlanta University and the wider community from white supremacist violence during the riots. Negotiation between Black and white elites helped to diffuse these standoffs and conceded the end of (white) violence in exchange for Black political and spatial marginality.[11]

Atlanta's mythologized biracial cooperation for urban governance has transformed over the years—from a pyramid-shaped community power structure in the prewar years to the more dynamic urban regime of the postwar era. But it continues to operate in the way it did immediately after the riots, with minimal white violent oppression in exchange for Black deferential cooperation. Biracial cooperation creates political opportunities for the biracial *elites* in power, while eliminating one of the many tools of the disenfranchised: direct action and other forms of vocal protest.

The biracial cooperation between Palmer and Hope to produce public housing was little more than good timing, and not indicative of a benevolent agreement between Black and white elites to produce safe and sanitary housing for impoverished Atlantans. The planning of public housing in Atlanta was yet another means of institutionalizing racial difference in the production of urban space. Segregated Black and white public housing developments were constructed as physical barriers demarcating Black and white spaces in the city. The rapid growth of Atlanta's public housing program suggests that it benefited from being an early adopter of the policy. The legacy of segregated public housing developments hardened into residential segregation in the postwar city.

Between 1936 and 1942, the Housing Division of the Public Works Administration (PWA), United States Housing Authority, and Atlanta Housing Authority constructed nearly five thousand units across eight developments. The four distinct phases of public housing construction are useful for understanding the larger shifts in Atlanta's racialized spatial production, or urban planning, in the city. The first phase was from 1935 to 1940, the second from 1955 to 1965, the third from 1969 to 1974, and finally the fourth phase of demolition and redevelopment from 1994 to 2011. These construction phases demarcate the different case studies presented in the following chapters.

In most American cities, the construction of public housing followed established patterns of racial segregation that were upheld through either legal racial covenants or deed restrictions. Atlanta, which received the greatest number of public housing units in the country before World War II, instead produced its city around the racially differentiating spatial logics of the segregated public housing program. Segregated since their construction in the 1930s, Atlanta's public housing developments remained that way until the city was forced to desegregate in 1968, four years after the Civil Rights Act mandated desegregation of public facilities and accommodations, and six years after President Kennedy signed an executive order barring segregation in federally funded programs. Long after segregation ordinances, zoning codes, and racial covenants were eradicated, the public housing development endured as a means of marginalizing races and spaces in the modern city.

The election of a Black mayor in 1974—the start of an uninterrupted tenure of Black mayoral leadership that continues into the present—did little to change the use of the public housing development to shape racial planning politics in the city. Black public housing developments—which were all public housing developments following the delayed desegregation in 1968—became crucial political campaign stops and rallying points for Black politicians in postindustrial Atlanta.

As Atlanta's public housing developments became all Black, so too did Atlanta's inner city, and this high concentration of a Black impoverished population near the city center disrupted Atlanta's downtown growth machine.

Yet this population also produced and sustained the Black urban regime, a majority-Black-led coalition of government and business interests that work in concert to implement growth machine policies. Growth machine politics prioritize policies that increase the value of properties in the center city, where, as noted, many of the early public housing developments were sited. In what Kraus and Swanstrom call the "hollow-prize problem," Black mayors elected in majority-Black cities faced difficult policy choices in the wake of declining populations and tax revenues and growing social welfare and antipoverty expenditures.[12] Thus, as early as 1980, Atlanta began examining the cost of selling off downtown units to remove Black public housing residents from the area and attract white businessowners back from the suburbs.

And so, when the city won the bid to host the 1996 Olympics, local, state, and federal officials worked together to facilitate the erasure of Black political geographies from the landscape and displace deviant interests from the renewing city. HOPE VI, the newest iteration of public housing policy, subsidized the demolition and private redevelopment and management of severely distressed public housing developments. Under the program's New Urbanism–inspired community planning, public housing was redeveloped into mixed-use, mixed-income, mixed-tenure spaces with suburban-style aesthetics. Although race is absent from virtually all planning documents, the goal of the program was to lessen this concentration of Black impoverished people, for whom the city no longer planned, and facilitate the movement of young, upwardly mobile or already wealthy residents into the city. That HOPE VI can facilitate gentrification demonstrates the ongoing role of public housing policy in structuring race, class, and land use politics in the city.

Public housing developments in Atlanta helped solidify the central role of race in urban land use and political decision-making. Throughout the program's existence, public housing developments shaped the racial geographies of the city, while also facilitating the inclusion of its residential population through the growing strength and legitimacy of tenant associations. Early private investors, such as Charles Palmer and John and Lugenia Burns Hope, helped establish the racial politics of cooperation of the regime, by shaping the racial geographies of the city through development siting.

The city's planning system continued to use racial segregation as a land use logic under both white and Black mayors who prioritized downtown business growth, slow racial integration, and minimal resistance by residents. Public housing tenant associations created political opportunities for those most likely to resist these planning logics: the economically disenfranchised, the spatially marginalized, and the politically deviant. The following section outlines how deviants are constructed and deconstructed through political geographies, such as racially segregated public housing developments.

Deviants

This book also traces the history of the "deviant" political (non)participant in the city slums and later in the public housing developments that replaced those slums. Deviant individuals are labeled as such because of their refusal to integrate and incorporate into the political mainstream. Deviancy, like other sociopolitical constructions, is sustained largely through the collective narratives of public policy debate and discourse.[13] These narratives legitimize the notion that deviants do not vote, do not engage in public debate or discussion, and are generally perceived as unable and unwilling to be organized or mobilized. Consequently, these negative sociopolitical constructions are reinforced by the state's allocation of fewer public resources and political power to politically deviant populations and places.[14]

This refusal to participate, normatively, is considered a character flaw and a personal choice as opposed to an outcome of a conservative political system that continually denies power and access to marginalized groups. Political deviancy is an intentional by-product of the gendered and racialized capitalist democracy, not a flaw. Thus, we would expect political deviants to reflect the intentional exclusionary structures of the mainstream political system.

In the 1930s, public housing developments were viewed as a solution to quelling social and political deviancy in the industrializing city, particularly the brand of deviant that resided in the urban slum. The production of the slum was twofold: slums were produced not only by a rapid urbanization that created substandard housing for low-income migrant populations near growing industrial districts, but also through a racialized urbanization that attracted cheap Black labor from rural areas yet refused to incorporate Black communities into the larger patterns of (white) urbanization.[15] Racialized language characterized the slums as the "dark recesses of the city," while white politicians accused Black slum communities of acting as safe harbors for criminals.[16]

Due to the higher crime, juvenile delinquency, and infant mortality rates in Atlanta's slum communities, as well as a growing Black population, slum inhabitants were constructed as politically and socially deviant. The marginalized spatial positioning of the slum in the city translated to marginalized political power and allocation of resources for its residents. Public housing developments were soon offered as a spatial fix to the dual crises of the slum: the provision of safe and sanitary housing would ease some of the supply pressures of the housing market, and the provision of segregated housing would serve as the new means to contain and segregate the growing Black population.

Changes in the public housing program at the onset of the 1970s urban crisis, such as the slow divestment from the federal government and the aggressive devolution to state and local governments, reduced public housing's ability to address the growing social and economic issues of its residents. This divestment also constructed a new form of deviant in the developments, as local authorities turned austere in response to reduced funding. Without strong support of social programs, involved management, and capital improvements for the developments, public housing residents became increasingly detached from and disempowered within the local political structure.

In *Double Trouble: Black Mayors, Black Communities, and the Call for Deep Democracy*, political scientist J. Phillip Thompson III's hypothesis on poor Black residents as deviants, with regard to decreased political participation in the 2000 and 2004 presidential elections, states:

> That the black poor are becoming increasingly spatially, and socially, isolated (Cohen and Dawson,1993; Wilson, 1987); that the black poor are distrustful of neighbors in dangerous and resource-deprived neighborhoods (Rosset et al, 2001); that they are not encouraged to join organizations; though they do participate where organizations are available to them (Berry et al, 1993, 95); and that they may, in fact, belong to informal organizations (such as gangs or street corner groups) that survey questionnaires looking for "good" forms of civic associations tend to ignore (Cohen, 2004).[17]

This contradictory idea of the poor Black political deviant—as those excluded and marginalized by politically legitimate Black civic organizations (such as the church, trade unions, and community-based organizations), yet who also participate when included in formal or informal organizations—mimics the contradiction of the Black woman in urban space. The *Black Woman* (a deviant) resident, like the *Poor Black* (deviant) resident, are "in [their] place when out of place."[18] The spatial difference borne by residential segregation produces a social difference that marginalizes the political legitimacy of these deviant groups.

This difference is further exacerbated for the *Poor Black Woman*, who is overrepresented in the public housing population. While socially constructed and politically and spatially marginalized as deviants in the urban political economy, low-income Black women were active shapers of their environment as politically engaged citizens who rejected the social difference borne of spatial difference. They thrived in the contradiction of deviance and, in many cities, reappropriated (or diverged) the space of public housing from the edge of the political margins into the center of Atlanta's political system.

(Black Feminist) Spatial Politics

Political geographer Margaret Kohn describes the emergence of radical democracy as an effort in collaboration, spacemaking, and collective redefinitions: "The radicalization of democracy can occur in several different ways: by linking diverse democratic struggles, creating new sites for more effective political participation, extending collective control into previously excluded domains such as the workplace, and expanding the definition of citizenship to accomplish meaningful inclusion of previously marginalized groups."[19] Linking diverse democratic struggles in the space of the public sphere, the creation of new spaces for more effective political participation, the extension of collective control into previously excluded spaces, and the expansion of the space of citizenship to include previously marginalized groups are all varying types of spatial practices that diverge and transform apolitical sites into politically empowering spaces for systemically marginalized groups.

This book demonstrates that public housing developments (particularly those with origins as segregated, Black developments), through their tenant associations, have the potential to diverge the space of the development to engage with the democratic process at multiple scales: community, local, state, and federal. The space politicized by the tenant associations allowed for residents to assemble and organize with other marginalized interest groups, to mobilize for collective control of public housing developments and policy, and to increase the legitimacy of the tenant association and thus of the public housing resident as a political interest.

That the public housing resident was increasingly more likely to be a Black woman, particularly after shifts in welfare and public housing policy included more Black female-headed households in the 1960s, links the importance of radical public housing spatial practices to the production of black feminist radical politics in the city. The 1960s and 1970s was a time of increasing social movements around Black civil rights, second-wave feminism, environmental politics, Indigenous peoples rights, and other historically marginalized interests. Yet within these diverse and often overlapping social movements, Black women felt increasingly isolated, excluded, and misrepresented. Within these single-axis movements, the refusal to understand and acknowledge the differential modes of oppression created a political opportunity for a politics explicitly centered around Black women's interests.

An example of this Black feminist spatial politics in public housing is the resistance to the public and private surveillance that has always shaped paternalistic public housing management. Public housing admissions and leasing required strict monitoring and documentation of tenant affairs, and thin operation margins mandated strict and uniform community and building aesthetics. The maintenance of a high moral environment, even as the welfare and admission policies of public housing shifted toward serving single-parent households, became the focus of national and local public housing policy in the 1970s. The changing residential population clashed with longstanding management and staff during this time. The response to this invasion of privacy, this increasing surveillance, was a Black feminist politics that was focused on increasing self-governance and decision-making for the most disenfranchised households.

In December 1966, the Atlanta Housing Authority evicted Ms. Josephine Williams of Perry Homes for misrepresenting her marital and familial relations—particularly having a child while unmarried and not reporting this new child to the staff and housing managers of Perry Homes. When Williams was evicted, she filed a lawsuit claiming her rent was paid and the eviction was unlawful; however, Georgia law required tenants to pay a bond that would cover the trial costs of the landlord before they could file a claim disputing the eviction.[20] Williams also filed a suit against the state claiming this bond payment was unconstitutional and in violation of the Fourteenth Amendment's due process and equal protection clauses. Per the claim, Williams stated this bond payment "deprives her of obtaining judicial review of her defenses in the courts of this State solely by reason of her poverty."[21]

Since poverty was a requirement for her admission into public housing, this policy created an effective legal mechanism to dispossess not only Josephine Williams but also thousands of other low-income women and men in Georgia's public housing units. The Georgia Supreme Court held in favor of the AHA, but Williams's claims put forth a new movement in Perry Homes—later codified and institutionalized in the citywide public housing tenant association—to install a grievance procedure that preceded a formal eviction, and gave tenants more opportunities to stay in their homes.

This type of political spacemaking for deviant interests in public housing developments is one of the ways of practicing a transformative Black feminist spatial politics. Centering Black feminist politics in the production of space is a divergence of the existing white supremacist spatial logics that guide modern citymaking. In taking up the causes of Black women produced by public housing policies and politics, public housing tenant associations were building cities hospitable to the modern deviant.

However, just as tenant associations, tenant unions, and nationwide tenant organizations were gaining momentum and legitimacy in the late 1970s, urban decline and nationwide deindustrialization produced a devolution of federal public housing responsibility and funding to state and local entities. Local governments with smaller budgets were forced to engage in austere measures that minimized the role of tenant associations, particularly as the streams of federal funding for antipoverty programs dried up. As the space for transformative Black feminist spatial politics shrank, opportunities for more conservative politics were produced in this increasingly ascetic environment. Yet even within this conservative turn, deviant interests and radical politics were *represented* although they did not always *dominate* tenant association politics. The eventual demolition and dispersal of public housing residents during the HOPE VI and Choice Neighborhoods

Initiative programs, and the concomitant eradication of tenant associations, all but removed Black feminist radical politics from the city.

Data and Methods

My interest in public housing is truly an interest in the city. Qualitative and quantitative methods and methodologies provide researchers with a range of tools to understand the production and contestations of space and place, from the collection and regression of macroeconomic data sets to the thematic comparison of qualitative case studies. Spatial analysis of urban forms and patterns have transformed the ways in which we can recognize problems and create efficient and equitable solutions in the pursuit of a spatial justice. Yet my data and methods primarily combine a number of archival documents to understand spatial production and spatial politics.

These macro- and micro-level processes are understood through analyses of policy documents, legislative session minutes, program evaluations, tenant association minutes, and personal communications such as letters and interoffice memorandums. Visual material and photographs are also useful to illuminate some of the performative notions of spatial production. Census data, economic data, and spatial data are included to illuminate how these qualitative and quantitative data interact and contest each other across space and time.

My conceptual framework for this project combines the theoretical understanding of Black participatory democracy described by Ella Baker with the practical strategies of participatory planning.[22] It also engages Epifania Akosua Amoo-Adare's concept of the critical spatial literacy produced by Black women in the city.[23] This critical spatial literacy is produced by Black women's daily routine practices that are rooted in the anticolonial and anticapitalist Black radical tradition of placemaking. In this work, I examine how tenant grievances about how Black women and their communities can and cannot move through the space of the city are mobilized into transformative spatial practices and policies.

These spatial practices make possible what I call *Black participatory geographies*. To trace these geographies, I examine how tenant associations and public housing developments created new spaces in which Black women residents and other deviantly constructed populations could remake spatial practices and logics in the city. These tenant associations and their members began asserting political power and identity through the participatory spatial practices of diverging segregated Black public housing *developments* into Black participatory *communities*.

Black participatory geographies allow for the expansion of traditional places and spaces of Black political engagement. Black participation in public and civic life is often relegated to established practices and hubs of the community. The

Black church, fraternal organizations, public sector and trade unions, and even the kitchen table of Black feminist politics are some of the acceptable modes and spaces of community engagement and participation. Voting, direct action, and legal tactics are some of the established practices of Black participation in urban life. Black participatory geographies engage both the traditional and nontraditional spatial practices of Black everyday life to account for more deviant interests and continue the Black radical tradition of countering dominant spatial logics.

Yet these geographies also challenge traditional notions of political participation that may account for its wider usage by deviant populations. In the spirit of Ella Baker's participatory democracy, these geographies transgress traditional hierarchies of leadership and employ horizontal organizing structures to maximize engagement, maintain inclusivity, and minimize the domination of one or more charismatic (male) leaders. This is an ideal version of a participatory geography and only appears in glimpses in the Atlanta public housing story. The struggle to maintain a Black participatory geography is difficult during times of neoliberalism, devolution, and austerity, and these challenges are well documented throughout this work.

My analytical framework for understanding the politics of Atlanta's public housing are also influenced by the Lefebvrian spatial triad.[24] My application of this triad of spatial production is the analysis of top-down or macro processes that produce representational spaces, bottom-up or micro processes, and finally lived realities and experiences—what I refer to as spatial practices in the text—that are also producing space. The triad guided my data collection of local, state, and federal policy documents, tenant association meeting minutes and development newsletters, and oral histories with tenants documenting day-to-day living around these macro and micro events.

I analyze the top-down production of the space of public housing developments—from federal legislation to city ordinances. The politics that produced public housing's physical and programmatic forms are crucial to understanding the political opportunities that are structured by these forms. I break down this legislation to include the testimony that preceded it, the program evaluations that restructured it, and the administrative documents that operationalize it. To look at spatial practices and spatial production—I look expressly at texts, words, and documents generated by Black women about their communities and daily routines. I then use Black feminist methods centering these narratives for analysis.[25] I have also employed oral histories and recorded interviews to further triangulate some of the historical documents into produced lived realities. In sum, the following chapters reconstruct the political tensions and opportunities that emerged in the production of public housing developments and Black participatory geographies.

Outline of the Book

The first chapter of the book details the history of Atlanta's public housing program, focusing on the interracial cooperation between real estate developer Charles F. Palmer and Morehouse College president John Hope that produced the construction of the all-white Techwood Homes and the all-Black University Homes. In detailing this history, I take a critical approach to understanding the public housing program as a spatial fix for both the unemployment crisis of the Great Depression and the racialized housing crisis of a rapidly urbanizing city with a growing Black population. This spatial fix was designed and implemented by several political interests in the city: real estate developers, "race" men and women, progressive housing reformers, bankers, building trades, academics, and, of course, elected officials. These political interests held a tenuous alliance that fractured over time, producing the contradictory and inchoate public housing policies in Atlanta.

Nonetheless, the involvement of Black Atlantans in the planning, construction, and management of the first Black developments was a transformative shift. Construction of Black public housing developments began during a period when Black residents were unable to vote due to the all-white Democratic primary, and the creation of this space was a major step toward Black political empowerment and citizenship. The program thus originates as a space of political empowerment for Black Atlantans, and subsequent chapters show the political evolution of public housing developments' tenant associations over the next seventy years.

Chapter 2 looks at the case of University Homes as an example of the form of racial uplift politics that dominated early Black political development at the turn of the twentieth century. As one of the first public housing developments for Black residents, University Homes enjoyed a prominent role as a positive example of what N. D. B. Connolly calls "Jim Crow liberalism" and the beginning of a formal Black self-governance.[26] Through a framework of spatial uplift, this chapter describes how Black elites repurposed Atlanta's and the public housing program's spatial logics to achieve their goals of Black racial uplift.

When Black Atlantans were enfranchised after the end of the white primary in 1946, University Homes increased its political education courses and its voter registration drives, and its auditorium served as a polling place. As the first public investment in Atlanta's Black community, University Homes management, staff, and tenant association all advocated for continued investment that would benefit both the residents and the wider community. With support from other prominent Black Atlantans, this coalition helped fund recreational facilities and staff for young children and a new library for the community, and it used the auditorium to host cultural and educational events. While these segregated facilities continued to harden the Jim Crow spatial logics of postbellum Atlanta, they also served to create more equitable spatial practices for the city's Black population.

Perry Homes, the thousand-unit development in northwest Atlanta, is the focus of chapter 3. Perry Homes was constructed in 1955, and its size, site, and tenant population marked a new era in the public housing tenant association as political opportunity structure. In 1951, to counter the increasing proportion of Black voters in Atlanta's electorate, the city approved the Plan of Improvement that annexed eighty-one square miles of land to the north and west of the city, along with over one hundred thousand mostly white residents. Perry Homes, and most subsequent public housing, was located in the underdeveloped northwestern quadrant of the city.

Perry Homes was also constructed with Urban Redevelopment and Urban Renewal funding from the 1949 and 1954 Housing Acts, which mandated that new public housing prioritize the rehousing of residents who were forcibly removed during slum clearance. These residents, unlike the carefully selected tenants for University Homes, were often poorer, with more precarious employment, and did not have to abide by the stringent application policies of home visits and minimum income requirements of previous tenants. As a result, Perry Homes had fewer men serving in leadership positions, which shifted the political opportunity structure toward Black women and their needs.

Black women's leadership and Black women's issues came to the fore during the mid-1960s. During this period, more inclusive forms of deviant politics, extending beyond the respectable race politics that dominated the first wave of public housing developments, shape the spatial logics and spatial politics of the tenant associations. The political mobilization of the Perry Homes tenant association during the 1950s and 1960s extends beyond the spatial uplift framework of chapter 2 and takes into account the institutional grievances experienced by this new resident population. The spatial practices of Perry Homes tenant association members, leaders, and residents can be collectively grouped into a methodological practice of Black feminist planning.[27]

Chapter 4 traces the latter half of the 1960s up to 1980 at Grady Homes, located in the Sweet Auburn neighborhood near downtown Atlanta. While Grady Homes was constructed during the first wave of PWA-inspired public housing construction and management and also was as spatially well resourced as the AUC-adjacent University Homes, its tenant population represented deviant populations comprised of the deserving and undeserving poor. This particular period is one of expansion for Atlanta's Black participatory geographies, as new scales for resource mobilization around tenant needs created political opportunities outside of public housing and the development tenant association.

Grady Homes was located across from Grady Hospital, Atlanta's public hospital that would serve many disabled and elderly public housing tenants. Several tenants were eligible to transfer into Grady Homes once they required constant health care, and the population shifted from two-working-adults-with-children households into single elderly or elderly caretaker households. This tenant population created a more intersectional tenant association that used the development to pursue political opportunities for elderly, disabled, and Black feminist interests.

The political opportunity structure of public housing and tenant associations again shifted under the newly formed Citywide Advisory Council on Public Housing (ACPH). The ACPH leadership used citywide and federal resources for citizen empowerment, workforce training and development, and public housing modernization to create more inclusive communities for the Black poor in Atlanta. This population became even more marginalized and constructed as deviant under Mayor Hartsfield's biracial elite regime. Although the election of Maynard Jackson as the first Black mayor in Atlanta was a success for many in a city where Black enfranchisement was virtually nonexistent three decades prior, even Jackson's approach to urban governance limited political opportunities for the working poor. This chapter also traces the shift in the political opportunity structures during Jackson's administration, and how decreasing political opportunities at the local, state, and federal levels led to increasing competition between tenant associations for limited resources.

Chapter 5 examines the conservative turn in public housing politics under a growing Black urban regime in Atlanta. Following Maynard Jackson's historical win and reelection, Andrew Young, the first Black congressman from Atlanta, succeeded Jackson for another two terms. It is during this uninterrupted reign of Black leadership that Atlanta's urban regime, Clarence Stone's theory of urban political development that characterizes postwar Atlanta politics, transformed from a biracial governing and electoral coalition to one that was becoming increasingly Black. The Black urban regime under Andrew Young continued the policies that supported the interests of minority business owners, often at the expense of the neighborhood-centered interests that carried Jackson electorally through two terms.

At the federal level, devolution of authority and budgeting to state and local governments during Ronald Reagan's New Federalism model quickly depleted the robust city funding streams that characterized the urban redevelopment, urban renewal, and urban empowerment programs in decades prior. Funding for (and spending on) police, property securitization, disposition, and demolition increased along with crime rates in urban areas—the crime rate in Atlanta tripled from 1965 to 1980. The chapter traces the forces that transform tenant mobilization from the start of the 1980s to the end of the decade. This analysis helps contextualize the politics of tenant associations that went from advocating for a self-imposed curfew during the Atlanta Child Murders to failing to resist a police-enforced curfew authorized by Mayor Maynard Jackson in response to increasing homicides near potential Olympic sites.

Chapter 6 builds off the conservative turn covered in chapter 5 to introduce the dual impact of the Olympics and HOPE VI on Atlanta's public housing politics—and the implications of the neoliberal turn in public housing policy on the spatial logics governing tenant associations. Politically, HOPE VI, a federal program that granted housing authorities funding to leverage for the demolition and private redevelopment of severely distressed public housing developments, was a modern-day New Deal for the fiscally insolvent public housing program. The legislation received testimonial support from a multitude of interests at the federal and local levels—including real estate developers, new "race" men and women, public housing reformers, bankers, academics, and, of course, elected officials.

Atlanta, ever the vanguard of public housing policy, was again one of the first cities to use HOPE VI grants to demolish the very first public housing development—Techwood Homes—to make way for athlete housing during the 1996 Olympics. The resistance to this demolition was folded into the development regime, facilitated by the conservative turn in tenant politics discussed in chapter 5. The chapter ends with a deconstruction of HOPE VI private managerial policies and practices and the limits to Black participatory geographies in a post–public housing city.

As Terrion L. Williamson says in her work on the apolitical spacemaking of Black feminist social life as a radical act, "Outside of all bounds—young, female, unmarried, poor, black—with the capacity to produce more of the same, the black teenage mother poses a threat that precedes and exceeds the field of representation and exposes the fault lines of capitalist (re)production. She codifies an unthinkable way of Being, a counter mythology, that alleges no commitments to law or order. And it is in this, her will toward rebellion, that she 'makes a crisis for dominant signification.'"[28]

With this work, I hope to build on this theoretical foundation to understand how this deviant political capacity is sustained and turned into political action through the public housing development. What follows is the application of this theory in Atlanta, from 1936 to 2011.

Chapter 1

A New Deal to
Plan the New South

The Politics of Atlanta's Public Housing

Our slum clearance program will take no note of race or creed or color. We are particularly glad that the requests from Atlanta for slum clearance have called for benefits for the entire population. Atlanta has been a pioneer among many progressive lines, and it is only fitting that the city which has been a leader in interracial cooperation should insist that all parts of its population should benefit from this new social venture. We know, from sad experience, that when one section or group of the population flourishes at the expense of others, it is not long before the whole country is the loser.

—**Harold L. Ickes, Secretary of the Interior at the October 1934 Inauguration of the Slum Clearance Program at Spelman College, Atlanta**

The modern public housing program is often viewed as a problem. By residents, who find the homes undermaintained and unsafe; by the wider community, who find the presence of public housing units depresses their housing values and community amenities; and by local, state, and federal officials who must balance the needs of an underserved population with public housing's often cumbersome bureaucracy and deteriorating infrastructure. Yet when public housing began as a New Deal initiative to finance slum clearance and low-cost housing construction in 1933, it was then regarded by its advocates as a solution to address the post-Depression crises borne out of rapid urbanization: substandard and costly housing, overburdened infrastructure that threatened public health, and unstable labor markets.

The federally supported public housing and slum clearance program that united the disparate interests of unionized construction trades with anti-labor real estate developers, garnered initial support from an untenable coalition of ur-

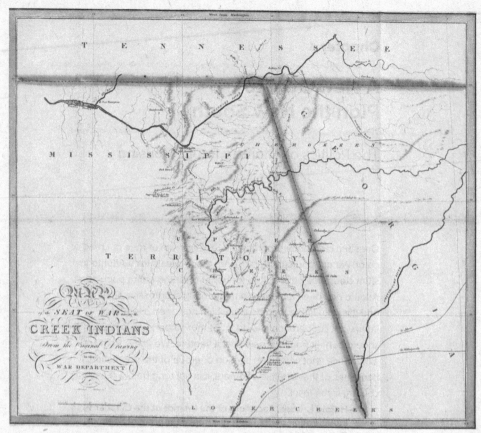

Map 1.1. The Seat of War among the Creek overlaid by Georgia, Alabama, and Tennessee state borders. Source: U.S. War Department, 1814, courtesy of the David Rumsey Map Collection.

ban interests. Public housing advocates included urban developers needing to shore up their investments by removing property-devaluing blight from city centers, housing reformers looking to morally uplift those residing in the slum areas to improve urban living, local elected officials wanting to boost the electorate's morale and employment through public works projects, and social reformers wanting to target the disease, vice, and crime districts that were often relegated to slum areas. These diverse political interests all allied in support of a federal public housing program as the solution to many urban crises.

Although the contributions of New York City and Chicago toward U.S. public housing policies are well documented, the origins of the national public housing system are largely the origins of Atlanta's public housing system. Atlanta was the site of the first federally financed housing development under the Public Works

Administration's Housing Division. The all-white Techwood Homes opened in September 1936, and the all-Black University Homes, the first public housing *approved* by the federal government, opened seven months later in April 1937.

In Atlanta, the crisis of urbanization produced new tensions between local and state elected officials, as Georgia's dwindling agricultural economy shifted capital and people from its politically powerful rural areas to growing, industrialized urban areas across the southeast. Between 1900 and 1930, the population in rural areas in Georgia's Black Belt counties grew about 18 percent, while more urbanized areas in counties such as Fulton, DeKalb, Richmond, and Muscogee saw their populations increase by about 168 percent during that same period.[1] Many of these migrants were Black tenant farmers who were looking to gain economic, social, and political opportunity in the developing city; but white farmers also migrated toward these higher wages and opportunities, creating interracial pressures within the urban labor and housing markets.[2]

In the chapter's opening epigraph, Secretary Ickes lauded Atlanta's progressive approach and interracial cooperation, while also pointedly addressing Georgia's tendency to regress into the racist parochialism that nearly destroyed the country during the Civil War. While Atlanta's local government largely supported the federally funded public housing program, Georgia's former membership in the confederacy produced a state government that was outright hostile to federal intervention. Further, Georgia's county-unit system that allocated one state representative for each county regardless of population, disproportionately favored rural interests over counties with larger urban populations. These scalar tensions between local and state officials, state and federal officials, and urban and rural interests would recur throughout the tenure of the public housing program, further contributing to the fragility of the political coalition advocating for public housing in Atlanta.

The racial politics of Atlanta continued to regress toward what political scientist Clarence Bacote referred to as the Black political "nadir," following the legal and extralegal rollback of Black civil rights in the post-Reconstruction era. In contrast, President Franklin Roosevelt established the nation's first "Black Kitchen Cabinet," an elite, all-Black group of presidential advisers including the Black economist and aide to Secretary Ickes, Robert C. Weaver. The cabinet signaled the first steps toward Black political incorporation into the federal government since Reconstruction.

However, Secretary Ickes's claim of interracial cooperation rang hollow here; Techwood and University Homes were planned independently of one another. The city's Jim Crow politics did not produce interracial cooperation toward local public housing policy, but rather the extension and expansion of segregated public institutions. The contradictory racial politics of the nation's public housing program were thus piloted in Atlanta: federally funded public housing developments were simultaneously used to institutionalize residential segregation into

the built environment, while also providing a host of social, political, and economic opportunities to Black communities that were often ignored by their local
governments.

Atlanta's public housing program, at the outset, allowed the city to create a spatial ordering through segregated developments that reflected the racial-political
hierarchy of the city. This Atlanta model of racial segregation for urban redevelopment was thus advocated for and spread across the country—albeit for different reasons—from many prominent Atlantans, including a white realtor turned
coordinator of defense housing, Charles F. Palmer, and University Homes' first
Black housing manager, Alonzo F. Moron.

Palmer, a local real estate developer and national advocate for slum clearance and public housing construction, was Atlanta's greatest champion for public housing. Palmer's contributions to Atlanta's public housing story have been
well documented, including in his own humble autobiography, *Adventures of a
Slum Fighter*. Palmer's aggressive lobbying at the local level helped secure buy-in
to sustain the program in Atlanta from the first PWA loan in 1934 through the
1938 founding of the Atlanta Housing Authority. In doing so, Palmer's charismatic leadership produced a local coalition of business leaders, real estate developers, elected officials, and academics, virtually all of whom were white men and
friends, that formally and informally advised elected officials on public housing
policy.

This select group established a public housing program that was an extension of southern patrician ideals of elite leaders as paternalistic caretakers of the
poor. The form and function of this group of business and political leaders mimic
that of the urban growth machine, another feature of the postwar city, where
landowning elite coalitions dictate and direct urban policy to prioritize growth
and wealth accumulation for themselves. The origins of Atlanta's public housing
program—and the nation's public housing program—suffer from this paternalistic, top-down approach to public housing siting, design, and operations, which
would ultimately lead to the program's demise.

While the clearance of slums and construction of low-cost housing provided
direct financial capital for landowning elites, and political capital for Black elites,
the programmatic aspects of public housing were largely structured to uplift a
submerged middle class. This uplift was differentiated across race and ethnicity,
with white ethnic public housing residents afforded opportunities to Americanize (or whiten) themselves through participating in pseudo-patriotic war efforts.[3]
Policymakers were also explicit in creating a path to single-family homeownership for public housing tenants, encouraging families to save with local banks
and take advantage of the new federally guaranteed secondary mortgage market.

Black elites, in their promotion of uplift ideology, also viewed the public housing development as a means of uplifting their entire race to achieve political, so-

cial, and economic equality with white residents. However, Black public housing residents were faced with different realities than their white counterparts in the Americanization experiment: the disenfranchisement of Black Georgians due to the white Democratic Party primary openly contradicted the citizenship goals of the public housing experiment.

The Jim Crow discrimination of separate-but-equal public goods and services and the individual discrimination against Black people by white private actors created different citizenship programs for white and Black public housing developments. Consequently, the goal of creating a politicalized class of homeowners as citizens, often described as assisting the submerged middle class from the Depression, also differed between white and Black public housing tenants. While the former could transition smoothly from public to private housing, the latter were faced with a private housing market that was spatially constrained by Jim Crow planning logics and reinforced by a white supremacist capitalist real estate industry.

Black public housing developments served to expose the contradictions of uplift ideology: no matter how high the race was lifted, Black citizenship with full political, economic, and social equality to white citizenship could never exist under the spatially restrictive Jim Crow conditions. Contrary to what policymakers and administrators espoused about the evils of slums and the benefits of public housing developments, the deviance was much less about class and much more about race. It is for those who live at the intersection of deviance—poor, Black, queer, differently abled women—that we see these dreams of citizenship were the most difficult to realize.

Atlanta pioneered not only the use of public housing developments as a spatial fix to fledgling downtown investment but also its use as spatial uplift for the deviant Black community. These spatial logics are derived from a land use politics that privileges the perspective of white, able-bodied, cis-gendered men of means and power. The history of the city's spatial construction and politics that facilitated these logics of fixes and uplifts are described in the following section.

Constructing Atlanta: A Citybuilding Project

Long before the city of Atlanta (1847) was called Marthasville (1842) or Terminus (1827), the place and area around it was inhabited by two groups of Indigenous peoples: the Muscogee/Creek and the Cherokee. The relationship between white Georgia settlers, Black free and enslaved people, and the Indigenous peoples who occupied the land based on inter- and intratribal battles and negotiations was cooperative and contentious in the early nineteenth century. Indigenous tribes fought with and against each other over land that was increasingly occupied by white settlers. At times, formerly enslaved and free Black people joined in these battles. Tribal leaders also worked with white settlers to take advantage of natural resources, such as extracting gold from tribal lands or participating in the plantation economy through the enslavement of Black labor for crop production.

The Creek nation (which split during the Civil War to fight alongside Confederate and Union forces) gave newly emancipated Black farmers an "equal interest in the soil" upon the end of the Civil War.[4] This equal interest was also bound with full admission into the nation, and Black Creek peoples fought alongside their Indigenous counterparts against white settlers to protect their land from further encroachment.[5] Examining the treatment of Cherokee and Creek peoples in the contemporary Atlanta area is useful to contextualize the modern State projects of land dispossession and political marginalization.

By 1827, the state of Georgia began seizing and dividing Cherokee lands into parcels and selling them through a lottery to white settler-citizens of the state. After Congress passed the Indian Removal Act of 1830, federal troops, with state assistance, forcibly removed the Cherokee peoples first into what is now Tennessee and then later into what is now Oklahoma. The Creek peoples were forcibly removed to what is now western Alabama. The act gave the federal government legal authority to "negotiate" with Indigenous groups on behalf of state governments, providing both the means of tribal nation sovereignty and the beginning of tribal land dispossession.

Two years later, Indigenous groups were excluded from dealing with state governments altogether in the *Worcester v. Georgia* case. The Supreme Court established the legal relationship between the federal government, state governments, and Indigenous tribes, such that only the federal government could negotiate with tribal representatives. This process of legislative othering and exclusion, of subsequent forcible displacement, and of white settler land profiteering would be repeated by the federal government, the state of Georgia, and the city of Atlanta on Black populations at least three more times over the next century and a half.

Cities in the southeastern United States emerged along the Atlantic coast, riverports, and later railroad lines, reflecting temporal shifts in chattel slave trade legality and technological advances in international and interstate transportation systems. Southern states were slower to urbanize than those in the North, generally, as the plantation economy did not require a heavy urban infrastructure. Black enslaved laborers turned "free" laborers in southern rural areas cultivated and harvested raw materials that were then processed by white women and children in dry good factories and textile mills located in towns adjacent to transportation hubs.[6]

The South had two distinct periods of urbanization. The first occurred between 1880 and 1940 when the percentage of urbanized populations increased from 9 to 35 percent (during the same period the nation's overall urbanization rate increased from 26 to 54 percent). The second period of high urbanization co-

Figure 1.1. *1827 Land Lottery.* Source: *1827 Land Lottery* by George Parrish. 20×30 in. drawing in watercolor. James G. Kenan Research Center, Atlanta History Center.

incided with the deindustrialization of cities in the Northeast and Midwest or the rise of the Sunbelt in the southeastern and southwestern United States from 1940 to 1970.[7]

Slow urbanization rooted Georgia's economic (and political) power in the rural areas, especially on large cotton plantations. Georgia's cotton history began in 1755, with the arrival of Sea Island cotton seeds from the Bahamas to the St. Simon's Plantation in St. Simon's Island, Georgia. Mass cotton production using enslaved labor began in the nutrient-rich Black Belt, north of the Georgia coast.[8] The Black Belt formed a U-shape from the center of South Carolina heading southwest to the shared border of Georgia and Alabama, before curving upward to the northwest, ending in the middle of Tennessee. Named both for its fecund, dark soil and its majority Black and enslaved population that planted and harvested crops from that soil, the black belt of any state mapped the power and wealth of a white, male, landowning class of political elites.[9]

Atlanta's political and economic fortunes would soon change. The cotton industry based in Georgia's rural areas took a major hit at the turn of the twentieth century, both from decades of profit-maximizing agricultural practices that degraded the soil as well as natural crop destruction from the 1915 boll weevil infestation. Consequently, Atlanta's population grew 37 percent between 1890 and 1900 and grew an additional 72 percent (to 154,839 residents) between 1900 and

1910. This rapid growth created pressures on the former outpost city to develop in a short amount of time. It also created a healthy labor market, with competition from Black and white rural migrants.

With a growing city came a growing need to systemically (and politically) plan for this growth. A resolution released in 1908 from the Atlanta Chamber of Commerce emphasized the need for

> the creation of a nonpolitical metropolitan improvement commission, made up of eminent citizens from the city and county, with well-defined powers which will enable it to formulate, adopt and carry out a comprehensive plan to beautify the city and the county. . . . Such commission, while working coordinately with municipal and county authorities, shall not be subject to their dictation, and the tenure of the office should be such as to preclude sudden or disastrous changes in policy. . . . The Chamber of Commerce hereby pledges its active support of the creation of such a commission . . . with their future efforts to beautify the city and county roads which, in these days of rapid transit, are fast becoming great residential boulevards.[10]

This resolution underscores enduring characteristics of Atlanta politics over time: the convergence of business interests to drive public policy and political arrangements; the externalization of core political functions (in this case, decisions over land use and development) into institutional arrangements not subject to transparency, election, or accountability; and the prioritization of business growth and accommodation at the expense of other social welfare needs.

Boosterism was another factor in Atlanta's rapid urbanization, and newspaper editors such as Henry Grady and owner Clark Howell of the *Atlanta Constitution* are considered major forces behind the growth and mythmaking of Atlanta as the capital of the New South.[11] The New South was a project to industrialize the agrarian South. After the Civil War, this state building project aggressively promoted the low cost of capital, largely through direct and native advertisements in local and national newspapers. Newspapermen and women took such a prominent role in promoting the South that they often became more closely associated with their cities than their publications. Both Grady and Howell heavily promoted Atlanta through their leadership positions in the business and political worlds.

Although not always present in the text, much of the subtext of this domination of the environment and rebuilding of the New South was the restructuring of the Old South to fit the new world order of slavery abolition. Members of the Atlanta Chamber of Commerce had made much of their money in rail, banking, and industrial manufacturing, industries heavily dependent on the stolen land and exploited labor of Indigenous and Black peoples. To maintain their domination in urban politics, business leaders and elected officials worked in concert to maintain close relations with the white working class and often did so by invoking white supremacy. Whether advocating for anti-labor positions that penalized the "fickle" Black worker or the zoning code that ranked and ordered land uses around the separation of races, white business and political elites used many of the tricks of the Old South in the New South state building project.[12]

Racial violence was also a poignant shaper of Atlanta, and none more so than the incidents that took place over four days in September 1906, often referred to as the 1906 race riots. After a false accusation of rape and attempted murder, Black persons were attacked and their homes and businesses were violated and destroyed, with over thirty dead (officially) and hundreds injured or displaced.[13] Racial zoning began in Atlanta in 1913, three years after the first documented case in Baltimore. The racial terrorism of 1906 loomed over the zoning discussions and certainly influenced those who supported the policy.

Zoning and comprehensive plans were late coming to the South, which urbanized later (and less densely) than the Northeast.[14] Racial zoning formally began in Baltimore, was perfected in Virginia and Atlanta, and then was exported across the country through real estate associations, business trade magazines, and planning conferences.[15] It was the bureaucratic implementation of the extra-legal and legal state violence that restricted nonwhite mobility. Prior to a formal racial zoning (as there was no planning body), Atlanta passed an ordinance stating: "It should be unlawful for any colored person to move into any house previously occupied by white people and where white people are still living in housing adjoining the same, without the consent of the white people in said adjoining houses."[16]

Although the city learned from Baltimore's and Richmond's ordinances to include these caveats for white people who purchase homes from Black property owners or that adjoin Black neighbors, this was still not enough to gain support from the Georgia Supreme Court, which struck down the ordinance in 1915. The majority opinion states, "Besides opening the door to numerous frauds, the situation might deny the owner all beneficial use and enjoyment of his property without a hearing and without compensation."[17] Much of the argument's support revolved around a hypothetical situation of a white property owner surrounded by Black property owners. The ironic implication is that this white property owner would be disenfranchised if they had to ask their Black neighbors' permission to sell.

The city revised the ordinance to exempt property purchased before 1917, only for the U.S. Supreme Court to abolish all racial zoning ordinances with the *Buchanan v. Warley* decision, when a white man was denied the "right" to purchase property from a Black property owner.[18] Here, professional planners create an opportunity to become advocates for racial segregation. They advocate for using racial zones (that, by definition, must surveil and track the race of property owners) to allow for the full growth of both races, separately, but equally. Segregation became a land use issue, a way of managing growth and race relations. The technical and bureaucratic language and function of planning became another means to organize cities around racially segregative spatial logics. By 1920, a planning commission soon had local support in Atlanta.[19]

The preservation of private property and property values also garnered support for zoning and a planning commission from the real estate industry. Following the annual convention of the National Association of Real Estate Boards (NAREB) in 1921, the Atlanta Real Estate Board hosted city planning expert Robert Whitten, who had been hired by the city to advise on the zoning plan. The takeaway, according to a local realtor, was "the sooner planning and zoning is started in our city, the sooner depreciation of values to our clients' properties will be stopped, and the sooner will our city collect taxes sufficient for its operation and that there is no necessity for allowing a citizen to build a garage or repair shop between private dwellings or to allow another citizen to put up a shack of a house among high grade apartments."[20]

In the fall of that year, Whitten gave a similar presentation to the Atlanta Chamber of Commerce, reinforcing the importance of converging business interests to advocate for a single set of policies.[21] Opposition to the plan was limited to the property owners who felt the imposition of zoning restrictions and housing codes was "equivalent to a confiscation of value, and is illegal, if not unconstitutional."[22] While NAREB was organizing nationally to appoint members supporting real estate interests to planning commissions and zoning boards, progressive reformers were also advocating for the social benefits of zoning, including the creation of a hierarchy of uses that "resulted in communities in which planned and orderly development provided a specific place for everything, and in which everything was kept in its place. . . . The progressive housing planners set up middle-class values as a societal paradigm . . . which included the desire for homes, order, and family."[23]

And so, the exclusionary politics of planning was created with widespread support. Pro-capitalist and pro-welfare interests converged around the need for a zoning code, at the expense of lower-class, nonwhite, and nonfamily or multifamily households. These convergences would later facilitate the use of New Deal funding and authority to rebuild the New South.

Planning consultants, local business interests, national progressive reformers, and white terrorists were not the only shapers of Atlanta neighborhoods of the early twentieth century. Bartow Elmore writes in a history of the city's water and sewage infrastructure, "segregationists wanted to control blacks' mobility in commercial spaces like movie theatres and train stations, but they also sought to regulate their access to key natural resources. Only by becoming masters of the natural world could they become masters in a world without slaves."[24]

Mastering the city's water and sewage management included running adequate infrastructure through white neighborhoods, while explicitly denying such infrastructure to Black neighborhoods. This mastery also intentionally routed wastewater into these Black communities from the publicly serviced white communities. The racialized sewage system and tainted water supplies in Black neighborhoods perpetuated an even greater danger: water-borne diseases in very dense neighborhoods that were underserved by health-care facilities. The disparity in Black and white tuberculosis rates in the city perpetuated the racist trope of the sickly—and thus indigent—Black dependent in a city clinging to a fading antebellum ideal of a white patrician class.

Water and sewage management also served to justify the early zoning code that ordered the hierarchy of Atlanta's land use through a racialized rubric that equated exclusively white residential communities as the highest and best use. As the city expanded, the quest to access clean water—out of reach of Black contamination and disease—extended into the streetcar suburbs, linking whiteness, status, and water through place-names: Sandy Springs, Springvale Park, and Lithia Springs.[25] The shaping of the New South to the Old South political order allowed for an explicitly racialized hierarchy of land use and space to take place in the Atlanta metropolitan area.

Early in 1920, the Georgia General Assembly passed legislation authorizing a planning commission for Atlanta. This entity had "authority granted . . . to recommend or make suggestions to general counsel and other public authorities covering the laying out, widening, extending or location of streets, sidewalks or boulevards, the relief of traffic conditions, development of housing and sanitary conditions and the establishment of zones or districts, suggestions concerning the use, height, area, and bulk of buildings and structures."[26] As noted from the order of this legislation, the focus of the planning commission was the growth, development, and maintenance of a comprehensive transportation system first and foremost. Shortly thereafter, Atlanta's recreation committee recommended that the mayor "appoint a commission of representative colored citizens to co-operate with the city planning commission in making investigations and recommendations concerning matters affecting the welfare of the negroes."[27]

In September, Mayor James L. Key appointed the six members of the planning commission, with representatives from different sectors of Atlanta's business community. Railroad and transport executives, academics, real estate professionals, and members of the media all held seats on the first planning commission. These sectors continue to represent the longstanding interests of Atlanta's planning politics. Black interests were externalized into an advisory committee, Indigenous representatives were outright excluded, and women—particularly Black women—were also not included. The anti-Black, anti-Indigenous, and anti-feminist planning body that prioritized (white) single-family household land uses, railways, and centralized commercial development (including in areas with Black residents) produced an exclusionary spatial logic in the city.

In February 1922, the city approved the zoning plan submitted by the planning commission. Earlier that month, the plan was endorsed by the Atlanta Real Estate Board and the local chapter of the American Society of Civil Engineers, who recommended committees to attend the city council hearings to advocate for the plan's adoption.[28] Once the antizoning realtors were assured of the forward-looking nature of the zoning code and comprehensive plan, they were happy to mute their resistance to any potential infringement on their existing property values. The original plan called for a radial-sectoral design, following the converging and diagonal tracks of the city's many railroads, that divided Atlanta into residential, commercial, and industrial sectors that radiated outward to accommodate the expected growth of the population.

The plan also called for racial zoning and corrected a potentially unconstitutional misstep from another southern city: "the zoning plan of a southern city had been declared unconstitutional because it was class legislation, prohibiting colored people from entering white sections but allowing white people to enter colored sections. This discrimination was corrected, and the law declared constitutional later on. . . . The Atlanta plan will no more allow a white person to build a home for his own use in a colored zone than it will allow a negro to do it in a white zone."[29]

These discussions around the separation of the races were framed as the natural, biological order of things. Whitten, in defense of his racial zoning, expanded on the residential segregation in an April 1922 interview:

> The zone plan for Atlanta is a logical outcome of that tendency. It subdivides residential districts into three race districts, white, colored and undetermined. No colored family may move into the selected areas reserved for whites; similar in the colored section no house not already occupied by whites may hereafter be thus occupied. Servants' quarters, however, in either case, are permitted to be inhabited by those of the other race if they are on the same lot as the resident of the employer. . . . It is essential in the interest of the public peace, order and security and will promote the welfare and prosperity of both the white and colored races. Care has been taken to prevent discrimination and to provide adequate space for the expansion of the housing areas of each race without encroaching on the areas now occupied by the other. . . . Nothing is to be gained, he thinks, by trying to promote a better mutual acquaintance of different groups by arranging for residential use areas that leave open the erection of home of unlimited variety as to the type of occupation. . . . The Atlanta plan is the first which makes a distinction by type of residents as well as type of residence. . . . It opens up the possibility of new zoning ordinances embodying restrictions against immigrants, or immigrants of certain races, against persons of certain occupations, political or religious affiliation, or modes of life. As such it deserves very serious consideration by all students of city development.[30]

Whitten's defense of racial zoning demonstrates that the need to constrain the expansion and mobility of Black residents was a priority not yet spoken before the plan was unveiled. In spite of the inclusion of the ad hoc advisory commit-

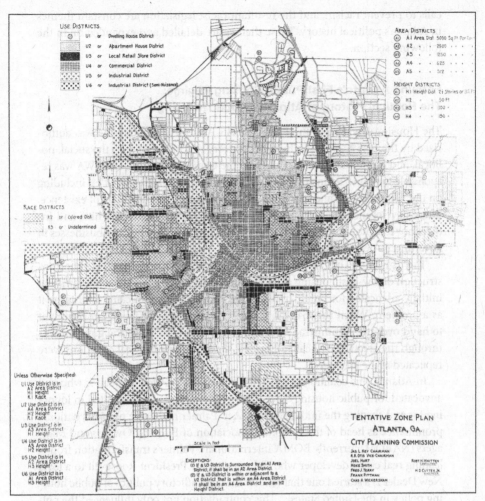

Map 1.2. Whitten's proposed 1922 plan. Source: Edward M. Bassett Papers, Division of Rare and Manuscript Collections, Cornell University Library.

tee on Black welfare, there was little to no consideration of the needs of the Black community. In fact, the approved zoning code appeared to only prioritize the needs of wealthy white business interests that would benefit from an artificially constrained residential market that explicitly tied land use to a racial ordering and hierarchy.

That "care" was taken to "prevent discrimination and provide adequate space" is emblematic of the biracial cooperation and consensus politics that defined Atlanta's Progressive Era. The expulsion of racial interests from the decision-making of resource allocation, the token inclusion of unenforceable calls to prevent racism, and the resultant racist legislation are constant themes in Atlanta's political history. These themes are detailed and expanded on in the following section.

Forming Atlanta's First Public Housing Regime: The Political History of Atlanta's Public Housing

The Housing Division of the Public Works Administration (PWA) was authorized by the 1933 National Industrial Recovery Act in response to the social, political, and economic crises produced by the Great Depression. The PWA was responsible for constructing fifty-one developments in thirty-eight cities, including on the Virgin Islands and in Puerto Rico, during its brief four years of existence. These developments housed nearly twenty-two thousand Black, white, and Indigenous tenants and cleared over twenty-five thousand homes and businesses in government-designated slum areas.[31]

The legislation that authorized both the clearing of the slums and the construction of low-cost housing created a diverse coalition of political interests that initially advocated for public housing as a solution but soon came to critique it as a problem. When the 1937 Housing Act authorized the federal government to hand over the administration of the program to state and local governments through the creation of local authorities, these tenuous political coalitions were replicated at the local level.

In Atlanta, this coalition was headed by Charles F. Palmer, a realtor who had advocated for public housing since the early 1930s and was influential in lobbying for and shaping the initial Housing Act. Palmer had some previous national prominence as head of the National Association of Building Owners and Managers (NABOM, currently BOMA International). Palmer's transformation from a leading real estate developer who did not vote for President Roosevelt to a loyal New Dealer is a storied one that reflects the contradictory politics of public housing policy in the United States.[32] This contradiction not only influenced the politics and policymaking of the design, construction, and operation of Atlanta's public housing developments but likewise shaped the political interests and organizing of its residents.

The advisory coalition that Palmer assembled to estimate the costs of and successfully lobby for a slum clearance and low-cost housing project accurately reflects the type of multi-industry coalition that would later come to define Atlanta's urban regime. Palmer recounts his motivation for doing so in his autobiography: "Promotion and group support were now the problem. Influential help was needed from a cross section of leaders who would understand the long-range benefits to the community. They must represent the views of capital, labor, local government, the press, and the social-service agencies."[33]

The political arrangement that favors this mix of elected, appointed, and civic policymakers is Clarence Stone's urban regime. The longtime focus of Atlanta's politics on growth—often for the sake of growth itself—has always positioned business interests and downtown property owners in places of power. From the pre-Depression loan from the Coca-Cola Company to cover the city's payroll to Coca-Cola president Asa Candler's successful bid for mayor, Atlanta's rail, real estate, and manufacturing leaders have held undue influence on the city's governance.[34] Atlanta's Black business interests and downtown property owners were able to take advantage of the regime, especially after the removal of the white Democratic Party primary in 1946. But even prior to that, in what political scientist Floyd Hunter called the community power structure, Black male leaders and property owners had some access to the regime and decision-makers, although in limited and often segregated or privately integrated forums.[35]

This project's critical approach to urban politics relies on Floyd Hunter's analysis of decision-making and power in early twentieth-century Atlanta and Clarence Stone's analysis of Atlanta's urban regime in the postwar era.[36] Hunter's study of power produced a hierarchical arrangement among Atlanta's business elite, composed of a narrow set of decision-makers at the top, supported by a broad base of professionals who were, in turn, advised by a select (elite) Black community. This pyramid-shaped community power structure effectively concentrated the power of decision-making at the top of the hierarchy, placing the major decisions of Atlanta's planning and policymaking in the hands of forty or so white, privileged businessmen.

While interests among decision-makers may have differed, the ability to influence was limited based on one's position within the hierarchy. Further, while the industries in which these forty men endeavored varied, the race, class, and cultural status (lineage—particularly the number of generations in one's family that were born and raised in Atlanta) remained the same: white, upper class, and long-time southerner. The community power structure theory remains an important framework for urban political analysis in early twentieth-century Atlanta as it captures the imbalance of political power across racial and economic differences.

Hunter's power structure hierarchy also contained an important spatial aspect to the decision-making dynamic. All meetings between the decision-makers at the top of the power structure were held in either their own homes, in private clubs, or in the segregated banquet halls of established hotels. Even the meetings for those in the professional substructure were held in segregated YMCAs, while Black leaders held their meetings in local churches and community centers. Unlike the congenial image of the public town hall that democratic decision-making often evokes, policymaking in postwar Atlanta was spatially segregated.

The spaces of power and decision-making in early twentieth-century Atlanta reflect the spaces of privilege and race in the city. Planning and policy leaders were concentrated in the wealthy, white northern neighborhood of Buckhead.

The professional understructure resided and congregated in the northeast of the city, in all-white enclaves that were less exclusive than Buckhead but nonetheless more exclusive than any address within the city limits. The leaders in the Black understructure resided east of the city center, along Auburn Avenue. The spatial dynamic to the power structure suggests the act of decision-making in postwar Atlanta remained concentrated in the north: in white, privileged spaces under the purview of white, privileged men. The fact that low-income Black neighborhoods were so far removed—both spatially and ideologically—from these spaces of power suggests a lack of political opportunities for this group.

Comparatively, Stone's regime—a governing coalition of decision-makers and an electoral coalition of voters—was composed of formal and informal relationships between porous and changing groups of decision-makers and voters. The porosity of these alliances created a context-dependent relationship between interests that were reliant on one another for progress, while also constrained by this dependence. Further, the multitude and diversity of interests acted as checks and balances for the governing coalition—preventing the complete domination of one group over the actions of the regime. The regime existed to protect privilege as an institution: who or what was privileged at the expense of greater redistribution of city resources was the result of intense struggle within the coalition.[37]

This struggle occurred both within and around the regime, as interests attempt to get into a coalition and, once in, to maintain an influential position within it. The inability of these coalition members to exert influence without the resources of others in the coalition suggests the struggle in power dynamics constrained the actions of the regime. Further, this incapacity to exert change without the coalition's resources suggests how interdependent the members were on one another, unable to exert change in city policy without coalition membership. The regime expanded political opportunities for those outside of the community power structure, a necessity in a growing and urbanizing city.

Academics were also involved in the emerging public housing regime. Dr. Marion L. (M. L.) Brittain, president of the Georgia School of Technology (Georgia Tech) enjoyed a close relationship with Charles F. Palmer. Brittain, with the increasing resources of his school, worked in concert with Palmer to provide early support for the public housing program. Housing studies, social work methods, health-care clinics, and other programs were piloted on the Techwood tenants by the faculty and staff of Georgia Tech, and provided additional means to ensure the success of the politically unpopular program.

Georgia Tech functioned as an anchor institution in that sense—using the ability of a multiscalar institution to attract a variety of funds from different sources (local, state, and federal funding, as well as private and nonprofit donations and grants) to make directed investments in the community where the institution was "anchored" in place. Palmer, in a July 1936 letter to Brittain, thanked Brittain for "devoting so much of [his] time to advice [sic] in connection with the opening of the Techwood Homes" and the following month noted that his "conscience constantly pricks [him] because of absence from the work you all are doing for Techwood right now."[38]

Georgia Tech also used its resources to influence the national public housing program, often obscuring its financial and political interest in the program with the presumed objectivity of an academic institution in pursuit of social science knowledge. In May 1935, Georgia Tech hosted the "Conference on Low Cost Housing," a three-day event covering rural, public, and urban housing problems, policies, and solutions, with particular attention to the recently passed New Deal legislation. On the evening of May 3, future AHA board member Marion Smith chaired the session on public housing, with the program noting the session was "non-technical for the general public."[39]

Maintaining class privilege was a shared goal between the races during this period of public housing policymaking. Both middle- and upper-class Black and white businessmen felt the introduction of public housing—and the clearance of slums that would precede this construction—provided a solution to a number of social and political issues in Atlanta. In framing the public discussion regarding slums adjacent to the Central Business District (CBD), political leaders ascribed societal ills to the slums' environmental and social conditions. The spread of tuberculosis, the lack of industry in the city, the decrease in tax revenue—all of these explicitly political-economic issues were absorbed into the public housing debate. The politics of public housing production in Atlanta simultaneously positioned public housing as the solution to poverty, discrimination, and redistribution.

Once public housing policy shifted toward redeveloping commercial properties and public buildings and spaces in later housing acts, the political interests and regime membership would also shift accordingly, further removing housing and social welfare advocates from the coalition. As housing reformer Catherine Bauer noted, the best thing to come out of the 1937 Housing Act was "the existence of some 500 local housing authorities run by Republicans and Democrats, business, professional and labor men, whites and negroes, and even a few females—all of them with at least some degree of knowledge and concern as to the housing problems of their communities."[40] Even among the local elite interests, the concern and knowledge about community housing problems differed across these stakeholders.

John Hope, the first Black president of Morehouse Bible College (now Morehouse University), first attempted to assemble land parcels for low-cost housing in the nearby Johnsonville neighborhood in 1932.[41] However, money and legal issues in assembling the parcels for the use of a limited-dividend corporation halted this initial attempt to provide affordable housing to the growing Black Atlanta community. The difficulty of land assembly for Black Georgians has a long history in white supremacist terrorism that continues into the present.

Figure 1.2. Two pamphlets: "Cozy Homes for Atlanta's Low Income White Families" and
"Modern Homes for Atlanta's Low Income Negro Families." Source: Atlanta Housing
Authority Archives. Note the differences between Black and white maximum incomes
(lower for Black families) for the same number of family members and the amenities
described in the first left panel of each pamphlet.

As early as 1890, an organized Black business community launched the Georgia Real Estate, Loan, and Trust Company, the first Black-owned land company in the state, out of the shoe shop of J. A. Schell. Schell and twenty-three others pooled together $1,000 in cash and created one hundred shares of stock valued at $10,000 to be sold via subscription books and public shares on the market.[42] There was a "great demand" for this type of enterprise, with returns for white and Black landowners still quite high in rural and urbanizing Georgia. Land assembly, investment, and development were viewed as a necessary step for the Black community's quest for equal citizenship.

Just two years prior, the *New Orleans Times-Democrat* lamented the lack of growth in Black landownership rates since 1860 but noted the race was making progress: "It takes more than one generation, however, to raise a race held in bonds of slavery to the condition of property holders. When the hundreds of millions of dollars paid to the negroes in wages and the millions wasted by them in veriest trash are considered it seems strange that so few dollars have been invested in land, houses, or any permanent property."[43] While white supremacists constructed the Black property-less as deviant and explicitly linked property ownership as part of the progression toward full citizenship, Black elite men organized toward land ownership and property investment as another pillar in their racial uplift politics.

Biracial convergence and consensus around Black land ownership and governance created political opportunities for Black elites to participate in the production and control of space in Atlanta, while white supremacists were able to maintain a strong color line that clearly demarcated the valuable white land uses from the devalued Black land uses. In 1901, Black and white investors purchased two hundred acres of land eight miles east of Atlanta that would have total Black governance. Intended as a governing laboratory, the town "will prove a great step in the advancement of the negro, as it will teach him how to better appreciate law and government and will show white people that he is capable of governing himself."[44]

These experiments in all-Black governance as progressive policy date back to the nineteenth century, when Moses Bentley was drawing up a prospectus to start a "Negro Colony in Georgia" for those who were "industrious and of good character."[45] Based around a town that had been decimated due to a malaria outbreak, the speculator was confident the "miasma has no ill effects upon negroes."[46] In both examples, Black and white support of self-segregation and self-governance for the profit-maximizing goals of property ownership were viewed as New South politics but clearly were Old South tactics reorganized under the new world order. The deviant character of the Black freed person, in need of training for self-sufficiency and governance, was reformed by the white supremacist spatial logics of private property ownership through segregated and racialized land production and ownership. The racial uplift was therefore dependent on the adoption of these spatial logics and politics.

To this point, Atlanta's biracial public housing regime members generated support for the slum clearance and low-cost housing construction program with direct displays of how this program simultaneously maintained the color line and supported the progress of the Black community. During the 1940 construction of the all-Black John Hope Homes, a 606-unit property adjacent to University Homes, articles highlight not only the estimated number of Black residents that would potentially be housed in these segregated areas of the city but also how the design, construction, and operation of these developments was virtually all Black. A full-page photospread of Black skilled tradesmen overseeing the construction of John Hope Homes covered a November issue of the *Atlanta Daily World*.[47] Reporting in Atlanta's non-Black newspapers often described the segregated developments and the populations each served. These open displays of both Black uplift and Black segregation were yet another means of creating convergence within the regime across Black and white elites. Pamphlets advertising public housing for Black and white residents demonstrate the material and ideological differences between the developments (see figure 1.2).

Deviants and the Spatial Fix of Public Housing

Public housing was also designed to address multiple forms of deviance. The clearance of slums, the construction of individual apartments with indoor plumbing and gas appliances, and the construction of water and sewage lines were all meant to address the deviance of slum living conditions. These conditions, often characterized as disorganized, were linked in the popular press and medical journals to high tuberculosis and infant mortality rates. Providing small and large greenspaces, play areas with recreational equipment, swimming pools, community centers, circumscribed pedestrian sidewalks and streets, and streetlights were design features of public housing developments that were intended to reduce crime and juvenile delinquency.

Yet deviance was not just criminal activity, youthful indiscretion, and public health. Race was also a form of deviance, and the approach to public housing differed for white and Black residents. In a 1938 article in the *Atlanta Constitution*, the benefits of public housing for whites, in addition to healthier children and a sense of obligation, include the "establishment of higher standards of housing by tenants in their contacts with real estate men (instead of accepting any apartment or house, as they once did, they now ask what conveniences are offered)."[48] On the contrary, the benefits of public housing—"a Godsend" to the Black community—include "a library, whose attendants are trying hard to interest their readers in some more serious things than fiction," and "a growing tendency on the part of the adults to stay home and enjoy their books and radios at night instead of visiting pool rooms and glorified lodge meetings."[49]

These disparate goals for Black and white public housing residents created different forms of programming within the public housing developments. Assimilating into single-family, homeowning, middle-class norms and "Americanization" were the primary focus of white public housing tenant associations, resulting in patriotic programming organized around the war effort.[50] In Black public housing developments, programming focused on creating and distributing many of the public goods and services not provided at the local level—or the basic benefits of urban citizenship.

The benefits of public housing developments to the Black community extended beyond the individual households and to the wider communities that surrounded them. The article continues to detail the value of the development to the larger area:

> More important to the negro problem in general is the project's value as an example in neighboring negro sections. Susceptible to the power of suggestion, near-by negroes have painted their houses and rebuilt their fences. Flower boxes have appeared on front porches where no flowers bloomed before. Community meetings in the project have drawn crowds from outside, and an educational influence is spreading rapidly. The negro is beginning to realize that if his condition is to be improved, he must help.[51]

In contrast to the white public housing residents, who—as individuals—were becoming better housing consumers and developing a greater sense of civic pride and duty, Black public housing residents were setting examples for the entire race. The apartments and developments would cure individual Black desires to wander and leave the home, stabilizing the deviant, broken family structure produced by disorganized slum life. In turn, these stable households would act as role models for the wider community, awakening a do-for-self civic spirit that would improve the neighborhood's character and property. Public housing for Black residents was not intended to cure the deviance of the slum dweller, or the individual, but the deviance of the entire race, or the Negro Problem.

The views of Blackness as deviance and public housing's role in addressing this deviance were held by both white and Black elites. As historian Karen Ferguson details in *Black Politics in New Deal Atlanta*, uplift ideology was a strategy of gaining full political and economic citizenship for Black people through the lifting up of the masses by the elite. This uplift project was a central organizing feature of Black urban politics at the turn of the twentieth century, a response to the influx of Black rural migrants into urban areas. Ferguson writes, "a key component of uplift ideology emphasized that the 'pathologies' of Black urban life stemmed from African Americans' supposed unpreparedness for the shift from 'peasant' to modern city dweller."[52]

Public housing served as a physical structure that could address the health deficiencies of the migrant, while programming could serve to address the social deficiencies, including classes in etiquette, housekeeping, and political education. In Atlanta, an experiment in 1912 created private tenements using capital from northern investors, in an effort to directly address the disinvestment and overcrowding occurring in Black communities. An advertisement for Atlantan investors took the moral approach that appealed to the patrician leadership: "Good environment stimulates better living. Good homes mean better citizenship for the future. Squalid surroundings encourage abandoned living and crime. The home is the nucleus of the state and the uplift of the one is the preservation of the other."[53]

Black elites were also interested in uplifting Black households into citizenship through improved housing. Historian N. D. B. Connolly calls this spatial dimension of uplift politics "spatial uplift."[54] In Atlanta, the racial project united Black and white elite interests around shared business goals that were cloaked in a false image of racial progress. Miami's Liberty Square, the first Black public housing development to open in the United States, as Connolly describes it, "helped many American and Caribbean colored folk believe in the possibilities of U.S. citizenship, some for the first time."[55]

While the use of Black managers and maintenance workers in public housing "helped give residents and the friends and family of residents hope that colored people could finally expect to achieve greater control over their destinies and their government," these hopes and expectations were limited by the Black elites selected to advise on the project.[56] Connolly notes that "many of the city's more influential middle-class Black folk were deeply in favor of relocating undesirable colored people and putting the state to work in the name of their *own* notions of race progress."[57] These contradictions within the space of the public housing development created political opportunities for those deemed "undesirable."

Connolly finds that Black elites who assembled the land and lobbied for the legislation *also* condemned Black property downtown, excluded the most indigent of Black applicants, and contributed to a resettlement of Black households for the hardening of Jim Crow spatial logics in developing Miami. Jim Crow spatial logics dictate a production of space that organizes land assembly and use by racial logics that conscribe nonwhite populations to the most marginalizing and disinvested areas of the city. These Jim Crow spatial logics prioritized the maintenance of a color line in the production of urban space, legitimizing the highest and best land use for the profit-maximizing real estate developer: the all-white, single-family residential neighborhood.

Through zoning decisions, racial terrorist violence, and legal instruments such as the restrictive deed covenant, Jim Crow spatial logics are probably better defined as *white supremacist spatial logics*, a systemic and entrenched means that organizes spatial production and use to benefit white men and women almost exclusively. The participation in spatial uplift politics fell in line with white supremacist spatial logics, as it privileged segregation and profit maximization for private Black and white investors and perpetuated segregated land uses that inherently marginalized and devalued all-Black communities.

The spatial uplift project was unsuccessful in decoupling deviance from Blackness because it furthered the spatial and political marginalization of an already disenfranchised community. Spatial uplift continued to benefit white and a few Black elites who participated in the decision-making processes. Many Black elites also benefited directly from the construction, legal, management, and financial cottage industry that sustained public housing construction and operations, while later others would indirectly benefit from the spatial containment of racially segregated developments as an electoral strategy post-enfranchisement.

Adhering to white supremacist spatial logics was a simple convergence politic that facilitated land assembly and public goods and service provision in Atlanta's Black communities. The public goods and land uses were often directly tied to Jim Crow and white supremacist productions of space that both isolated and marginalized Black spaces and people. An example of this convergence occurred in 1903, when Black and white philanthropists assembled enough land and capital to build the first reformatory for Black youth in the city.

The *Atlanta Constitution* notes that "the building of the negro reformatory at an early date seems now assured, since the cause of the movement has been espoused by the best element of the colored race and is indorsed [sic] by the leading white citizens.[58] This cause was articulated as: "something must be done in rescuing, from themselves and the community the hundreds of little negroes swarming the streets in certain sections of the city."[59] While Black elites, including W. E. B. Du Bois, financially supported these spatial uplift interventions, the spatial logics that equated Black children to a "swarm" and deemed the Black community that cared for them as "in need of rescuing" only further serve to marginalize Black residents and communities, particularly low-income ones.

Black elites in southern urban politics were not as paternalistic as their white southern counterparts, nor as vocal as their Black northern counterparts. Legalized disenfranchisement, white supremacist terrorism, and delayed urbanization contributed to what C. A. Bacote and others have termed the nadir of Black politics, from roughly 1909 to 1932.[60] While unable to participate in the formal political institutions designed to grant access to power due to the white primary election, Black elites developed other institutions to formalize collective organizing efforts.

The Atlanta Housing Authority

Two years after the opening of Techwood Homes, the Atlanta Housing Authority (AHA) was established through a resolution from the Atlanta Board of Aldermen's Special Housing Committee on May 18, 1938, and was approved by Mayor William Hartsfield on May 27. At the time of the AHA's incorporation, the Georgia Supreme Court was hearing arguments between an Augusta resident and the Augusta Housing Authority about the constitutionality of the housing authority holding dual roles: issuing bonds and acquiring property for clearing slums *and* constructing low-rent housing.[61] Similar arguments were heard in the state supreme courts of New York, North Carolina, Kentucky, Alabama, Louisiana, Pennsylvania, and Florida, all of which granted powers of clearance and construction to local housing authorities.[62]

In Atlanta, Mayor Hartsfield unsurprisingly named Charles Palmer as chairman of the five-member AHA Board of Commissioners. The aldermanic resolution establishing the AHA board included a residency requirement linking board members to sections of the city—one from the southeast, southwest, northeast, and northwest and an at-large member.[63] However apolitical the origins, the policymaking body was geographically diverse (although not representative), suggesting that there should be some spatial equity for decision-making about the federal slum clearance and housing program.

The role and membership composition of the AHA board is one of the earlier formalizations of Clarence Stone's urban regime. The AHA Board was appointed by the mayor and approved by the Board of Aldermen, with staggered five-year unlimited terms that exceeded the four-year limited terms of elected officials. The members of the board from 1938 to 1970 were a rotation of the downtown elite.

Palmer retained his position for two years until he was appointed as the U.S. coordinator of defense housing. Hartsfield appointed Palmer's successor, Marion Smith, son of a former Georgia governor, U.S. senator, and secretary of the interior, Hoke Smith, and himself, an established leader of Atlanta's business and political elite. During Hoke Smith's tenure as governor of Georgia (1907–9, 1911), he established some of Georgia's more regressive Jim Crow legislation, such as literacy and property ownership voting requirements. Hoke also contributed to the hateful environment preceding the 1906 Atlanta Race Riot and campaigned on a platform that used state violence to further disenfranchise and exclude Black residents.[64]

Following Smith's 1947 resignation was the appointment of one of the board's longest-serving chairmen, John O. Chiles.[65] During his twenty-year leadership, Chiles was also the owner of one of the largest real estate firms in the south. The persistent domination of real estate and white supremacist interests within the board created a habitus, or a unified way of thinking independent of board membership, which influenced the board's policies until the early 1970s.

The AHA existed in name only for the first four months. On Thursday, September 22, 1938, the Georgia Supreme Court affirmed the judgment of the Richmond Superior Court, dismissing the petition against the Augusta Housing Authority and city council for overextending its powers by undertaking slum clearance and housing construction.[66] By Saturday, September 24, the AHA board had named Philip Weltner, the former chancellor of the University System of Georgia, as the first executive director of the AHA. Weltner's leadership experience and connections to the state legislature paired well with Palmer's strong local and federal connections.

That day the board also signed contracts with architects to begin designing four new projects, two for white families and two for Black families, one in each quadrant of the city. An estimated $900,000 in bonds were needed to match the $9 million in expected funding from the U.S. Housing Authority. The Sunday newspaper headlines captured the swift action of the AHA leadership: "Slum War Spurred" and "10 Millions Slum Projects Mapped" over photos of Palmer and the architects with furrowed brows, studiously signing contracts.[67]

Atlanta's mayors and the AHA often had a tense relationship depending on the city's coffers. When federal spending was abundant, and the regime was able to shape the downtown with the security of government lending, the AHA was a welcome member of the regime. When federal support weakened, such as the years between the late 1970s through early 1990s, the AHA became a problem that the city was supporting. Due to the political relationships between the (rural) Georgia State Assembly and the (urban) Atlanta Housing Authority, federal intervention to support AHA activities was often met with lawsuits and resistance at the state level. While the existence of the AHA continued to exacerbate state and local tensions in Atlanta, it also provided the multiscalar political opportunities that the city (and its Black residents) would not have had otherwise.

Public Housing Developments as Political Opportunity Structures

Enfranchisement was a major victory for the Black community. However, in the three decades following the 1946 *King v. Chapman* decision, Atlanta's housing market grew more segregated, and the labor market shifted into a bifurcated model of high-skill professionals and low-skill, low-wage workers.[68] Atlanta's poor and disenfranchised Black residents had only token political participation with the vote, yet the "Black vote" was still a powerful resource in a majority-Black city.[69] Atlanta's politically marginalized Black residents required their own political spaces, or a political opportunity structure that would leverage their resources in exchange for alterations to the urban and political environment.

I posit that disenfranchised Black residents used the capacity of their own marginalized spaces, the public housing developments, as political opportunity structures in postwar Atlanta. These political opportunity structures provided the visibility and legitimacy for marginalized Black residents to advance their own political interests. However, the nature of these political opportunity structures made them dependent on the vulnerable or instable political environment.

Elite division, which is captured during the changing racialization of Atlanta's urban regime, provided the best set of political opportunities for deviants.[70] Changes, particularly stabilizations (or agreement) in the political environment, could limit the developments' functioning as political opportunity structures for marginalized groups.

Political opportunity theory is a means of conceptualizing how social movements are able to mobilize resources—including people, funds, and campaigns—to effectively achieve transformative social change.[71] These political opportunities are structured by both internal organizational resources such as leadership and collective consciousness, as well as external resources such as neighborhood institutions and civic capacity. These political opportunity structures thus evolve over time to account for the spatial transformations of resource availability, political stabilizations, and collective consciousnesses. This evolution also structures the success and failure of political opportunities for marginalized groups over time.

Public housing developments functioned as political opportunity structures in postwar Atlanta using the organizational capacity of its tenant associations. The tenant associations allowed the public housing residents to effectively mobilize their resources (such as people and voters, funds, ideas, interests) for political leverage and visibility within the changing political structure. The organizational infrastructure of tenant associations provided access to a large member base (tenant populations ranged from five hundred to five thousand per development), an established structure of solidary incentives (organizational membership as political legitimacy), a communication network (formally, a newsletter or tenant association board meeting minutes; informally, gossip), and residential leadership (see figure 1.3).

Stronger tenant associations evolved from the earlier iterations of the associations from the PWA Housing Division developments, which emphasized leadership qualities to Americanize ethnic, working-class residents with middle-class values.[72] Thus, one would expect the older developments to have stronger memberships, solidary incentives, communication networks, and leadership. The organizational capacity of tenant associations is a key component of the public housing development functioning as a political opportunity structure for disenfranchised Black residents in the city.

The ability for public housing developments to function as political opportunity structures is also the result of the external organizational capacity of people and place-based community development organizations. Public housing developments tend to rely on a wide network of social service organizations to provide social welfare programming for residents. These organizations range from local economic development organizations to nationwide tenant and housing groups. The organizational capacity of these groups is the same as that ascribed to tenant associations in figure 1.3.

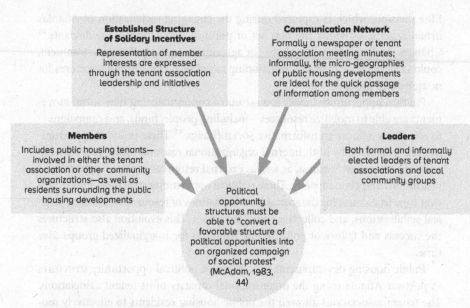

Established Structure of Solidary Incentives

Representation of member interests are expressed through the tenant association leadership and initiatives

Communication Network

Formally a newspaper or tenant association meeting minutes; informally, the micro-geographies of public housing developments are ideal for the quick passage of information among members

Members

Includes public housing tenants—involved in either the tenant association or other community organizations—as well as residents surrounding the public housing developments

Leaders

Both formal and informally elected leaders of tenant associations and local community groups

Political opportunity structures must be able to "convert a favorable structure of political opportunities into an organized campaign of social protest" (McAdam, 1983, 44)

Figure 1.3. Organizational capacity of tenant associations in political opportunity structures.

Tenant association members often had memberships with both local and national organizations—ranging from the local church to the National Association for the Advancement of Colored People (NAACP). Shared membership had the benefit of expanding the scope and magnitude of group demands, while also lessening effectiveness of these demands from intergroup fighting and turf wars—battles concerning which group has the right to make claims on the state. The synergistic effects of shared membership allowed for these groups to mobilize resources both outside and within the developments, enhancing opportunities while also reducing opportunities from the group organizational dynamics that produced the turf wars. The external organizing groups both benefit from and contributed to the public housing development as a political opportunity structure.

The public housing development is uniquely situated in the political landscape to function as a political opportunity structure. As a federally financed, state-legislated, and locally administered program, public housing is a public space that is the responsibility of the government as proscribed by the 1937 Housing Act. Any failure or disparity in the provision, maintenance, or management of this public space is a political decision, an outcome of policy decisions or administration. As a result, the daily lived experiences of most public housing residents are inherently politicized, as their inability to live in housing that meets the standard described in the 1937 Housing Act ("decent, safe, and sanitary housing for families of low-income") is the responsibility of the state.[73]

It is this collective struggle, and collective interest, that characterize the unique political positioning of the public housing development as a political opportunity structure. The spatial consciousness and self-determination of public housing residents are a result of the state's intentional political arrangements and failures.[74] These outcomes produce an inherently political response through residential grievances to and claims on the state, which are actualized as a legitimate everyday politics.[75] Over the course of the program's lifetime in Atlanta, public housing residents would organize in response to the state's failures as landlords, as employers, and later as contractual partners.

Conclusion

Land taking and city building in Atlanta are rooted in a long history of othering, displacement, and spatial marginalization that began with the removal of Indigenous groups from the state of Georgia. This sociospatial process created segregated Black communities in early Atlanta, and racial violence and racial zoning maintained these twentieth-century areas as spaces of marginalization and disinvestment. Political opportunity was limited to elite Black women and men, and segregated political spaces emerged to support Atlanta's community power structure, a pyramid-shaped network of Black and white elites who drove Atlanta's early urban policy.[76]

The New Deal and the PWA created the first shift in Black political opportunity by offering a new space of political power, legitimacy, and assembly through the public housing program and development. The public housing development as a political opportunity structure has evolved from a cooperative extension of the state in the 1930s into one of the last spaces to engage in class-based political activism in the twenty-first-century city. During the early days of public housing, tenant associations were used both as a means of controlling the activities of the less fortunate (providing supervised and limited access to communal meeting rooms, for example, to limit labor organizing) and as a means of shaping the activities of the less fortunate to mimic those of the middle and upper classes (by providing courses in good housekeeping for women and etiquette for teenage girls).[77] Public housing functioned as a state intervention to support working-class employment and develop a middle class through the encouragement of savings and home purchases.[78]

Yet Black political incorporation was not advancing at the same pace across the country, as residents struggled to gain access to local and state governments during the Great Depression. This spatial disparity in Black political incorporation created political opportunities through federal intervention from Roosevelt's kitchen cabinet toward Black communities across the nation. The transfer of political opportunity across scales of governance was a defining characteristic of these new Black political geographies and structured the resource mobilization capabilities of the public housing development as a political opportunity structure.

Tenant associations promoted the tools for lower-class and working-class assimilation into middle-class norms and values. Segregated white tenant associations promoted Americanization via citizenship and language courses.[79] Black tenant associations promoted accommodationist tactics, determined to preserve the patronage benefits of New Deal funding.[80] Black housing managers promoted high standards of cleanliness, work ethic, education, religion, and civic participation among their tenants and staff. They carefully selected tenant association members and organized tenant association activities.[81]

Thus, public housing developments began as top-down political opportunity structures, gaining much of their political opportunity from the federal level, with trickle-down effects emerging following changes at the local level. With stricter standards of public housing tenant selection that favored the two-parent heteronormative nuclear family structure, men, particularly those affiliated with the church, were elected to lead the early Black public housing tenant associations in Atlanta.[82]

In spite of the political opportunities afforded to Black residents through public housing developments, the program also served to reify and perpetuate race and racial differences. The use of public housing developments as a physical "closing off" or "opening up" of neighborhoods from or to Black urban residents in the city is described by Rhonda Y. Williams in Baltimore, N. D. B. Connolly in Miami, John Arena in New Orleans, D. Bradford Hunt and Arnold Hirsch in Chicago, Nicholas Dagan Bloom in New York, Lawrence Vale in Boston, and Larry Keating in Atlanta.[83] Public housing is a thread in the racially segregated fabric of U.S. cities.

The programmatic differences of the tenant associations, as evidenced by their events and newspapers, suggests that Americanization in white developments went beyond language and citizenship classes. Racist op-eds, photographs of racist carnival games, and contests sprinkle the issues of both the *Techwood News* and the *Atlanta Constitution* and *Journal*. While these games and contests are intended to improve citizen morale during the war, public housing advocates relied heavily on these visible displays of patriotism—such as a carnival game that targeted a racialized depiction of a Japanese solider during Word War II—to maintain ongoing political support for the program.

A propaganda tool for the citizenship project, early editions of public housing newspapers are filled with false op-eds from housing managers (who were often the newspaper editors) advocating for ideal residential behaviors. This was true for both Black and white developments. For the *Techwood News*, this often

PIGGLY-WIGGLY SUPER MARKET
376-378-380 TECHWOOD DRIVE
ATLANTA, GA.

August 5, 1940

To Our Techwood Friends:

"Thank You" . . . is ordinarily a poor expression of APPRECIATION . . . however, in our particular case, "thank you," is an expression of our SINCERE EXPRESSION for our GRAND OPENING SALE . . . last Friday and Saturday!

We are grateful to the HUGE CROWDS who attended our OPENING! To those of you not having the opportunity of attending this opening, we extend an invitation to inspect our NEW, MODERN, 1950-Style Piggly Wiggly Super Market! This new store is completely stocked with FRESH GUARANTEED MERCHANDISE, and EVERY ITEM is PRICED as LOW or LOWER! Every Item is SUPER MARKET PRICED! You'll SAVE REAL MONEY on GUARANTEED FOODS!

If it's NEWS in the WORLD of FOODS . . . it's Piggly Wiggly! And our Piggly Wiggly Na-Bor-Hood Super Market has a WELCOME mat at the door for you and your friends! So don't delay . . . start a thrifty, pleasant habit of shopping with us each week!

Cordially yours,

CHARLES D. STANLEY, GROCERY MANAGER

HUGH M. McGARITY, MARKET MANAGER

On the Tennis Courts

The Tennis Sub-Committee of the Committee on Recreation, TTA, will hold a meeting this week, announced as the final meeting for adoption of court rules. The courts are being put in shape, having suffered severe damage from the recent prolonged rains, and some players continue to slip in with heeled shoes, which of course is ruinous to the playing surface. When the rules are adopted the number one rule will be placed in large letters above the present rules board and the other rules will have a protecting cover from the weather. The number one rule will be, we understand, "Regulation tennis shoes, or their equivalent as to heels and soles, are positively required on the playing surface." A registry will be provided for those who play, but there will be no charge for playing.

Welcome, Mr. Dial!

Since July 21st Dr. Ralph Dial has been one of the pharmacists at Baldwin's Drug store. Dr. Dial is a graduate of the Southern College of Pharmacy in Atlanta, and the nephew of Mrs. J. J. Sollar of 467 Techwood Drive. We hope that everyone will drop in the drug store to meet Dr. Dial and make him welcome to Techwood.

Woman's Club Executive Board

The Executive Board of the Techwood Woman's Club met with Mrs. R. F. Moss last Friday. Reports of the different committees were given and it was voted to have no general membership meeting in August. Plans for a fall campaign were discussed and approved. Committee members present were: Mrs. J. G. Thigpen, President; Mrs. John W. Lloyd, Vice President; Mrs. J. L. Kelly, Secretary; Mrs. Charles English, Treasurer; Mrs. Homer Agnew, Mrs. A. G. Sullivan, Mrs. Pat Padgett and Mrs. Moss.

Another Letter from Willie

Editor and People:

Techwood parents should shore feel proud.

Yaw'l know—Willie was sorta saunterin' back towards the office 'tother afternoon, had 'bout four more minits on his lunch hour an' takin' 'vantage of it, (was walkin' up the driveway of cose, sorta short cut you know—) I was just a fixin' to cross Pine St. on account I live on Hunnicutt an' has to head due North to get to the office, when a leetle mite of a fellow 'bout fo' year old stopped me.

"Red lite!" he said, and held out his pudgy hands. I wants to be a good aitisen, so I halted. In due time he said, "Cautin" and then "Green. Now you kin go, Willie." But I dint wannt go—I sorta hung 'roun' watchin'.

Yaw'l won't believe me I kno', but that leetle kid had yore chillen, pert nigh up to fo'teen years old a mindin' him . . . They were really obsarvin' his traffik rules, an' like a real leetle traffik casifer he 'sisted on them a carrin' his orders out.

Well, I got to sorta thinkin', after watchin' for about half hour an' seetin' that leetle fellat orderin' them big kids aroun' that this here safety game was a pretty swell game.

So I thot I'd write this here letter to Mr. F.D.R. on account as this is the fust of these wonderful low cost housin' units, and that this here 'vironment he give'd us has created such a gorjus movmint toward safety. Now I realise that he has all these scrumpshus Nashnul defince consels, and all these billion dollar propeashun bills back of him but I feels that if he wood sorta make this here traffik game a sorta nashnul movmint 'mong all his housin' projects thet he'd have sompin!

I make them statemints on account of—while thet fella Adolf over in 'Urope makes his chillen play wit' toy guns, and our Mr. F.D.R. makes his chillen play safe-ty games—why heck fire, thet's plain ole country sense, our'ns gonna live longer.

God bless America!

Your'n,

Willie, the office boy.

P.S.—Hope the boss don't dock me fer thet extra half hour.

Diamond Ball

The Techwood Cubs, our diamond ball lads, after losing to the E. P. Howell school in their first tilt of the season, turned in a win this week to balance their percentage at .500 for this year. They were somewhat disappointed, however, in having won the game the easy way as they were all set for a glorious triumph over Calhoun School. As it was the Calhouners turned out to be the little boys who weren't there, with the consequent score of 9 to 6 in favor of our side. The line-up follows: Ed. Allen, 2b (Mgr.); Harold Allen, p; Don Hargrove, 1b; Benny Carlton, 3b; Sonny Baldwin, cf; Ben Holmes, lf; Charles Oxford, sf; James Thompson, rf; Bobby Boddie, ss; Charles Witt, c; Bub Tietz, sub; Jerry Parker, sub; Jerry Spier, sub.

In Georgia last year 31 babies died from smothering from bed clothing and overlying by mother.

"GEORGIA'S HEALTH."

Figure 1.4. Undated issue of the *Techwood News.*
Source: Atlanta Housing Authority Archives
Oversized Scrapbook, no. 3 of 4, p. 15.

came under the guise of "Willie the office boy," who would write lengthy letters to the editor advocating for a letter-writing campaign or fundraiser about public housing policy. An example in figure 1.4—written in the linguistically inconsistent style of a white supremacist mocking African American Vernacular English (AAVE)—manages to advocate for a progressive nationalized public safety initiative that would benefit Black and white public housing residents and their wider communities, while also clumsily dropping illogical Black stereotypes about laziness. While the *Tab*, the newspaper for University Homes, was advocating for greater savings in the local credit union and stronger participation in political education courses, the *Techwood News* was sustaining white supremacy through "Willie."

These differences are why the next three chapters focus on the political development of public housing tenant associations for Black residents in Atlanta over the next half century. From 1937 to 1968, legally segregated Black tenant associations fought for social, economic, and political inclusion through the political opportunities afforded by the public housing development. At times, the development produced and sustained radical politics in response to white supremacy, capitalism, patriarchy, and ableism as the range of deviant interests was included in and represented by tenant associations. These divergences of the public housing development, and the political opportunities afforded therein, were temporary appropriations of the space intended to function as a pass-through for a submerged middle class.

Chapter 2

University Homes

The Spatial Uplift of a Deviant Slum

University Homes, Atlanta's first approved public housing development and the first Black public housing development built in the city, was conceived of at a time when Black residents were unable to fully participate in Georgia's elections. The white Democratic Party primary—a common tool of the South for privatizing political parties in order to legally bar nonwhite residents from participating in state primaries—was legal in Georgia from 1892 to 1946. It disenfranchised nearly one million Georgians, and, unsurprisingly, this lack of direct electoral representation led to Black communities that were disinvested, underserved, and vulnerable. Politically and spatially, Black residents were deviants, unable to participate and marginalized to the least desirable areas of the city, in part from legal and extralegal violence by the white community.

The inability to vote severely curtailed the availability of political space for Black citizens in Atlanta, particularly for low-income and otherwise marginalized city residents. Consequently, conservative Black and liberal white elites firmly controlled the public spaces for Black political debate and critique, as their social and economic status provided them with the greatest legitimacy and ability to access these spaces. The most popular—or highly utilized—spaces for Black political debate were publications (the *Atlanta Daily World*, or *ADW*, was the leading Black publication), community and political organizations (ranging from established churches to the NAACP), fraternal organizations, and women's clubs.

Political scientist Adolph Reed Jr. states, "disenfranchisement raised the cost of popular participation by eliminating the most accessible forms of political speech—voting and other aspects of electoral action."[1] The legal disenfranchisement of Black voters from Atlanta's influential Democratic Party primary removed an accessible political space, particularly for non-elite Black residents. Further, until 1946, the conservative and accommodating Black elite restricted community political discourse in the city to spaces under their ownership and control.

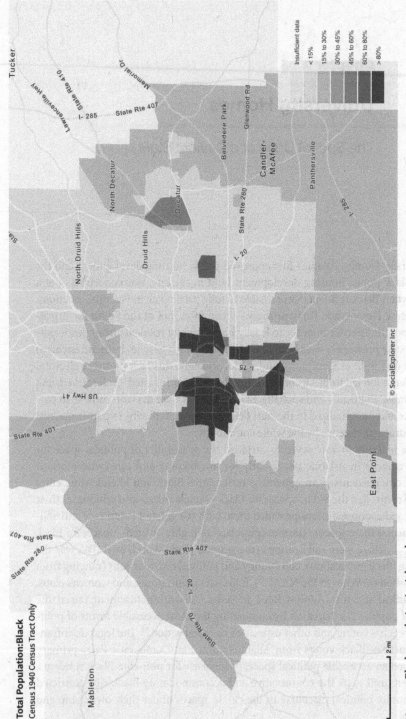

Total Population: Black
Census 1940 Census Tract Only

Insufficient data
< 15%
15% to 30%
30% to 45%
45% to 60%
60% to 80%
> 80%

© SocialExplorer Inc

Map 2.1. Black population in Atlanta by census tract, 1940.
Source: U.S. Census Bureau, Social Explorer.

This chapter discusses how in the years leading up to the postwar era, elite Black Atlantans were able to mobilize resources of both human and economic capital to make impressive political gains in terms of representation and control. Notwithstanding these political achievements, the changing political environment simultaneously constrained working-class and working-poor Black political actions, mobilization, and spaces in new ways. The construction and planning of University Homes demonstrates the growing political power of Black elites, and how this power shaped political opportunity for working-class and working-poor Black residents in Atlanta.

Black Political Spaces

Despite the constraints of Black political spaces in postwar Atlanta, historically, non-accommodationist interests were able to participate and mobilize politically at the local level.[2] After the Great Depression, the growth of interracial labor organizations and groups committed to communist efforts presented opportunities for Black political participation at the local, state, and national levels. Interracial, class-based organizing remained an alternative venue for Black political participation, even if the organizing principle was not explicitly oriented toward the improvement of the race's social, economic, or political standing.[3] However, the domination by white supremacist interests in Atlanta's prewar governing coalition (in both elected positions and positions of enforcement, i.e., the police) suppressed pro-labor political expression and legitimacy.

While interracial labor organizations were attacked with equal aplomb, white supremacist organizations—with the support of the Ku Klux Klan–dominated Atlanta police force—targeted organized Black laborers. As white unemployment rose in the 1930s, white Atlantans organized to suppress Black employment in the city. The Order of the Black Shirts, a white supremacist group formed to intimidate Black employees and the firms that employed them, freely terrorized Black laborers as the police department and local government turned a blind eye.[4] The violence of the Black Shirts against Black union members and pro-communist activists increased the cost of working-class Black political participation in interracial labor unions. This political environment of white terrorism in prewar Atlanta produced few productive spaces for Black political action.

At the time of the planning and design of University Homes, Atlanta's Black political participation was at its "nadir," according to esteemed Black political scientist C. A. Bacote.[5] The nadir's origins reach back to 1892, when the Georgia Democratic Party Executive Committee, as a private political organization, adopted a whites-only primary. This restriction prohibited Black voters from participating in the influential Democratic primaries for municipal and state offices. The end of Reconstruction meant the end of federal protections supported by the Military Reconstruction Act of 1867. For about a decade, federal troops provided some level of protection against white terrorist violence during the initial years of Black male emancipation and enfranchisement. Black voters immediately demonstrated their power and legitimacy in urban governance. In 1870, two Black Republicans were elected to the city council to represent Atlanta's third and fourth Wards.

By 1890, there were two Black members on the powerful citywide Democratic committee, which was now splintered in factions. The populist movement increased in representation as national issues of the unstable economy and temperance movement dominated urban politics.[6] The fractured Democratic Party divided (and devalued) the Black vote, while waning support from the federal level curtailed the strength of the local Republican Party in the post-Reconstruction South. Black resistance to white supremacist political alliances was limited. White Democrats and Populists rallied to support the white primary in 1892, and again in 1897 after it was temporarily repealed in 1895.

The white Democratic primary had the dual purposes of consolidating white political power while also redefining the social construct of race in the postbellum South. In the years following the end of the Civil War, white and Black residents grappled with new social and political dynamics in the southern urban political economy. The election of Black candidates William Finch and George Graham to the city council in 1870 demonstrated the power of a harnessed and targeted Black vote. This powerful political force continued to support the Republican candidates in local elections until the withdrawal of federal troops that marked Reconstruction's end in 1877.

White political elites feared the potential of Black population majorities taking control of southern legislatures, and they utilized a number of political, economic, social, and cultural tactics to promote and maintain white supremacy. The growing power of this new Black voting bloc was quickly curtailed by the diffusion of white supremacist laws across southern states. Georgia's transformation into a one-party state post-Reconstruction through the physical removal of the Republican Party and the electoral removal of the Populist Party virtually stripped Black voters of all electoral power until the 1946 *King v. Chapman* decision declaring the state's white Democratic primary unconstitutional. The legacy of the white primary was the ability of white southerners to consolidate their political power around the social construct of race, while relegating Black southerners to virtually the same political and social rights they had during bondage.

Despite this second-class citizenship, Black residents were as politically active as possible during the period of Bacote's political nadir.[7] Although Black Atlantans could not vote in primaries, they were permitted to vote in general and special elections and redefined their citizenship through this political action. In 1921, a $4 million bond issue was on the general election ballot to construct new schools for Atlanta's white children (there was always difficulty finding money and land for the construction of Black schools). Black voters organized both reg-

I STAND
ON MY
RECORD

YOUR SUPPORT
WILL BE
APPRECIATED

WM. B. HARTSFIELD

RE-ELECT

WM. B. HARTSFIELD

MAYOR OF ATLANTA

WHITE PRIMARY, SEPTEMBER 5, 1945

VALUABLE EXPÉRIENCE · PROVEN ABILITY

Figure 2.1. White primary postcard for William B. Hartsfield, September 1945. Source: William Berry Hartsfield Papers, Stuart A. Rose Manuscript, Archives, and Rare Book Library, Emory University.

istration drives and voter education drives to reject the bond issue twice.[8] When the bond issue finally passed on the third try, $1.25 million was allocated to the construction of schools for Black children. With this repetitive and focused political action, Black residents redefined their citizenship through cohesive electoral participation.

Using electoral participation exclusively to redefine racial status and citizenship had its limits as a sustainable strategy.[9] As free Black citizens struggled with whites over political, economic, and social power in the postbellum period, white supremacy as an overruling ideology was enforced outside of a legislative structure. Legal and extralegal violence permeated all facets of postbellum Black southern life, and urban race relations were often framed by the degree state-sanctioned violence was tolerated in the open against Black people. Cities perceived as having good race relations had little visible violence against Black residents, while those with poor race relations had significant visible violence against Black communities.

Feminist political theorist Iris Marion Young noted that violence as a form as oppression is systemic and is often used as one of many tools of the dominant group to keep another group subjugated.[10] Violence in the post-Reconstruction South was a tool to support a white supremacist political, economic, and social structure that marginalized Black life. An example of this is an editorial published in the *Atlanta Constitution* in the months following the 1906 race riot. The editorial, titled "A Negro's Protest," implicitly and explicitly threatens Black Atlantans against "heartily protesting against the false and incendiary advice proffered by their misguided alleged friends at the north, knowing that it only confuses and further complicates the issue."[11]

I frame the actions of Black men and women during the planning, construction, and management of the University Homes developments as a new political strategy to gain local control through spatial production and as a means to complicate the nadir narrative. Black Atlantans bypassed the white supremacist local and state power structure that oppressed Black political interests with legal disenfranchisement (the whites-only primary) and state-sanctioned violence (unequal protection of Black residents and enforcement of laws by all-white local police forces) by accessing the federally supported New Deal resources.[12] Although Bacote claims that Black political action was at its nadir during the 1930s in Atlanta, by readjusting the scale where local Black voters gained political power, we see the Black elite who comprised the local advisory committee for University Homes were quite engaged and active and acquired political legitimacy for Black residents in the city. This political capital structured political opportunities by providing residents access to federal benefits and space to pilot social welfare programs over the next half century.[13]

University Homes: Planning and Design

Morehouse College president John Hope's pre–New Deal attempts to create quality, low-income rental housing near his campus failed due to the administrative and legal difficulty of assembling large tracts of land in Atlanta's racialized real estate market. Atlanta's exclusionary and unstable urban planning administration that funneled resources to all-white neighborhoods and redirected waste from this resource provision into overcrowded Black neighborhoods contributed to this racially disparate real estate market. Hope's Corporation for Improvement of Negro Housing (CNH) advocated for a planning and development process that would lessen the barriers to Black land assembly and real estate development. The CNH hoped to take advantage of the federal loans offered to limited-dividend corporations building subsidized housing.

In the "Planning and Related Data" section of an early development proposal, four points articulate these racial land politics:

(a) The project is an attempt to meet the housing problem of the negro and it is contemplated that an enlargement of the development will be made on adjacent properties or in the other sections of the city.

(b) There is a planning board in the city and while this plan has not been submitted officially due to the necessity of maintaining secrecy until all

   properties are acquired, it has been reviewed by members of the Board
   and they have pledged their support.
   (c) It is in harmony with any plan of metropolitan development
   (d) It has the support of the community and it is contemplated that the equity
   will accrue to the Negro colleges.[14]

Secret land assembly—often leading to higher prices with greater transaction
costs—was one of the direct costs of Atlanta's racialized urban planning. Increasing Black populations—and expanding Black geographies—remained a
threat to white elites as long as spatial dispersion was linked to greater political
representation.

In addition to its role in limiting Black enfranchisement, legal and extralegal white supremacist violence constrained Black residents to the same handful
of neighborhoods such as Summerhill and Darktown in the years following the
1906 Atlanta Race Riot (see map 2.2). Civic associations, neighborhood groups,
and citizen associations were just some of the euphemisms for white residents
to formally organize against expanding Black geographies.[15] These groups often
incorporated, created charters, elected board members, and collected dues as a
means of institutionalizing white supremacy and violence against Black mobility.

In the months after the secret plan for CNH's University Homes was made
public, the president of the Garden Hills Corporation civic association, Phillips
Campbell (P. C.) McDuffie, sent an enumerated list and petition to Dr. Robert D.
Kohn, the director of housing at the Atlanta Public Works Administration. Mc-
Duffie, who also served as president of the Guaranty Mortgage Company and
chairman of the Atlanta Committee on Slum Clearance and Low-Cost Housing,
wrote that he was not against public housing in Black and white areas in general,
but merely the specific areas that were currently receiving federal funding. Particularly, he was against development in the "Spellman [sic] area" because it is "on
the whole much superior to the average negro community in this City."[16] Further,
he asserted, "apartment houses have not heretofore seemed to be desired in this
community."[17]

McDuffie asked Dr. Kohn to reconsider both Techwood and University
Homes projects in favor of projects in Darktown and the area surrounding the
state capitol building. Both of these areas were located in the Central Business
District (CBD) and would most certainly benefit downtown (white) business interests. Darktown ran along Auburn Avenue, the main thoroughfare of the Black
business district, but was also adjacent to the white business district. Unlike other
in-town Black communities such as Vine City and Beaver Slide, railroad tracks
did not physically divide Darktown from the CBD and white districts.[18] McDuffie's request was a direct plea to create hardened boundaries of racial segregation
in the city through slum clearance and the siting of subsidized housing.

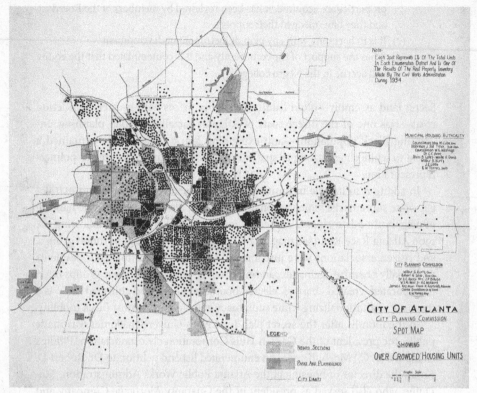

Map 2.2. Spot map showing overcrowded housing units and Negro sections, 1934.
Source: Planning Atlanta City Planning Maps Collection, Georgia State University
Library.

In his letter, McDuffie invoked the white supremacist spatial logics that
equated concentrated residences—particularly concentrated Black residences—
as spaces of vice, deviance, crime, and immorality. Darktown, in its three-square
blocks, had "a population of one thousand negro families. . . . The houses very
nearly cover the lots on which erected, leaving no open spaces for gardens or
playgrounds. No other section has given law enforcement officers so much trouble. For twenty years it has been a breeding place of disease and crime."[19] That
these one thousand families were confined to three-square blocks adjacent to
downtown is written as if the households had the choice and mobility of similarly situated white families. That these one thousand families were squeezed into
these three-square blocks is stated without the context of the 1906 race riot that
left many Black residents dead and made Black spatial isolation risky. McDuffie,
in his assessment of the housing needs of Darktown, invokes the spatial practice
of slum clearance as a social control for individual Black deviance and collective
community disorganization.

To underscore his points on morals and wholesomeness, McDuffie pointed to the support of Atlanta's white women groups for the petition as proof that morality, not capital, underscored the need for federal funding to demolish Darktown: "Certain woman's organizations of this City have made the objection (whether a valid one or not, I do not venture an opinion) that if low cost apartments are constructed in this area [Techwood], many persons of doubtful reputation may gain admittance to the apartments whose presence would be demoralizing to the students of the Institute [Georgia Tech]."[20] The petition was signed by representatives from the following Atlanta civic and political organizations: the Atlanta League of Woman Voters, Atlanta's Board of Education, the Association for the Grand Jurors of Fulton County, the Woman's Democratic Club, the Atlanta Apartment House Owners Commission, the Civic Improvement Committee, the Atlanta's Woman's Club, the Atlanta Woman's Civic Council, the fifth district of the General Federation of Women's Clubs, and the Fulton Loyal League Volunteers.[21]

The organization and mobilization of these seemingly disparate interests against Techwood and University Homes provides yet another example of the forms of political opportunity afforded by public housing policies. Women's groups, civic associations, educators, and private developers were all able to converge around the interest of upholding white supremacy through control of the city's spatial production and the spread of spatial equalizers such as public housing. Black feminist theorists have long linked the perpetuation of white supremacist capitalist patriarchy through the upholding of white feminine morality.

The assistant director of housing for the Federal Emergency Administration of Public Works, Charles E. Pynchon, forwarded the letter and petition to John Hope to provide him a chance to respond. In his letter of February 6, 1934, Hope highlights the other form of political opportunity that can emerge from public housing policy: "It seems to me that for present advantage and for guaranteed future advantage no Negro neighborhood in America is quite so promising for a Negro housing project as the one in the neighborhood of Atlanta University."[22] Hope believed that the spatial proximity to the predominantly Black-occupied (and partially Black-controlled) institutions of higher education, philanthropy, and religion could produce an outcome of Black progress and advancement that complied with the uplift political ideology held by many of the Black elite.

This spatial uplift strategy meant that University Homes could provide a permanent space of Black progress in the community that extended beyond existing institutions and could serve as a means of promulgating Black political, economic, and social power. Similar to early arguments in favor of public housing emphasizing the ability to "Americanize" ethnic working-class families into white middle-class citizens, public housing served as a laboratory for Black elites to uplift Black working-poor and working-class communities.[23] While the rationale underlying these early public housing policies was paternalistic, top-down, and focused entirely too much on behavioral and cultural trainings, these politics did produce a space that countered the white supremacist spatial logics and supported Black agency and control.

Creating a Black spatial politics in 1930s Atlanta was an ongoing challenge for the Black elite. In Hope's letter to Dr. Kohn, he focused explicitly on the spatial proximity to Black institutions and organizations that could provide uplift to future tenants of University Homes. He claims: "Spelman College, Morehouse College, Morris Brown College, Atlanta University, and the Atlanta School of Social Work; and four of the better Negro public schools of Atlanta are in this section, one of which, the Booker T. Washington School, has an enrolment of 2,954 pupils. . . . I do not believe in the entire South as far as present and future are concerned there is a better place to make an experiment in Negro housing."[24] Hope and other Black elites in Atlanta were directly challenging the dominant spatial norms that racialized land into productive (white) and unproductive (nonwhite) spaces. And they made sure to share these strategies with other groups across the country.

In March 1934, John Hope received a letter from the Colored Civic and Improvement League of Montgomery, Alabama, about the racial makeup of the local advisory committee for the new public housing project. Secretary C. W. Lee, who later served as treasurer of the Montgomery Improvement Association that would lead the yearlong bus boycott in 1956, wrote: "Can you advise if the government's requirement in connection with this movement provides for the local supervising board to have Negroes thereon? We raise these questions because our local city government is undertaking to sponsor a similar project to the one now in process of construction in your city, but no official Negro representation is contemplated on the official board, notwithstanding, the project is to be an entirely Negro project for Montgomery."[25]

The response from Florence M. Read, the white president of Spelman College and secretary of the University Homes advisory committee, who was answering correspondence for John Hope in his absence, was swift and direct. It highlighted the political urgency of public housing policy and the need for Black progressives to seize this opportunity for local power and control:

> As I understand the matter, the procedure for construction and management has not yet been finally determined by the Government. There has always been included in the plan, however a representation of Negroes in the advisory committee or board and there has been assurance given to us by the men in the Housing Division that Negroes would receive fair consideration in connection with employment on the job. . . . I think by all means there should be Negroes on the local board. If you wish to raise the question with the Government, I would suggest that you write directly to Mr. Robert D. Kohn.[26]

Read, a white Mount Holyoke alumna, served as president of Spelman College from 1927 to 1953.[27] In her tenure as Spelman's president, Read worked

Figure 2.2. John Hope, undated. Source: *Atlanta University Photograph Collection*, Robert W. Woodruff Library, Atlanta University Center Consortium.

as a vital middleperson between the Black and white power structures in Atlanta.[28] Inherent in, but often understudied, the white middlepersons that linked Atlanta's segregated racial political structure fostered inclusion of Black decision-makers while also propagating white supremacist practices of power and legitimacy.

However, in her role on the advisory committee, Read provided a great deal of practicality and humanity when structuring the first federally financed public housing program for Black residents. Read often advocated for housing policies that provided economic allowances for women, nontraditional family structures, and other groups most susceptible to the structural causes of poverty and discrimination. An adept politician, Read was able to fight for these marginalized groups while navigating the raced and gendered political environments of Washington, D.C., and Atlanta.[29]

Between May and December of 1934, Lugenia Burns Hope, John Hope, and Dr. Clark Foreman exchanged correspondence about the hiring of Black laborers during the construction of University and Techwood Homes, as well as designing spaces within the housing development that could be of economic use for its residents. Foreman, the grandson of *Atlanta Constitution* founder Evan Howell and former member of Atlanta's Commission on Interracial Cooperation (CIC), was the adviser on the economic status of Negroes for the PWA.

Foreman was raised in a southern bourgeois family. Several events during his time as a student, such as witnessing a lynching in Athens as an undergraduate at the University of Georgia, attending an integrated dinner with W. E. B. Du Bois as a student at Harvard, and reading about the CIC as a graduate student in London, steered him toward a lifetime of racially progressive causes. During his time on the CIC, Foreman became aware of the charitable works of Lugenia Burns Hope's organization, the Neighborhood Union.

Foreman's ideologies wavered between providing equal opportunity to Black residents and providing political opportunity for Black residents, with the former motivating his correspondence with Lugenia Hope in January 1934: "It seems that there is a possibility of including, in the government housing projects, facilities for improving the economic condition of the inhabitants. . . . The kind of project which could be included is a laundry, where the women could not only do their own clothes but do, in a sanitary way, the clothes which they may wish to do for other people. . . . Also, a carpenter shop, bake shop, and sewing room could be included."[30]

John Hope, in response to inquiries from not just Foreman but from other white elites about the needs and capacities of the Beaver Slide community currently occupying the space of the future University Homes development, commissioned a study by W. E. B. Du Bois and six of his Atlanta University graduate students. Du Bois's study is comparable to the modern existing condition studies used in urban planning, but with an added qualitative element of interviews. In this early example of Black urban sociology, Du Bois and his team conducted a survey of 315 residences and businesses during the week of May 4–10, 1934.

The survey noted the householders' composition, size, and occupations, number of rooms in the home, amount of rent paid weekly, amount of income earned weekly, length of time at current residence, and residential plans during the construction of University Homes. The research team also recorded the number of rooms needed in the new development for each household, along with the estimated weekly rent each household could afford to pay in the new apartments. Researchers also conducted interviews with residents, and several quotes appear to contextualize the quantitative data analyses.[31]

Of the 315 surveys, 247 were completed by Black families, 1 by a white family, 67 recorded vacant residences, and 6 were completed by local business owners. Finally, the study documents the name, address, condition ("Character"), and race of the owners for the 29 businesses within the University Homes federal project area.[32] In sum, this study's method and findings challenge the status quo of white supremacist spatial logics that consider Black communities as deviant, disorganized, or unproductive spaces.

The first page of the report refutes the notion that the Black slum is a product of individual deviance, vice, and laziness. Challenging the dominant racial science thinking, Du Bois worked to decouple the structural positioning of Black residents from their phenotypical features and cultural expression. Du Bois writes, "It is a slum area because of the poverty, and not by reason of vice or crime."[33] Here, an almost radical Du Bois turns away from conventional social science frameworks that equated spatial disorganization with social disorganization and immorality.

The characteristics of the slum that were visible in the University Homes study area (e.g., some gambling and drinking, some numbers, old and dilapidated housing stock, little green space, and commercial activity) were more a reflection of the intermittent and artificially devalued wages of the Black working-class community during the Great Depression. Further, Du Bois noted that there were comparatively few lodgers, and that most families were "normal."[34] The spatial disorganization of the neighborhood did not emerge from, nor did it contribute to, the social disorganization of the Black household.

The study also reflects some of the early tensions of the public housing program, namely the social, economic, and political disparity between those who lived in the space before and after the slum clearance and public housing construction. From a social aspect, the residents of the University Homes study area had more in common with a submerged working class than a submerged middle class. Most of the men were unskilled to semiskilled day laborers, and most of the women were washwomen and servants.

Of the 255 surveyed men who were over the age of fifteen, nearly 46 percent (116) were unemployed, and only 3 percent (8) could be classified as a skilled laborer or professional. Similarly, of the 357 women over the age of fifteen surveyed, over 47 percent (153) were unemployed at the time of the survey. Excluding the sole schoolteacher, none of the women could be classified as a member of the submerged middle class, the target population for Hope's spatial uplift experiment.

Economically, the households in the University Homes study area reflected the unstable and cyclical income of the average Great Depression–era Black household. Du Bois notes, after his summary of weekly incomes by household size: "In many cases, this present income lasts only part of the year. In some cases, this income for part of the year is small. In other cases, the weekly income is large, because of the temporary character of the service. This statement of income is, therefore, in some respects an overstatement. . . . The usual tendency to overstate the actual income is balanced in the present crisis by the widespread knowledge that most people are suffering, and by the hope that some aid may be forthcoming."[35] At the time of the study, roughly 30 percent of the households were on public relief or had no income at all. Another 30 percent of the households

Table 2.1. Literacy populations and rates for persons over 10 years of age, by county and race, 1930 decennial census

	DeKalb County	Fulton County	Total
White literate population	45,939	177,024	222,963
(rate)	(98.8%)	(98.8%)	(98.8%)
Black literate population	7,371	74,762	82,133
(rate)	(78.0%)	(89.1%)	(87.9%)

were earning over $12 weekly, for an annual median income of $600 to $1,300 for a household of two to five people. The data shows a wide disparity and clustering between the two ranges of incomes (the 30 percent without any source of income and the 30 percent who were comfortably working class at the time), and the high rent burden, or portion of income spent on rent, for those in the former cluster. The report's findings suggest that Hope and Du Bois accurately understood the connection between the lack of stable, safe, and sanitary housing options for Black Atlantans and the lack of a stable labor market for Black workers.

High unemployment rates were not directly tied to low skills and educational attainment but more likely were the result of racial employment discrimination that marginalized Black workers into semiskilled and unskilled labor markets. While the literacy rates of Black Atlantans lagged those of white Atlantans (see table 2.1), there was a surge in literate Black residents who began settling in Atlanta during the second decade of the Great Migration. Despite the misgivings of the Black elite that Black migrants were poor, uncultured, and in need of uplift, this migration (like most migrations) was only increasing the skill, wage, and economic diversity in receiving communities.

In spite of the mismatch between current residents and future housing options, Hope and Du Bois solicited letters and funds from local educational, philanthropic, and religious institutions to support the case that the Beaver Slide area was the best place to sustain the development's larger social goals. Through the provision of steady employment, nontraditional education for nontraditional students, and social and political spaces for the community to meet, the public housing development could function as a new redistributor of resources and power for the Black community. Middle-class and elite Black residents benefited the most from this arrangement—whether through their involvement with the planning, construction, and administration of the developments or their preferred status in the application process. Overall, public housing was an important first step to countering the white supremacist spatial logics that had long dominated the construction of Black space, place, and opportunity in Atlanta.

Figure 2.3. Aerial view of John Hope Homes during construction, 1939.
Source: Aerial view of Atlanta, University and partially completed
John Hope homes, 1939—Atlanta History Center.

Galvanizing Support in the Local Community

The eight members of the University Homes local advisory committee were
tasked with building support at the local level; however, two of the eight committee members resided in New York and Washington, D.C., and none of the committee members resided in the Beaver Slide neighborhood that was demolished
for the construction of University Homes.[36] These committee members all had a
vested interest in the public housing development, and eradicating the slums that
preceded it, as they were all affiliated with the surrounding historically Black colleges and universities (HBCUs) in Atlanta. From the outset, the working-poor
Black residents who resided in the Beaver Slide community prior to the slum
clearance, and the working-class Black Atlantans who would reside in University
Homes after its construction were virtually excluded from the planning and policymaking processes.[37]

After the untimely death of John Hope in 1936, Spelman president Florence M. Read was named as interim chairperson of the local advisory committee. As committee chairperson, Read took her leadership responsibilities seriously, organizing, running, and taking the minutes of each of the biweekly committee meetings. On March 23, 1936, in the Administrative Building at Atlanta University, Read convened the local advisory committee to discuss the candidates for the housing manager position.[38] Examining the meeting minutes from these committee gatherings is helpful in understanding the power dynamics of the biracial coalition. Local knowledge of the limited resources of the Black community was important, yet white supremacist ideologies of Black inferiority and corruption were also shaping these discussions.

The two candidates for the job were Alonzo Moron and Albert W. Dent.[39] Dent was preferred to Moron, as Dent was from Atlanta and had returned after an unsuccessful foray into Houston's real estate market in the 1920s. In 1931, Dent returned to Atlanta to work as alumnus secretary for Morehouse College, thereby developing a close relationship with the late advisory chair John Hope.[40] White committee member Kendall Weisiger suggested the development hire both men, an option that Read thought Secretary Ickes and the Housing Division staff would consider:

> I think that is one thing they have been working on up there, they told me. If through employing two pretty high-class men—I talked with the acting head of the management division about this—you could get more resources that wouldn't cost you anything in other ways, it would merit it. If we make use of the University resources, it's going to need somebody to coordinate them with the community. Take the things that students might do in their leadership—dramatics, and music, and in the nursery school even, the whole range of activities might come from the University. It is going to take somebody there.[41]

Read and the other committee members understood that in order to maximize the resources available from the New Deal, there would have to be strong local involvement to coordinate and mobilize these resources at the local level. Moron had the stronger background and qualifications (he was a trained social worker), but Dent was favored among committee members for his local ties. According to white committee member Eugene Martin (executive at the Atlanta Life Insurance Company): "Between the two, I think Mr. Dent would be the better man from a civic standpoint. Moron is not an Atlantan and Dent is. So far as getting cooperation, that has some bearing. I do not mean that a person from out of the city could not get cooperation. Moron's home is the Virgin Islands. At least he was born there; I guess he spent most of his life here. Mr. Dent would be able to get more cooperation from the city at large, of doctors, etc., than someone out of the city.[42] Despite these discussions favoring Dent, Moron was offered, and accepted, the job.

"Cooperation" with existing resources in the city required both intimate knowledge of the local scene and the proper social background (a middle- or upper-class Black man with a college education, preferably with an advanced degree). It was a code word for not troubling the racial order established following the 1906 race riots, by making demands of white elites. The push from the advisory committee for someone who could facilitate cooperation was consistent with the use of uplift ideology, both within and around the University Homes development. Federal resources as political opportunity were still structured by the local biases administering these political opportunities.

The same March meeting continued with discussion of the development's construction activities.[43] The committee members discussed the difficulty a group of Black painters had in organizing as a legal trade union.[44] Black painters were denied incorporation papers by Fulton County administrative departments, in addition to experiencing racial discrimination and violence from white building trade unions. The two groups (union workers and bureaucrats) worked in concert across class lines to promote and maintain the difference between white and Black work. These acts of civil disobedience within the southern white supremacist power structure sustained the marginalization of Black citizens by snubbing federal legislation and privileging local and state interests. Without full enfranchisement, southern Black residents had little recourse to these open acts of local and state defiance.

Florence Read and the committee, however, were using the new federal relationship and the visibility of University Homes to suppress this civil disobedience and begin redefining the racial politics in the South. Read had taken it upon herself to visit national labor heads when she was in Washington, D.C., in an effort to get the Black painters unionized.[45] Her efforts were stymied as local unions in Atlanta accused one Black painter of having communist affiliation. Communist accusations took on new meaning after the conviction of Black labor organizer Angelo Herndon in 1932, who was charged with organizing Black and white laborers and leading an insurrection against the state.[46] However, Read remained optimistic that the Black painters would triumph in the union battle, increasing the already impressive number of Black laborers working on the project. Per Read, two-thirds of the plasterers were Black workers, as were one-third of the brick masons.[47]

Black men and white women advisory members were critical to incorporating the Black lived experience into local housing policy. In January 1937, the advisory committee (and the recently hired Moron) met with the district supervisor for University and Techwood Homes, and a PWA Housing Division staff member.[48] The committee was meeting to set rental rates for the 675 units in University Homes, which would in turn set the federal minimum and maximum income limits for the development. Table 2.2 shows the proposed monthly rent schedule for University Homes, both with and without a utility allowance.

Table 2.2. January 1937 proposed rent schedule for University Homes units

Number of bedrooms	Monthly rent ($)	Monthly rent with utility allowance ($)
2	12.32	17.37
3	16.32	22.12
4	20.32	26.77
5	22.82	29.77

Committee members debated whether these rents were too high for Black Atlantans, and whether it was feasible to set rents at this rate if they required income limits that would only include "the top 2%" of the Black population.[49] Some committee members did not feel the rents were particularly high, as the average rent for a wooden four-bedroom house in a Black neighborhood was approximately twenty to twenty-five dollars per month depending on its proximity to downtown. Black professor and pharmacy owner L. D. Milton argued that it was not sustainable for the Black population to continue renting homes at such high rates, while wages remained artificially low for Black workers. By reducing the rent burden for Black families, these renters could potentially save for a home down payment, gaining equity in the housing market. Using political capital to gain economic capital in the Black community was yet another benefit of the public housing development as a political opportunity structure.

Nontraditional family structure and the role of working women as household leaders were also discussed during this meeting, and it was at this point we see the racial and gender politics within Atlanta play out. PWA district supervisor D. A. Calhoun argued with Florence Read about nontraditional family and gender roles, as Read advocated for more flexible admittance procedures than those at Techwood Homes. While Calhoun indicated that each unit must contain one "legal family"—defined as a married heterosexual couple and their children—Read countered that Black families were often composed of dependents outside of direct offspring, such as a cousin or aunt: "I think you will find quite frequently that colored families are very generous about helping friends and relatives. Perhaps they have just taken in a girl of high school or college age who got her living and helped with the children."[50]

This common survival strategy in the Black community created resiliency within Black households in spite of the economic, political, and social disparities with white households. Black families, due to low wages for Black workers, often were composed of at least two working adults, with other family members or close friends exchanging childcare services for room, board, or other goods and services.[51] Read also advocated for nontraditional family structures and gender equality with a suggestion to make allowances for single-person applications:

I want to ask whether you have allowed for one person. I wish to make a stand for that. When the Advisory Committee talked about the 2-room units, it seems to me we didn't have in mind the question of the lone female. I don't see why it isn't performing a useful service to society to permit her to occupy a 2-room apartment in the housing project. There are some schoolteachers, for instance. They cannot have a home of their own if their income does not permit it. If they live with another family it is a hard life. I do not see why a housing unit should not be—why they should not be permitted to live in a housing project.[52]

The topic of Black single women struggling to carve out their economic and social independence in the post-Depression South was close to Read's heart, as she was a single woman educator herself. Her plea was met with immediate dismissal during the meeting, with Calhoun indicating it was better to help "three or four people" than just help one, and Moron going so far as to suggest permitting single persons into the development would promote the dissolution of Black families.

These protests fell in line with the heteronormative, middle-class mores that privileged nuclear family structures and homeownership for social and spatial reproduction. The progressive ideology that guided the PWA Housing Division policy prohibited single persons and strongly discriminated against single-parent households. One purpose of public housing was to help low-income families out of poverty by allowing them to save for down payments to purchase single-family homes. The project was intentionally exclusionary to nontraditional family arrangements.

What Read suggested was politically impossible at the time, particularly for the first Black public housing development. Nonetheless, Read, with the support of the advisory committee, issued a resolution to the director of housing that "other families shall be given preference by holding in abeyance the applications of one person families for a reasonable length of time to determine whether there will be space available for one person families."[53] This resolution for single women and nontraditional family structures did not go unheard. The PWA Housing Division staff allowed the University Homes Tenant Selection Committee to place single-family households on a special waiting list. Married couples were given priority for the apartments, and single-family households were given an opportunity to apply for the unclaimed units.[54]

University Homes:
Management and Tenant Associations

The elite influence and privileging of middle-class norms and behaviors was not limited to the planning processes. Implementation of public housing policy was subject to this top-down mentality as well, as evidenced by Alonzo Moron's activities during his tenure as housing manager. This elite, top-down approach was favored by those who practiced uplift politics and distributed to other Black public housing managers across the country due to Moron's outsized influence as one of the first to hold the position.

Moron's years of social work experience and the symbolic and political importance of University Homes' role as one of the first Black public housing developments in the nation, placed this development at the forefront of housing and social policy in the United States. As the manager of this nationwide social experiment in public housing, Moron carefully, and somewhat paternalistically, oversaw the social activities of the tenant association and public housing residents. However, Moron's guidance provided the structure for residents to take advantage of the unique space and position of the public housing development in the evolving urban political economy, mobilizing these new resources to sustain the development as a political opportunity structure.

Three months after the April 1937 opening of University Homes, the public housing development was 80 percent occupied.[55] One-, two-, and three-bedroom units were full, and the less popular (at least, for the income requirements set by the PWA Housing Division) four- and five-bedroom units remained available.[56] The vacancy of four- and five-bedroom units—that is, the units for the larger, and likely poorer, Black families shows one of the early biases in U.S. social and housing policy—rewarding the deserving poor. In the case of the University Homes Tenant Selection Office, applicants for four-bedroom units needed a monthly income of at least $66 (or, $1,230 in 2020 dollars); conversely, the income for a family with three or more children could not exceed $216 per month (or $4,026 in 2020 dollars).[57]

In spite of this early example of cream skimming, or separating the upwardly mobile working class from the intransigent poor, Moron was eager to make examples of the University Homes residents for the city of Atlanta, as well as the nation. Moron wanted to show that the model citizenship found in public housing tenants extended to Black families as well, in the hopes of refuting some of the deviant images and stereotypes of Black people circulated post-Reconstruction. Much like the role-modeling goals of the modern, mixed-income approach to public housing policy, these programmatic desires are regressive and further serve to marginalize deviant interests in public housing politics.

Nonetheless, the emphasis Moron placed on getting University Homes residents to organize and assemble was still risky at the time. The developments of the PWA's Housing Division faced rampant accusations from the real estate lobby as being hotbeds of communism and fostering communal living and proletariat organizing via tenant association meetings.[58] These accusations were heightened in Atlanta when the Herndon case of 1932 equated virtually all Black political activity with that of insurgent, communist activity.[59]

Figure 2.4. University Homes management and staff, with Alonzo F. Moron
front row, center. Source: Atlanta Housing Authority Archives.

During the 1930s, even the elite philanthropic Black organizations (such as Lugenia Hope's Neighborhood Union) faced police harassment and raids in an effort to suppress any form of Black assembly and organizing.[60] This suppression effectively eliminated political spaces for working-class Black Atlantans. Moron, aware that the local authorities were wary to interfere with University Homes activities given the federal status of the residents, took advantage of this positioning by frequently organizing assemblies, parties, and political speakers for residents.[61] Just as Florence Read subjugated the local biases of labor unions by advocating for Black interests to national labor leaders, Moron utilized the perceived federal status of University Homes residents to rebuff local and state police efforts to suppress Black assembly.

The first block party organized for University Homes residents by the management-selected tenant association was intended to recruit more (particularly, male) residents to join the tenant association, and to raise money for a library within the University Homes development.[62] It is unclear whether Moron or the tenant association was responsible for deciding what the receipts from the block party funded. However, it is clear that the number of attendees at the block party exceeded the number of residents living in University Homes, suggesting that residents of the surrounding Beaver Slide community partook in the festivities.[63]

This first tenant association event raised about $140 (approximately $2,520 in

2020 dollars) toward furnishings, books, and periodicals for the library. It also generated several photographs (sent to the PWA Housing Division's publicity office) showing thousands of Black people gathering and socializing peacefully, respectfully, and without incident. Moron would often send these types of publicity photos to Washington, D.C., attempting to showcase the University Homes residents as role models for all poor and working-class Black Americans.[64]

While the funding and creation of a University Homes library may not have been driven by the residents, it had far-reaching effects for both residents and the community. Libraries, like all public facilities in Atlanta, were segregated by race, with Black facilities intentionally subpar to those of whites (either through construction materials, availability, location, staffing, or other resources). Although a public library system had been available to white Atlantans since 1902, Black Atlantans were unable to take part in this system until the Carnegie Library was constructed in the Sweet Auburn neighborhood in 1921.[65]

Andrew Carnegie donated money for both libraries in 1902, but local leaders, unable to find a suitable site in a Black neighborhood, refused to utilize these funds while denying Black residents' access to the white library system. Thus, the entire Black community had only one public library in Atlanta, and it was primarily accessible to those who lived on the more affluent east side of the city. For those in the southern and western districts of the city, the library at University Homes would have been a welcome resource. The issue of poor Black and public housing residents' access to public libraries in Atlanta would remain a relevant and pressing topic—thirty years later.[66]

Another much needed facility in the University Homes development was the large playground that was shared by all of the housing blocks. Each apartment building had a smaller, centrally located play area that allowed small children to play while their mothers (or neighbors) monitored them from the apartment unit windows and steps. The larger playground was a space for preteen and teenage children. Beyond the standard play equipment, this playground was equipped with a baseball field, a workshop for woodworking, and the development's recreation center. Moron wrote to the PWA Housing Division staff: "Following out the principle of using at University Homes whatever existing services the community offered, we requested a Playground Director from the City's Department of Parks and Playgrounds. The request was received very graciously and referred to the Works Progress Administration who promptly supplied us with a very good Playground Director, Mr. Scott Edwards."[67]

Moron's request from the city first and the subsequent referral to the Works Progress Administration show the development's ability to formalize new racialized public spaces in Black communities. Prior to University Homes, there were fewer than ten parks and playgrounds in Black Atlanta communities, and the number of Black playground directors is unknown, if any existed at all. Hiring Edwards as the playground director at University Homes created new institutionalized Black spaces in the city and allowed for Black residents to continue rede-fining their citizenship through New Deal programs.

Moron continued in his memo to the housing division about the use of the large playground and the activities offered by Edwards in the context of the sur-rounding Beaver Slide community:

> An interesting question arose as to whether or not this large playground at University Homes should be closed to children from the neighborhood. To date this has not become a problem and the tenants have not raised the ques-tion of their children playing with outsiders and the Management has taken the position that as long as no friction develops between the two groups and as long as the playground has not been fenced in, it will be well to let matters re-main as they are, for it would be difficult to keep outsiders from the grounds unless there was a fence with gates which could be controlled by the Director. Within the next few weeks, however, a fence will be erected around this large playground and it is our hope that we shall gradually be able to restrict use of this space to adults and children living in University Homes. This will be with some regrets as this particular play area is the only play space available for col-ored children within this neighborhood which is about one and a half miles square.[68]

The residents of what remained of Beaver Slide were still much poorer than the residents of University Homes. In order to prevent a negative externality from more children using the facilities than anticipated, the fence provided benefits for those who were considered deserving, and the undeserving poor continued to go without. This appeared to be the only divisive decision during Moron's tenure at University Homes, one that exacerbated the class divisions in the wider commu-nity. Moron shifted the blame for this decision to erect a fence away from the lo-cal advisory committee and the Black elite and instead insisted that federal em-ployee Scott Edwards requested limiting playground activities to the children of University Homes residents only.[69]

In a September 1937 letter to Chief of Police M. A. Hornsby and Chief of At-lanta's Traffic Bureau Captain T. J. Malcolm, Moron followed up from a previ-ous week's meeting about traffic signals and signage in and around the devel-opment.[70] One of the qualifiers that made Beaver Slide a "slum" was the lack of formalized streets and sidewalks, in addition to the lack of public services in the area. The PWA installed the necessary infrastructure to provide utilities for the neighborhood, but recognition from local authorities to provide public services to its communities in spite of the residents' race did not occur immediately af-ter the April 1937 opening. The city had installed sidewalks and paved streets as agreed in the original lease between the PWA and Atlanta, but traffic control and police enforcement of traffic regulations in the neighborhood were insufficient according to Moron.[71]

Moron requested a traffic light outside of the development, at the intersection of Fair and Chestnut streets, to curb the speeds of commuters and allow neighborhood children to safely cross the street to the local school. Moron also requested a stop sign at the intersection of Leonard Street and Greensferry Avenue, the latter of which had recently been widened and transformed into a main artery between the east and west sides of the city. At the intersection of the new stop sign, Moron also wanted motorcycle police stationed to deter speeding "bugs" or private bus lines that were repeated offenders of traffic laws.[72]

Police presence in Black communities was a contentious subject in Atlanta and throughout the South after the end of Reconstruction's federal troop protection. Police officers in Atlanta were all white, and the secondary status of Black citizens in the city prohibited equal application of the law and its penalties. Inviting more police scrutiny into the University Homes community seemed antithetical to the theory of public housing as a political opportunity structure for Black residents.

Moron was hoping that engaging the police with the support of the federal government (the letter that he addressed to the two chiefs was on official Department of the Interior stationery) would legitimize his requests and help legitimate the citizenship status of the Black community.[73] He offered to work in concert with the police and traffic bureaus, indirectly suggesting that management would not interfere if arrests were made of residents of the development and surrounding community.[74] The hiring of Black police officers was still a decade away, but the steps Moron took started redefining the relationship between the local white power structure and *some* of Atlanta's Black residents.

One of Moron's final and most ambitious projects was the construction of an auditorium within the development. There was only one city auditorium for Black communal use—again, located in the affluent Sweet Auburn neighborhood. Church basements and privately owned homes frequently acted as spaces to gather and orate throughout the city. Placing an auditorium for public use in the middle of the Beaver Slide community would strengthen the public housing development as a political opportunity structure, particularly in its capability to mobilize resources. Immediately following the opening, Moron pleaded with housing division staff in Washington to allocate more funding to construct an auditorium. In a July 1937 letter (three months after opening day), Moron requested "an auditorium which can be used for large group meetings and which will give the tenants an opportunity to express themselves and allow us to abandon gradually the idea of having all activities originate from the Management or from the steering committee. It is our sincere hope that the plans for an auditorium at University Homes now being considered by your office will be approved at an early date and then we can engage in more worthwhile activities than an occasional party or dance."[75]

This request was not immediately acted on, and over the course of the development's first year, Moron and the tenant association collected money during parties and raffles to construct the auditorium. There appeared to be an agreement among both management and residents that an auditorium would greatly improve residents' social and political life, by allowing for larger and more inclusive parties and more distinguished speakers interested in orating to a larger group. After much hard work, the auditorium was opened in 1938, and most of the development's events took place within the building.

During the massive voter registration following the *King v. Chapman* decision in 1946 when 18,000 Black voters were registered in fifty-one days, the auditorium at University Homes acted as a registration space. On the first day of registration at the auditorium, 750 Black citizens were enfranchised in three hours.[76] Again, the political opportunity structure of the public housing development spatialized the resources of the federal government for the production of local Black citizenship. The space of the developments created social and political benefits for residents of both University Homes and the surrounding community.

The 1946 municipal election was not the first time University Homes tenants were able to cast a vote to directly elect their mayor. In 1942, Mayor Roy LeCraw resigned after he was drafted to serve in World War II, and the Atlanta Civic and Political League, led by Republican John Wesley Dobbs, headed a door-to-door campaign to register voters before April 27. Black voters would be eligible to elect the mayor through a special election not subject to a white primary.

The campaign to support a mayoral candidate was done as an open secret. In the month leading up to the election, Dobbs and other members of the Black elite refused to endorse any candidate to the wider community until the night before the election. Through this noncommittal approach, Dobbs hoped to put pressure on the candidates to agree to neighborhood improvements, new schools, and attention to local Black labor market conditions—that is, respond to the Black electorate. An article in the *Chicago Defender* notes, "It is believed that the Negro vote may easily prove the deciding factor in the election since to date seven prospective candidates have indicated their desire to run for the vacant post."[77]

After the passage of the Wagner-Steagall Housing Act in September 1937 authorizing local housing authorities, University Homes residents, management, and staff were fearful of losing the protection of federal ownership, and the political capital that accrued in the five months of the development's existence. Moron discussed his fears in a memo to Florence Read and members of the advisory committee with regard to different ways of transferring ownership from the federal to the state and local levels:

> While these first fifty-two projects [constructed by the PWA] are more or less a novelty and have that appeal at the present time, it must be recognized that the changes in policies after they have been in operation for a period of time

will have a very definite effect on the demand for housing of this type from the group of people most in need of it and also upon the ability of the Authority to secure and keep qualified personnel for the management of the projects. . . . Those of us who are living in the south should be aware of the possible danger to Housing for Negroes if management of these projects is turned over to local Housing Authorities. At present the Housing Authority would be a creature of the state which means that to some extent it would be dominated by the same views and prejudices which characterize the actions of the state affecting Negroes. There would also be a tendency to depart from National standards of maintenance and operation and sink to the levels of local standards of administration and maintenance of public property.[78]

In several letters found among Moron's papers, residents sent pleas to the local advisory committee, the management's office, and even to the housing division in Washington, D.C., in an attempt to keep Moron as housing manager after the development was leased to the newly formed Atlanta Housing Authority. Moron's guidance in establishing and maintaining the tenant association, the men's, women's, girls' and boys' clubs, the credit union, the account for tenant activities and supplies, and the entertainment and political speakers was noted in these letters. One resident spoke of how a lease to Atlanta for sixty years should require the mandate of Black management and supervision for sixty years.[79] Despite this resident-led rally to keep Moron as housing manager, he was let go in 1940.

Conclusion

The University Homes case helps illustrate both the capabilities and the limitations of the public housing development as a political opportunity structure. The capabilities of the structure are evident—with the creation of the structure at a time when popular enfranchisement was limited to white Atlantans, the public housing development provided the resources and attention of the state for the disenfranchised Black population. The University Homes library would serve the larger Black population that was only permitted to borrow books from the Auburn Avenue branch just east of the CBD. Further, the installation of traffic lights, paved sidewalks, sewer lines, and the University Homes power plant provided public goods and services to everyone in the Beaver Slide neighborhood. Yet clearly these gains were not permanent: one can note the similarities in the requests from Alonzo Moron and the requests in the modernization statement from the Techwood/Clark Howell tenant association described in the introduction.

The spatial divergences of assembling land for Black public housing developments were a means to mainstream the deviant Black communities in Atlanta. Following the 1906 riots, the racial zoning ordinances, and the stereotypes of slum disorder and Black social life, Black communities were demonized in the press and devalued in the real estate market. The reappropriation of slum communities in public housing developments was a means of incorporating the spatially and politically deviant Black community. With the end of the white Democratic Party primary and the success of voter registration drives, the ability to use the space of public housing developments for both political assembly and electoral participation embodies the true meaning of spatial uplift.

However, the top-down approach to political mobilization limited the inclusiveness and representation of tenant and community interests that were largely shaped by an elite housing management and advisory committee. In spite of being included in the first tenant association that Moron selected, women were largely excluded from making decisions and determining grievances for the tenant association. Lugenia Burns Hope, Florence Read, and members of elite women's groups held some decision-making power in the planning and design of the developments, but their work was largely relegated to the background, to the point where President Read was taking notes during her own advisory committee meetings.

No members from the Beaver Slide community were invited to participate in any aspect of this process outside of the survey administered by Du Bois and his team. In limiting what was truly considered deviant, the political opportunities of the early public housing developments were available only to those who were living in or proximate to these developments. The changes in tenant selection, public housing development sitings, and private housing availability would all shift the political opportunities of future public housing developments. These shifts are discussed in the following chapters.

Chapter 3

From Production of Place to Production of Space

Spatial Justice in Perry Homes

Following the construction of the first eight public housing developments in Atlanta and the creation of the Atlanta Housing Authority, new urban crises mandated new forms of public housing policy. The urbanization trajectories of the Great Migration's receiving cities (including Atlanta) and the end of the Second World War put unprecedented growth pressures on urban housing and labor markets. The policy response at the federal level was the passage of legislation subsidizing the movement of residences, businesses, and public works projects into the suburbs. In cities, new "slums"—designated in the 1949 and 1954 Housing Acts as "blight"—were the targets of federally funded demolition and redevelopment. Although the 1949 and 1954 Housing Acts were considered extensions of the 1937 act, neither the coalition of interests nor the policy goals remained the same.

In 1953, the Georgia Supreme Court declared the city's urban redevelopment plan unconstitutional, stating the city did not have the eminent domain powers to take land for redevelopment. Several cities faced this dilemma, and the U.S. Supreme Court ruled in 1954 that federal and state legislatures had the power to authorize slum redevelopment. In order to overrule the Georgia Supreme Court decision, the state legislature had to amend its constitution, granting redevelopment powers to local entities.[1] Local housing authorities were granted power over redevelopment programs, and in Atlanta, biracial cooperation continued to shape its policy design and implementation.

Racial representation was included in the process through separate commissions and boards appointed by the mayor. These boards were tasked with maintaining "race relations" at a neighborhood scale, minimizing the inherent white supremacist spatial logics of postwar land use to a series of conflicts between Black and white residents. In creating these race relations committees for every city initiative and agency, the city externalized racial considerations—and de-

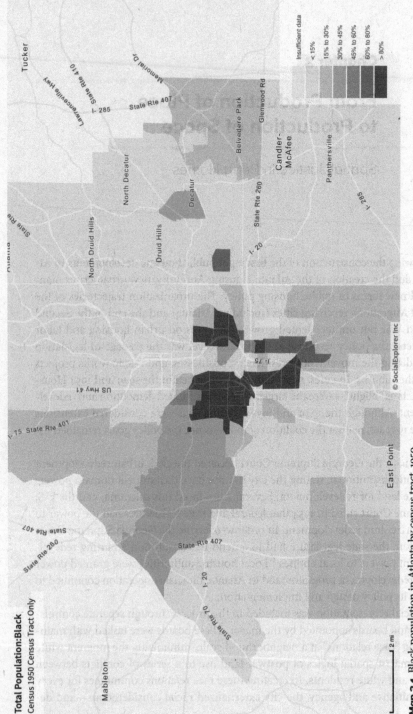

Total Population: Black
Census 1950 Census Tract Only

Insufficient data
< 15%
15% to 30%
30% to 45%
45% to 60%
60% to 80%
> 80%

© SocialExplorer Inc

Map 3.1. Black population in Atlanta by census tract, 1950.
Source: U.S. Census Bureau, Social Explorer.

mands of Black residents—outside of the planning, decision-making, and imple-mentation processes of urban governance.[2]

Urban planning with and around race provided limited representation for the interests of the Black elite who were rewarded for their accommodation and up-lift politics with minimal inclusion in the regime. Yet the Black working poor and disenfranchised continued to face exclusion and marginalization from this mode of political participation. The use of public housing developments as a space for more deviant Black interests who were—intentionally or not—excluded from other forms of political participation led to the construction and maintenance of what I refer to as *Black participatory geographies*. The inclusionary nature of pub-lic housing tenant associations toward political interests not typically considered in the biracial coalition was a means of empowering and expanding the existing political geographies for Atlanta's Black residents.

I utilize the concept of spatial justice to understand both the grievances and interests proffered by Black residents at this time, as well as the procedural trans-formations of the political opportunity structure that accommodated these in-terests. Geographer Edward Soja's definition of spatial justice identifies transfor-mations to democratic principles and practices that center the inherent spatiality in the pursuit and implementation of socially just outcomes.[3] For Black partic-ipatory geographies to be effective, socially just spatializations of political par-ticipation are amended to or outright replace existing political structures of marginalization.

Using the case of Perry Homes as an example, this chapter further examines the impact of exclusionary planning on the welfare of working-poor Black resi-dents, and how the development's tenant association responded to these local challenges over time. At the state and federal levels, the battle over the 1954 Hous-ing Act's funding and administration and the simultaneous ruling on the *Brown v. Board of Education* case prompted spatial and institutional rearrangements in Atlanta. These spatial rearrangements include the annexation of eighty-one square miles of land to the north and west of Atlanta to create the city's modern boundaries. Atlanta's 1951 Plan of Improvement was a spatial rearrangement to counter the political emancipation of Atlanta's growing Black population follow-ing the 1946 *King v. Chapman* ruling.

The plan increased Atlanta's population from about 330,000 residents to 490,000; the proportion of Black residents decreased from 41 percent to 33 per-cent, and white residents were able to maintain their strong electorate majority status. This shift in land area, political geography, and population reshaped the city's racial geography. To counter the enfranchised Black population, Atlanta's white supremacist political elite manipulated the means of land production to spatially, economically, and politically marginalize Black Atlantans over the next two decades (see table 3.1).

Table 3.1. Atlanta's increasing hypersegregation, 1940–1970

Year	Total number of census tracts	Number of tracts 99% white	Number of tracts 99% Black	Total number of hyper-segregated tracts	Percent of total (%)
1940	75	9	6	15	20
1950	75	16	9	25	33
1960	109	35	11	46	42
1970	119	26	22	48	40

SOURCE: Howard Openshaw, "Race and Residence: An Analysis of Property Values in Transitional Areas, Atlanta, Georgia, 1960–1971," Research Monograph no. 53, Georgia State University School of Business Administration Publishing Services Division, 1974.

NOTE: Hypersegregation defined as tracts that are 99% Black or white.

As a result, Perry Homes and other developments built during Atlanta's second phase of public housing construction between 1955 and 1964 differed from those in the first phase. Tenant associations in the public housing program's early years had strong managerial influence shaping the political opportunities available. In the second phase, residents began taking on a more independent political identity that was reflected in tenant association initiatives and organizational formations. The end of the white Democratic Party primary created Black political legitimacy and power, and in the 1949 mayoral election, the Black population comprised 27 percent of the total electorate.

This newfound political and social identity within the city briefly shifted power relations, and directly led to the token inclusion of a cooperating elite Black coalition into Atlanta's urban regime. But the growth of the disenfranchised public housing population during the second phase of construction produced tensions in the once-unified Black vote. Using this growing political power as leverage, tenant associations gained legitimacy as political spaces and public housing developments provided a platform for the interests of the Black working-poor population. The case of Perry Homes demonstrates the typical postwar Atlanta public housing development, from its segregated origins at the planning stages to its radical responses to the spatial, social, and economic disparities that resulted from these exclusionary planning process.

Changes at the federal level enabled local authorities to create more segregated geographies within the city using public housing developments, as well as spatial inequities between denser urban areas and the newly developing, sprawling suburbs. The 1949 Housing Act was a shift to a more conservative ideology of housing policy. Title I (slum clearance) removed the equivalent elimination clause, which replaced one demolished slum home with one new unit of housing. Title III provided funding for the construction of eight hundred thousand units of public housing. Due to propaganda campaigns from the real estate, banking, and construction industries, very little public housing was actually built in the 1950s. The campaigns focused on the xenophobic Red Scare that equated the communal modernism experiment of politically engaged public housing developments with "hotbeds of socialism."[4]

While Titles I and III proscribed and constructed fewer public housing units relative to the number of cleared homes, Title II of the Housing Act further increased spatial inequities between cities and suburbs by increasing funding for the Federal Housing Administration (FHA). Because of the 1934 Housing Act, the FHA had explicit guidelines that enforced residential segregation through the provision of mortgages to neighborhoods and properties with restrictive covenants. Although this language was removed from the Housing Act after the 1948 *Shelley v. Kraemer* U.S. Supreme Court ruling, the 1949 act did little to ameliorate the past spatial inequities established in the 1930s. The multiple private actors in real estate, banking, and construction continued to privilege and prioritize projects in racially homogenous neighborhoods.

The 1949 Election and the Limits to Atlanta's Jim Crow Liberalism

Atlanta's 1949 municipal election was a significant moment in the political development of the Black community. In the first election since the end of the white primary, Democratic incumbent mayor William Hartfield was running against Democrat Charlie Brown. That year, new institutions were established, such as the Atlanta Negro Voters League (ANVL), led by A. T. Walden and J. W. Dobbs. Headquartered at 28 Butler Street, N.E., in the Walden Building, the organization had entirely male leadership, the result of joining the boards of the Black Democratic and Republican clubs led by Walden and Dobbs, respectively. The ANVL was a continuation of the all-male, all-elite political spaces of the community power structure that fostered exclusionary and marginalizing politics.

The group's initial correspondence with mayoral candidates suggests that spatial uplift remained a top political priority. On Friday, August 20, 1949 (less than three weeks before the primary), Dobbs and Walden sent an invitation to Mayor Hartsfield inviting him to speak with ANVL's general committee on the following Tuesday. Walden and Dobbs notified the mayor that "members of the Committee . . . will be interested in your discussion of the following matters: (1) Increased Negro Policeman (2) Fire Station on the West Side Manned by Negro Firemen (3) More and Better Parks and Playgrounds (4) Improvement of Facilities at Washington Park (5) Expansion of Public Housing (6) Use of Vacant Land for Building Homes Adjacent to Fairview Terrace with Facilities (7) Continued Rent Control (8) Upgrading of Negro Employees in the City Government."[5]

The group's demands were overwhelmingly spatial, and the focus on upgrading neighborhood conditions suggests that the production of space remained a contested, racialized issue. Spatial production became an issue of convergence due to the increasing discrimination, dispossession, relocation, and containment that was transforming the racial geography of Atlanta. However, ANVL's aggressive voter registration push, alongside the increasing Black migration numbers, gave the group a great deal of electoral leverage. In August 1949, Black voters were 41 percent of the population and 33 percent of the electorate. The Black population continued to increase between 1950 and 1970, growing by 16.1 percent and 53.9 percent each respective decade.

The 1949 election was pivotal because race was at the forefront of the campaign, exposing the contradictions of the New South—mainly, its failure to reconcile with the past and the ongoing role of state violence in maintaining the color line. While each mayoral candidate reached out and met with the ANVL and other "Influential Negroes," as Hartsfield's notes indicate, the candidates also used the incumbent's past racism to discredit him to the Black community.[6] Weaponizing and exceptionalizing prior acts of racism is a longstanding characteristic of political campaigns in postwar U.S. cities. In many of Atlanta's races, candidates pointed fingers at each other while eliding and obscuring institutional acts that structured racially disparate outcomes, particularly when it came to housing and city planning.

Notes from William Hartsfield's files during his contentious campaign against Fulton County commissioner Charlie Brown show a point-by-point comparison of how the two men fared on race issues. The statement "Mayor Hartsfield issued no permits for masked parades in Atlanta, and when anti-mask law was passed in Council signed it within 30 minutes thereafter" suggests Hartsfield's condemnation of masked parades for white racial terror groups such as the Ku Klux Klan. However, "in 1948, under Commissioner Brown masked men paraded on Howell Mill Road, led by County Police. No protest by Mr. Brown." The speed of Hartsfield's signature on an anti-mask bill is compared to Brown's silence on a masked parade, but the support and participation of the Fulton County police in a "masked men parade" is mere context for Brown's exceptional racism.[7]

Hartsfield's positions on public pools, libraries, and federal housing for Black citizens were in the Jim Crow liberalism tradition—maintaining a separate but unequal color wall that inscribed Black marginalization into the physical space of the city. Brown, a hardline segregationist who had little power as one of the Fulton County commissioners, was accused of building no libraries for Black residents and enforcing separate windows for Black and white people in the county courthouse. He also did not advocate for hiring any Black policemen, which Hartsfield had done the year prior, receiving nationwide press as the first southern mayor to do so.[8]

Throughout this postwar period, the politics of race in the city were internally unstable but externally presented as collegial and progressive, with Mayor Hartsfield notoriously declaring Atlanta as the "city too busy to hate."[9] The formation of the biracial coalition and the relegation of Black participants to the electoral coalition as opposed to the governing coalition of Atlanta's urban regime created strong intraracial divisions within the city spatially, socially, economically, and politically. Black elites held some level of spatial, social, economic, and political control as key participants in the electoral coalition, while working-class and middle-class Black residents were used as the treasured Black vote without much representation. Black elites privileged patronage and land use for middle-class homeowners, as their working-class counterparts suffered inadequate rental housing and labor market conditions.[10]

The hiring of Atlanta's first Black police officers make plain the limits of Jim Crown liberalism and its usefulness as a strategy to appease Black voters. The eight men were segregated into their own police station at the Butler Street YMCA and initially were discouraged from arresting white citizens. The officers were a source of pride and demonstrated the political legitimacy for the emerging Black electorate, a visible declaration of Atlanta as the capital of the New South. Yet their hires also signaled the sort of compromises that would come in the emerging biracial urban regime. The continued segregation, isolation, and marginalization of the Black police officers also serves as an example of the new racialized production of southern urban space—as a process, form, and imaginary. Black Atlantans would be incorporated into the fabric of the city, but only at the pace and comfort of white (and Black) elites.[11]

The capital of the New South appeared as a shining example of racial cooperation, with Hartsfield traveling to virtually all public events with the eight Black police officers. Photos of the group leading up to the election show a jovial white mayor in front of the ceremoniously solemn Black policemen. As lynchings, KKK parades, and police brutality incidents rose in Georgia and were widely reported in the national press, these pictures presented a strong counterimage to the negative perceptions of southern race relations, obscuring the racial violence that structured the everyday lives of Black Atlanta residents. In Atlanta, economic growth for both Black and white elites—white elites who profited directly from this growth and Black elites who saw their cooperation as a means to political and social equality—superseded the need to express overt white supremacy that dominated traditional images of postwar southern cities.

Political incorporation and Black patronage came at the expense of spatial mobility and control, which helps to explain the focus on neighborhood conditions and improvement found in the ANVL's demands. The Black police officers' appointment was a direct act of patronage from the mayor in 1948, yet they were not permitted to patrol white neighborhoods and were explicitly forbid-

Figure 3.1. Atlanta's first Black police officers. Source: James G. Kenan Research Center, Atlanta History Center Digital Collections.

den from arresting the well-to-do residents in the northern part of the city. They were, however, free to arrest and ticket Black residents. These trade-offs between Black middle-class patronage and Black working-class and working-poor mobility would continue in the postwar period.

Three weeks before the primary, on September 2, 1949, the ANVL sent out its letter to the 21,963 registered Black voters on the county registrar list, officially endorsing William B. Hartsfield. The letter states:

> He has stated that he is a Christian gentleman, a wise statesman, an efficient administrator and courageous fighter for principles and policies promoting the welfare of the community and particularly the Negroes by:
>
> 1) Fearlessly advocating Negro policemen and increasing the number
> 2) Promoting parks and playgrounds for Negroes resulting in establishing one each for the Pittsburgh and Butler Street sections
> 3) Supporting Public Housing and continuing Rent Control in the interest of citizens who cannot buy homes
> 4) Fighting for expansion of the city to reduce the tax burden and increase opportunities for the Atlanta community at large

5) Favoring measures to reduce inequalities among citizens, such as fire
protection, employment, equal education and salaries.[12]

The mention of Christianity as a virtue was no doubt the influence of the sixteen
clergy who sat on the ANVL's executive and campaign committees. The strength
of the church in the Black community was not just demonstrated by its ubiqui-
tous presence in every neighborhood, but also by the strong representation of its
leadership in Black public affairs.

While the Black church continued to play a dominant role in the new biracial
regime, women (elite or not) had fewer seats at the decision-making table. Some
Black women had roles on the ANVL's campaign committee, but there were none
on the executive committee. The newly emergent spaces of Black politics were
mimicking the spatial logics and structural exclusions of white political spaces. In
both cases, minorities are relegated to ad hoc, nonessential positions that could
be activated and deactivated when the political opportunity arose.

In Atlanta, ANVL Black women members such as Ella Clark and Grace Towns
Hamilton had long, impactful careers. Hamilton led the local chapter of the
NAACP before eventually winning the first seat for a Black woman in the Georgia
legislature. However, women without the social capital and middle-class backgrounds of Clark and Hamilton were often excluded from these token ANVL appointments that could lead to further political opportunity.[13] The ability to participate in Black politics as a Black woman shifted with the expansion of the city's
public housing program in the 1950s.

The Postwar Housing Acts and the
Creation of the Northwest Ghetto

Heman E. Perry Homes, one of the largest public housing developments constructed and managed by the Atlanta Housing Authority, was built when the racial geography of Atlanta was shifting. The 1951 Plan of Improvement, the 1954
Alley Dwelling Act, and a 1957 bond referendum for $1.5 million in urban re-
newal funding granted unprecedented land use control and authority to the politically unaccountable Atlanta Housing Authority Board of Commissioners.
Black rural-to-urban migration and the return of white and Black soldiers at the
end of World War II both created new pressures on Atlanta's labor and housing
markets.

After the passage of the 1949 Housing Act authorized 800,000 new public
housing units throughout the country, the Atlanta Housing Authority immediately began constructing high-density, high-unit developments for Black tenants
and low-density developments for white tenants. Between 1953 and 1957, some
2,500 public housing units were constructed: 1,990 units across two Black developments on the west side of the city and 510 units for white residents in the

southeast.[14] The planning process for these projects had a different aim than the housing developments constructed in the prewar era. Instead of linking slum clearance to the redevelopment and improvement of people and areas through constructing low-cost housing, the 1949 Housing Act permitted the AHA to clear slums (and, to an extent, clear poor residents) independent of where low-cost housing was sited.

There are other differences between public housing developments constructed before the 1949 Housing Act and those constructed after. During the first phase, the AHA and the Public Works Administration constructed eight public housing developments in the city; four each for white and Black families. Under the influence of Charles Palmer and the real estate interests on the AHA Board, 80 percent of the first phase of public housing construction occurred in areas within or adjacent to the central business district (CBD). The purpose of the developments was to clear the existing slums and construct housing developments and communities that induced further investment around the CBD.

To create stable neighborhoods where slums once stood, tenant selection for these first developments was a multistage process. First, applicants had to meet income requirements (a minimum annual income based on family size that was not to exceed a maximum annual income), and then were subject to a series of interviews and home visits to determine whether the current home was substandard and observe the stability of the family. A stable family dynamic was defined as an employed head of household with all children enrolled in school. These early developments attracted the submerged white (and Black) middle class— those who were unable to save enough for a home down payment as a result of an unstable economy or tight capital markets, but who might be able to ascend to the middle class with government assistance. Single-parent households were not eligible to apply, and the entrenched poor (the chronically unemployed and disabled) were also excluded by income minimums.

Planning documents and political memoranda make clear that Atlanta's shifting racial geography through public housing construction was in direct response to the increased political enfranchisement of its Black population. In the context of a deepening Black political divide, declining tax base, and decreasing and depoliticized white population, Mayor Hartsfield proposed a Plan of Improvement that would annex eighty-one square miles to the city. Hartsfield's close ties to the white upper-class business community to the north of the city limits (the Buckhead neighborhood), coupled with the end of the white Democratic primary in 1946, created an opportunity to adjust the city's political geography. In exchange for a smaller proportion of the electorate, Black elite middle-persons accepted the increase in available residential land to address Black housing needs. The proposed annexation included several unincorporated Black communities in west Fulton County.[15]

Hartsfield worked for over a decade on the expansion plan, sending this plea to a friend in 1943:

> This annexation movement is not for revenue purposes at all. It is a move-
> ment for better government. We want voters, not money. At the same time, we
> can perform the city services cheaper than the county. But the most import-
> ant thing to remember, cannot be publicized in the press or made the subject of
> public speeches. Our negro population is growing by leaps and bounds. They
> stay right in the city limits and grow by taking more white territory inside At-
> lanta. Our migration is good white, home owning citizens. With the Federal
> government insisting on political recognition of negroes in local affairs, the
> time is not far distant when they will become a potent political force in Atlanta
> if our white citizens are just going to move out and give it to them. This is not
> intended to stir race prejudice because all of us want to deal fairly with them,
> but do you want to hand them political control of Atlanta, either as a majority
> or a powerful minority vote?[16]

Black political inclusion warranted the need to annex additional land for not only the white voters, property taxes, and suburban amenities, but also for Black res-
idential expansion and containment.[17] Paranoia of racial mixing, racial purity, and sexual violence continued to dominate the social and political imagination of Atlanta's white citizens, even if it did not manifest into the racial terrorism of the four September nights in 1906. Tracking Black mobility, residence, and leadership was the quotidian infrapolitics of the white silent majority. The codifica-
tion and institutionalization of these practices led to the hardening of Jim Crow, and the demobilization of radical acts of resistance.

Maps 3.2 and 3.3 visualize some of the postwar policies that shaped Atlanta's racial geography long after *de jure* segregation shifted into *de facto* segregation. The 1951 Plan of Improvement created the space for Black relocation, isolation, and containment. The 1954 Alley Dwelling Act created the mechanisms to clear, relocate, and marginalize predominantly poor Black residents into undeveloped and underdeveloped tracts of land in the annexed western areas.

Despite the strong federal support for cities, the funding for suburbanization policies was even stronger. Urban planning scholar June Manning Thomas notes that in Detroit, the relatively low funding for urban redevelopment and renewal created structural tensions that inhibited the success of these programs: "People were leaving the central city by the tens of thousands, a process that redevelopment did not slow."[18]

The federal shift from urban redevelopment to urban renewal occurred when governments were unable to recoup the high costs of demolition, and private investment continued to flow toward the suburbs. A profitable transformation of slum housing into middle-class and working-class housing was not possible with

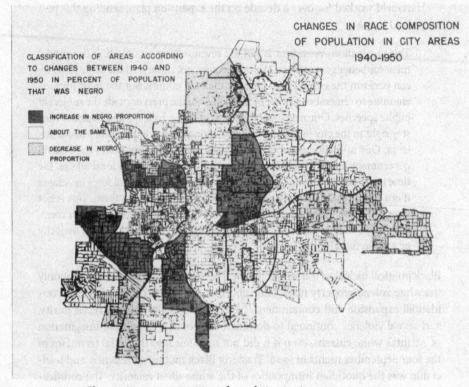

CHANGES IN RACE COMPOSITION
OF POPULATION IN CITY AREAS
1940-1950

CLASSIFICATION OF AREAS ACCORDING
TO CHANGES BETWEEN 1940 AND
1950 IN PERCENT OF POPULATION
THAT WAS NEGRO

INCREASE IN NEGRO PROPORTION

ABOUT THE SAME

DECREASE IN NEGRO
PROPORTION

Map 3.2. Changes in race composition of population in city areas, 1940–1950.
Source: atlppo153_33b, Planning Atlanta City Maps Collection,
Georgia State University Library.

the targeted specificity of the 1949 Housing Act Title I funds. Real estate developers were weary of investing in the unstable city, particularly when returns on suburban residential development were so lucrative.[19] Urban planners ameliorated those fears by calling for a more comprehensive redevelopment program, one that would implicitly account for the individual and institutionalized racism of the urban political economy.

Per Harold Kaplan, in his study of urban redevelopment in Newark, this federal redevelopment program would reconcile the contradictions of Title I and urban race relations in the following way: "The ideal solution, from NHA's [Newark Housing Authority's] point of view, was to tear down the entire ghetto and build a 'city within a city.'. . . . [The locus and contours of a redevelopment site] were dictated by a search for natural boundaries (a railroad, a park, and a major thoroughfare) to contain the project as a community within itself and protect it from its immediate environment."[20]

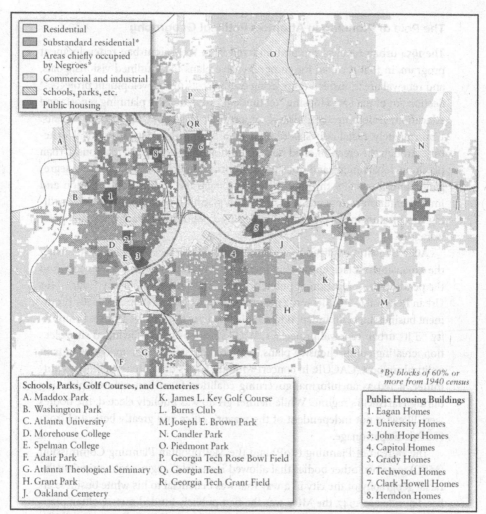

Residential
Substandard residential*
Areas chiefly occupied by Negroes*
Commercial and industrial
Schools, parks, etc.
Public housing

*By blocks of 60% or more from 1940 census

Schools, Parks, Golf Courses, and Cemeteries

A. Maddox Park
B. Washington Park
C. Atlanta University
D. Morehouse College
E. Spelman College
F. Adair Park
G. Atlanta Theological Seminary
H. Grant Park
J. Oakland Cemetery
K. James L. Key Golf Course
L. Burns Club
M. Joseph E. Brown Park
N. Candler Park
O. Piedmont Park
P. Georgia Tech Rose Bowl Field
Q. Georgia Tech
R. Georgia Tech Grant Field

Public Housing Buildings

1. Eagan Homes
2. University Homes
3. John Hope Homes
4. Capitol Homes
5. Grady Homes
6. Techwood Homes
7. Clark Howell Homes
8. Herndon Homes

Map 3.3. Land use map of Atlanta prepared by Atlanta Housing Authority, 1940. Source: Redrawn from atlpm0503, Planning Atlanta City Planning Maps Collection, Georgia State University.

As the passage shows, the longevity of urban renewal and redevelopment plans for processes of urban growth and urban race relations stem from the use of existing urban boundaries to naturalize the division of the races. Separating and segregating communities across rivers, creeks, railroads, public housing developments, and cement walls are means of physically inscribing separation between the race as a feature of the built *and* natural environment.

The Role of Planning in Atlanta's Political Geography

The 1954 urban renewal program differed from the 1949 urban redevelopment program, in that it called for comprehensive plans that outlined visions, goals, and renewal areas, instead of focusing on the costs of redevelopment projects.[21] Section 701 of the 1954 Housing Act funded comprehensive planning reports and education, scaling up the political opportunity of local planning departments. Unfortunately, racial issues were externalized from the postwar political structure through the creation of ad hoc committees overseeing race relations. Urban planning departments and housing authorities implicitly sustained racial segregation and inequality through the exclusionary and technocratic creation and implementation of renewal plans.[22] Urban planning departments became willing conspirators in the creation of a racialized political geography in many postwar cities.

Atlanta institutionalized its ability to create a new racial geography following the expansion of Black enfranchisement, the prohibition of racial covenants, and the pending desegregation of public schools. The Citizens Advisory Council for Urban Renewal (CACUR) was a mayoral-appointed committee of socially prominent businessmen, an independent body to advise the Atlanta Housing Authority on its urban renewal projects. CACUR's responsibilities included site selection, creating comprehensive plans, and holding stakeholder meetings to gain political support. CACUR, in concert with the AHA's urban renewal policy committee, acted as an informal governing coalition for urban renewal planning during Hartsfield's regime. While neither group was publicly elected, the bodies were likewise not independent of the mayor's office and greatly benefited from Hartsfield's patronage.

The Bureau of Planning (BoP) and the Metropolitan Planning Commission (MPC) were two other bodies that allowed Hartsfield's regime to manipulate the racial geography of the city in a way that was beneficial to his white business allies. Founded in 1947, the MPC was the first publicly funded metropolitan planning group in the nation—funded jointly by Fulton and DeKalb counties.[23] The MPC focused on race relations and racial transition within Atlanta's neighborhoods. MPC's all-white governing body assembled biracial groups composed of white residents and Black real estate brokers to negotiate the racial transition of communities (neighborhoods only transitioned from white to Black, not the inverse). The commission also worked to expand the availability of residential land for both Black and white residents within the city, following the expansion of city boundaries in 1951.

By 1956, the MPC had drafted a plan for race relations in Atlanta that took into account the dual housing markets and mass displacement of poor Black residents in the city from urban renewal projects.[24] The entire plan revolved around the housing market and reaching a consensus with representatives of both races

Figure 3.2. Southwest Atlanta planning and zoning meeting, 1954.
Source: James G. Kenan Research Center, Atlanta History Center.

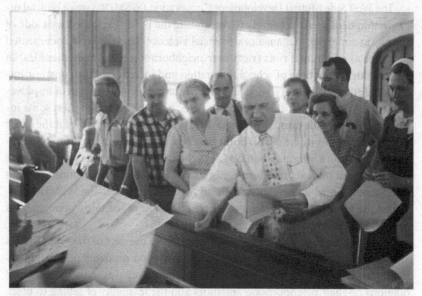

Figure 3.3. Southwest Atlanta planning and zoning meeting, 1954.
Source: James G. Kenan Research Center, Atlanta History Center.

within the "home building, financing, and selling businesses in the metropolitan area."[25] The plan sought to eliminate the violence inherent in transitioning neighborhoods, as urban white residents across the country resisted the influx of Black residents after the war. Unfortunately, tasking the all-white MPC with designing this plan created an exclusionary planning process that virtually prohibited citizen participation and limited Black working-class interests to only token inclusion. Planning meetings slowly transformed into another all-white political space (see figures 3.2 and 3.3).

All-white planning bodies dominated the governing coalition, but Black leaders were not completely excluded from the planning processes in the postwar city. In addition to the Black real estate interests invited to participate in the MPC's plan for race relations, Black leaders lobbied to get appointed to CACUR's many advisory subcommittees, leveraging the Black electorate for improved goods and services in Black communities.[26] The Perry Homes Advisory Committee, an appointed external committee similar to the University Homes Advisory Committee discussed in chapter 2, listed J. B. Blayton Sr., Bishop J. W. E. Bowen III, Dr. Benjamin E. Mays, William A. Scott, and R. A. Thompson as its members.[27] However, these men represented a similar cross-section of the Black community that was thus far overrepresented in Atlanta politics—businessmen, academics, and churches.

The West Side Mutual Development Corporation (WSMDC) was a biracial organization dedicated exclusively to integrating the newly expanded west side of the city in a manner that ameliorated racial violence. There are few documented incidents of communal riots (riots over neighborhood space and amenities) in Atlanta during the time of school integration and increasing Black postwar migration. Established in 1952, soon after the city implemented the Plan of Improvement, the WSMDC provided a space for Black business leaders to exert some influence on the creation and planning of Black communities throughout the city.[28] Representatives from the all-Black Empire Real Estate Board, in addition to representatives from Atlanta's banking, development, and insurance companies headquartered on Auburn Avenue, negotiated with their white counterparts to safely transition white neighborhoods on Atlanta's west side. The WSMDC continued the legacy of elite biracial cooperation that afforded more opportunities for decision-making and governance to Black elites.

Surveying Black communities had changed since the days of the 1934 Du Bois study in Beaver Slide. In 1954, the WSMDC surveyed residents in a neighborhood targeted for transition. The purpose of the survey was to gauge residents' opinions on their neighborhood amenities and the feasibility of selling to Black residents.[29] The WSMDC also met with working-class and low-income Black residents, particularly those facing displacement from urban renewal projects. Unfortunately, the group often advocated for and usually secured the best concessions for middle- and upper-class Black residents. Black WSMDC leaders leveraged the power of the electorate to "provide a number of public improvements, such as street widening, paving, drainage, lighting, and the construction of a park and a golf course."[30]

The Temporary Coordinating Committee on Housing (TCCH) preceded the West Side Mutual Development Corporation and served as an interesting counter to the production of postwar racial geographies. The TCCH was an all-Black group that assessed the housing needs of Black residents in postwar Atlanta. Created by the Atlanta Urban League and led by Black real estate developer W. H. Aiken, the TCCH controlled the racial geography of Atlanta by purchasing and building homes in vacant west side neighborhoods.[31] This organization was actively involved in creating a political geography for Black middle-class homeowners that was independent from white control and spatial proximity.

Constructing Postwar Black Geographies in Atlanta

It was in this exclusionary and segregated planning environment that city leaders designed and planned Perry Homes and its surrounding neighborhood. Urban redevelopment authorities—often public-private endeavors that institutionalized real estate interests into urban governance—began to deepen existing residential segregation patterns by incorporating local prejudices into federally financed plans. Working counter to the production of new spaces for Black communities that was established during the PWA and early AHA construction, this phase of public housing construction was focused on reinforcing and hardening spaces for Black and white Atlantans. This new form of spatial production was containing and confining Black residents into areas of the city that would not interfere with white spatial supremacy in the CBD and northern suburbs.[32]

White spatial supremacy included the creation and maintenance of white spaces that had amenities—both public and private—that excluded Black people or marginalized them within it. Legal and extralegal harassment, constant surveillance, and even outright violence threatened Black interlopers in white supremacist space. Spaces produced for Black residents were intentionally underdeveloped and isolated to reinforce spatial and political marginalization. In the FY 1953 Atlanta Housing Authority Annual Report, the board of commissioners described the site for Perry Homes: "On April 26, 1953, the ground was broken for the second multi-million-dollar post-war housing project to be developed by the Atlanta Housing Authority. This project, containing 1000 units for Negro occupancy, is scheduled for completion by the winter of 1954. It is located on previously undeveloped land in the Sweat Road area of northwest Atlanta, not far south of the Southern Railroad's Inman Yards, approximately midway between Marietta Road and Hollywood Road."[33]

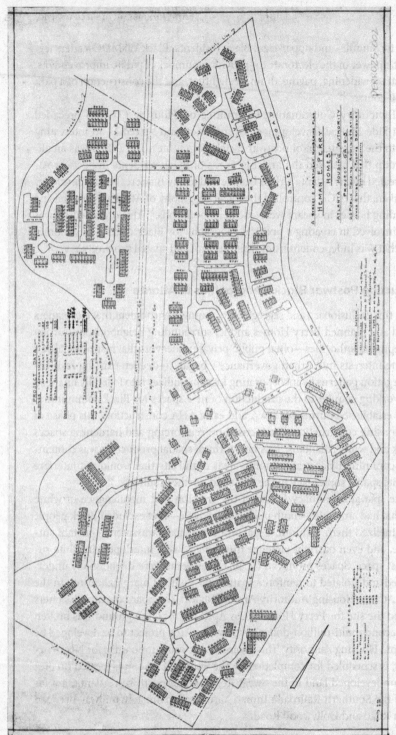

Map 3-4. Perry Homes site plan. Source: West Highlands at Perry Boulevard Records, Atlanta Housing Authority Archives.

The site plan demonstrates the isolation of this undeveloped tract of land for Perry Homes (see map 3.4). Note the natural barriers (Proctor Creek and Rockdale Park) that separate this area from the larger northwest community, preventing easy access through Perry Homes from downtown. Further, manmade barriers (the Southern Railroad Inman Yards) limited access to the growing employment opportunities in Atlanta's prosperous northern suburbs. The use of natural and man-made physical barriers echo Kaplan's suggestions for how to get local buy-in in Newark for urban renewal projects.

Downzoning industrial land into residential land was an improvement in the land use, but the city did not make any effort to implement the infrastructure necessary for that zoning designation. From a design standpoint, public housing developments were becoming increasingly landlocked, designed with circuitous streets with limited outlets onto main roads. Designers privileged constructing massive superblock structures that literally isolated the developments from the larger community.[34]

In spite of this reduced state support for developing community in and around public housing, the design for Perry Homes was comprehensive and comparable to that of University Homes. Paved roads, new sewage systems, and fully modernized amenities (electric stoves and refrigerators) were included, in addition to multiple play areas for children. Centralized laundry facilities would limit the water usage in each unit, and individual dry lines in backyards would not interfere with the uniform appearance of the property.[35] Social and economic spaces, specifically a community center and commercial spaces for rent, created an intentionally insulated community.

What the plan did not include, however, was accommodation for the increase in students in the undeveloped area. By 1969, Perry Homes would house 3,350 school-aged children. The plan also did not include accommodation for increased public transit use by this isolated population with few car owners. Even though Perry Homes was the first residential development in this area, designers still managed to bisect the community by designing it around a railway thoroughfare. Approximately forty buildings were constructed between a railway and a creek. Despite (or perhaps because of) this deficiency of public goods and services, city planners continued to increase residential development for low-income Black residents in the northwest, particularly after the passage of the 1961 Housing Act.

Section 221(d)(3) of the Housing Act of 1961 funded mortgage insurance to construct multifamily rental housing for residents with income above public housing income limits. In Atlanta, this program allowed for Black families to leave public housing developments and enter another subsidized housing program that also provided limited socioeconomic mobility. Turnover in Black public housing developments was low, and the two-tiered mortgage market largely prohibited Black buyers from qualifying for government-guaranteed mortgages.[36]

Working-class and middle-class Black residents whose potential homes were less likely to secure guaranteed mortgages yet who were still financially able to purchase private housing in cash were equally stymied. The land available for Black residential development was limited to select areas of the city, mostly in the northwest. During the site selection for Perry Homes, the AHA and MPC intentionally chose a site that would accommodate the housing needs of multiple socioeconomic classes of Black residents, thus creating a racialized space in one of the most undeveloped and marginalized areas of the city:

> The project site occupies only a portion of the above-mentioned tract of land. The remaining portion, wooded and rolling, extends northwestward to the Brownsville Road Settlement on Hollywood Road. It is bounded generally on the southwest by Proctor Creek and on the northeast by Sweat Road. Paved access roads and main utilities lines will be brought into the area in conjunction with our project. The Atlanta Housing Authority has worked closely with civic and private groups who have expressed an interest in developing the remaining portion of the tract. Well planned private developments here, adjacent to Heman E. Perry, would add up to a balanced, model community.[37]

Advocates for preventing such racialized planning were few and far between. Reports by the Metropolitan Planning Commission illustrate the hypocrisy of the urban regime, and the limits to challenge deviance from within. Although Black elites were participating in these planning processes, they were only contributing to the ongoing spatial injustice promoted by the city's postwar white supremacist planning logics:

> Top level program to create general agreement between leaders of both races about the need for planned expansion of housing space for Negroes, avoiding community disruption wherever possible. . . . Work to modify the FHA's policy of refusing approval to projected Negro developments in outlying areas. Dispersion of Negro communities throughout the area will help to avoid the high densities conducive to so many social problems, will make exploitation of Negro voters less likely, and will help preserve the economic strength of the valuable central business district.[38]

The result of this empty rhetoric and token, exclusionary participation for elite Black gatekeepers was a spatial justice that focused on outcomes, and not one that focused on processes. The biracial coalition worked in favor of middle-class and upper-class Black residents, providing for new parks and golf courses in their subdivisions. Conversely, working-class and working-poor Black residents were confined to underdeveloped areas without amenities or political representation in the planning processes.

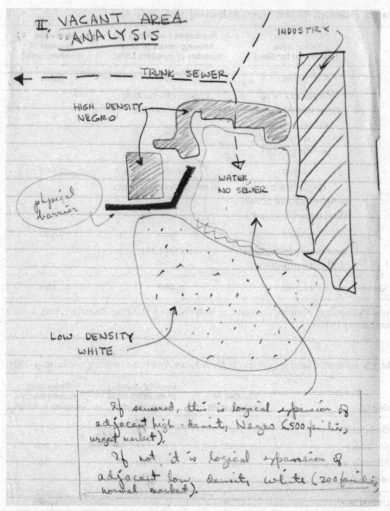

Figure 3.4. Bureau of Planning vacant area analysis, ca. 1960. Source: Bureau of Planning Papers, Atlanta History Center. The note reads: "If sewered, this is logical expansion of adjacent high-density Negro (500 families, urgent market). If not, it is logical expansion of adjacent low density white (200 families, normal market)."

A vacant area analysis from the Bureau of Planning illustrates the approach to planning for Black residential neighborhoods. Figure 3.4 shows a vacant area just south of a white neighborhood that was slowly transitioning to a Black neighborhood. The Bureau of Planning predicted this neighborhood would transition to all Black residents within five years. The bureau conducted the vacant land analysis to appease demands from resistant white residents.

Table 3.2. Estimated African American housing needs, 1959–1963

	Gross need (number of families)	Resources committed to housing needs to date (number of dwelling units)	Net need (number of dwelling units)
	9,100 displacees of all government action (urban renewal, expressways, public buildings, etc.)	2,500 turnover to existing public housing	6,600
	2,600 displacees by nongovernment action (fire, demolition, etc.)	4,500 in urban renewal areas	−1,900
	10,000 new family formation and net in-migration	500 Section 221	9,500
TOTAL	21,700	7,500	14,200

SOURCE: Metropolitan Planning Commission Archives, James G. Kenan Research Center at the Atlanta History Center.

Table 3.3. Estimated land requirements for African American housing needs, 1959–1963

Housing type	Number of dwelling units	Density (number of dwelling units per gross acre)	Gross land requirements (number of acres)
Public housing	1,200	10	120
Single family	3,000	3	1,000
Multifamily and duplex	6,400	10	640
Transitional	3,600	—	—
SUBTOTAL	14,200		1,760
Ex.			880
TOTAL			2,640 the equivalent of 12.75 land lots

SOURCE: Metropolitan Planning Commission Archives, James G. Kenan Research Center at the Atlanta History Center.

The maintenance of the "city too busy to hate" reputation required control of the pace and extent of desegregation through planning methods and tools. Surveys from the WSMDC indicated that while most white residents were amenable to ceding the neighborhood to Black residents, others were resistant to such change.[39] The political implications of this resistance—that is, the possibility of white terrorism that would shatter the city's New South image—required painstaking planning from city leaders, with Black residents making the most concessions.

Figure 3.4 demonstrates these concessions: the vacant area analysis suggests that if the proper sewage infrastructure is constructed, both Black and white residents could reside in this area. The white residential units were planned as low density, suggesting single-family homes to accommodate the "normal" white housing market. Black residents, given the "urgency" or high demand of their housing market, would be forced to reside in high-density or multifamily residential units. The neutrality of the planning process ignored the racial discrimination that created two housing markets and thus contributed to the processes and promulgation of segregation and difference.

The city planned to construct a physical barrier to separate the two races living in an "integrated" community. If the city did not install the sewage infrastructure, they would designate the area for white residential use only. Racial zoning has been illegal since 1913, yet these practices of racialized planning continued through the postwar period. These exclusionary processes limited Atlanta's 35.6 percent Black population to only 16.4 percent of its residential land.[40]

The severity of Atlanta's artificially controlled and racialized housing market was outlined in the Metropolitan Planning Commission's 1960 "Report from the Departing Housing Coordinator." The MPC calculated that the city had netted 14,000 housing units for Black residents between 1950 and 1960, yet this number barely satisfied the number of residents displaced by government and nongovernment action (estimated as 11,700). Tables 3.2 and 3.3 show the estimated housing needs of Black residents between 1959 and 1963, following government and natural displacement, in addition to natural in-migration and existing population growth. The report notes that neither estimate accounts for the existing overcrowding and substandard living conditions of the current Black population. The estimates were later reduced by 75 percent to account for Black residents "that were displaced for so long, they left the City."[41]

The report identified white resistance—and underreported communal violence—as the greatest "stumbling block" to relocating the increasing and displaced Black population. The "unlikely, but not impossible" solutions to such resistance included the following:

- Some form of minimum price assurance by local government to whites selling their homes to Negroes. Bonuses or help with moving expenses might be another form of financial assistance.

- Something like "221 eligibility certificates" for whites "displaced" by Negro expansion
- Special assistance for widows and elderly people who frequently do suffer financial hardship when "forced" to move because of the Negroes
- An intensive interpretation program by newspapers designed to attach "civic virtue" to selling a house to a displaced Negro family in an appropriate community.
- For the die-hard race haters, the idea might be sold negatively, in terms of saddling Negroes with old houses and big mortgages containing their expansion to avoid general dispersion. This, of course, could only be done on an individual basis.[42]

With the northwest providing the only vacant land available to Black residents, the city created a low-income neighborhood without sufficient public goods and resources and even less political representation. Within the first few years of Perry Homes' existence, the tenant association worked quickly and effectively to remedy the deficiencies in their development and the community at large.

Perry Homes and the Greater Northwest Community

Six months after Perry Homes' January 1955 opening, 904 families moved into the development after undergoing the stringent tenant selection process of the Atlanta Housing Authority.[43] In spite of the urgency of the Black housing market, tenants were selected following an initial screening of income requirements, an inspection of the current home to verify whether it was substandard, and housing manager approval. Minimum income requirements (except in the case of government relocation) and employment verification limited the selection of tenants to the deserving poor.[44] The Perry Homes tenant population was initially similar to that of University Homes and other prewar developments.

However, while the residents themselves were Black working-class and middle-class tenants, the northwest neighborhood into which they moved did not reflect their political capital. Compared to the neighborhoods inhabited by their white counterparts, the public goods and services of the northwest neighborhoods were considerably inadequate.[45] This section describes how the Perry Homes tenant association, in conjunction with local and citywide organizations, mobilized the resources of their residents to correct the racial and economic inequities in the city's allocation of public goods and services. This is an initial way the development was able to mobilize its resources in pursuit of spatial justice.

The disparity of public schools, libraries, and parks between white and Black neighborhoods was significant in 1954 Atlanta. A city map shows there were three libraries designated for Black use: a University Homes branch (discussed in chapter 2), the first branch constructed by Andrew Carnegie on Auburn Avenue, and the West Hunter branch, located in the southwest quadrant of the city.[46] Eventually, another library branch was constructed in the northwest—Dogwood Branch on Bankhead Highway—for Black residents' use, but was largely inaccessible to Perry Homes children lacking transit fare.[47]

When Perry Homes opened there were no high schools for Black students in the area, except for the overcrowded Turner High School—one of three Black high schools in Atlanta.[48] Construction soon began on the Samuel Harper Archer High School, which accepted its first students in 1957, while construction of the classrooms were still ongoing.[49] Within a decade, this high school would also face serious overcrowding issues; the 1,661 students attended the school in double shifts, while the night school for adults further strained the school's limited resources.[50] In spite of the *Brown v. Board of Education* decision to desegregate public schools in 1954, Atlanta schools were not desegregated until 1961.[51]

Parks, recreational facilities, and green spaces were underresourced and also difficult to access for Black residents in the northwest.[52] At the time of Perry Homes' construction, there was one large park for Black residents in the southwest, compared to ten large parks for whites throughout Atlanta. The two large parks located in the Central Business District were restricted to white use only, even though Black residents lived in many of the neighborhoods adjacent to the CBD until the start of the city's Urban Renewal program. There were also ten white community parks—smaller parks that included playground equipment—compared to three community parks for Black residents. Neighborhood parks and green spaces, designed to accommodate neighborhood children and provide open space throughout the city, were located exclusively in white neighborhoods. In 1954, there were approximately twenty-nine neighborhood parks and sixteen green spaces for white Atlantans.

In addition to insufficient libraries, schools, and parks, the development's first decade was marked by complaints of poor public services and infrastructure. The trunk line sewer installed during Perry Homes' construction could not accommodate the concomitant growth in 221(d)(3) multifamily homes over the next decade. By 1965, the population of Perry Homes and its surrounding community totaled over ten thousand residents. Due to this state neglect, residents complained frequently about sewage backup in their yards and their homes.[53]

Further, sewage overflow ran into Proctor Creek, the northern boundary of Perry Homes, creating an environmental hazard and unpleasant odors for residents. Residents complained about unpaved areas around front and back entrances that left floors and drying clothes caked in a fine red clay dust.[54] Further, there were few sidewalks throughout the development, which limited the walkability of the area for all residents, but particularly for children going to school. Similar to University Homes, there were no traffic lights installed at the major intersections on the southern and eastern entrances of the development, creating difficulties for children walking to school and adults walking to bus stops.[55]

The white supremacist spatial logics that dictated which areas were suitable for Black neighborhoods meant that many were adjacent to or wholly contained in areas once zoned for heavy industry. The formation of community organizations around environmental justice has long been a part of the Black radical tradition.[56] Black women took the lead in this and many other movements serving politically deviant interests in postwar Atlanta. The multiple movements at the local level pushed tenant associations to be more responsive to these interests.

Black Women at the Fore:
Black Feminist Planning Methods
as Spatial Justice

Working-poor Black women in Atlanta had been organizing for a long time. Dating back to the late nineteenth century, Black and white washerwomen organized one of the earliest interracial strikes in the South as they protested for higher wages.[57] They also organized in the Neighborhood Union, for the Gate City Day Care. Later, they worked the polls, mimeographs, and ovens and did other spade work that sustained the long desegregation movement for public schools and other public goods.

When the schools finally desegregated and Black students on the south side of Atlanta were legally able to enroll in schools on the north side, Black women who worked as domestics organized to get higher wages from their north side bosses to cover the bus fare for them *and* their children. Dorothy Bolden, founder of the National Domestic Workers Union, was one of the women to connect the public and private spheres through her lived experience, which informed her political organizing. Bolden, who was born in Newnan, Georgia, and moved to Vine City by the age of six, had been employed as a domestic worker since the age of nine.[58]

Black women like Bolden, who have long had to work inside and outside the home (and often, working outside of the home meant working inside of someone else's home), are well positioned to articulate the common interests between the public and private spheres. The social positioning of Black women, with race denying them the fragility of white femininity and gender denying them the authority and wage (however depressed) of Black men, doubly oppressed them in ways that produced a more inclusive politics. Bolden herself states: "We [working-class women] are in the best position to know the struggles. We have all given up a lot. I stomp the ground for Black and white."[59]

Bolden's ability to stomp the ground is also a by-product of her social positioning. When Bolden campaigned for Julian Bond, he noted that her network of domestic workers put her in many communities, many times a day:

> I think she just walked and talked in the neighborhood. We would give her a small bunch of campaign literature and . . . depended on her to walk around

in the neighborhood and influence her friends and associates. It was almost as if she was the center of an informal network. Now the other people who were at the centers of formal networks—political clubs—some of them were more imaginary than real. But I just had the feeling that she had this web of influence. . . . She was in touch with all these maids, and they were people who moved through the community twice a day. They left and they came back; they left and they came back. And I just had this image of this kind of talky bunch of women who, if they're talking about you in a good way, can only help. So she was into that loose, loose network. That was my picture of her, as well as her non-maid friends and neighbors and associates and so on, so she was just a good person to have on your side.[60]

Just as the demographics and politics of the community were shifting, the political opportunity structure was also adjusting to accommodate the increasingly converging needs and decreasingly available resources of residents inside and outside the public housing development. Instead of the traditional relationship where the public housing development funneled state and federal resources outward into the local community to produce new Black geographies, tenant associations were formally partnering with local organizations to increase capacity and autonomy outside of the increasingly racist housing authority. They worked to expand and maintain new Black participatory geographies.

The Council of Neighborhood Organizations (CNO) was formed to "stimulate the organization of Neighborhood Improvement Groups . . . coordinate the activities of these groups through the Council . . . conduct neighborhood Social Welfare Projects . . . sponsor city-wide Social Welfare Programs . . . discover unmet Social Welfare needs affecting Negroes and help organize for community action."[61] The CNO was taking up the excess produced by the city's approach of externalizing racial inequality into ad hoc committees and patronage-heavy boards and commissions. By centering racial inequality and the needs of those discriminated against, the CNO was mobilizing for those not included in the interests of the class-centered biracial urban regime.

There were seventeen organizations in the CNO membership, including elected tenant association leaders and managers from Carver, Eagan, Grady, Herndon, Perry, and University/John Hope Homes, representatives from eight neighborhood associations or civic leagues, and leadership from three citywide organizations. Religious groups, established political groups, and white "advisers" are notably absent from the membership list. Without the restrictions of uplift ideology, religious morality, and respectability politics structuring political opportunities, more deviant Black interests had the ability to assert power through public housing developments. New political norms, tactics, and strategies emerged to complement this more radical assemblage of interests for Black social and spatial justice.

Perry Homes Tenant Association and Goals

The first elected tenant association at Perry Homes reflected the residential population: three men held the leadership positions (Reverend C. A. Samples, president; Reverend Jerome Graham, vice president; Mr. Willie Schofield, treasurer), while three women held the remaining positions (Mrs. Helen Grimes, secretary; Mrs. Louise Williams, publicity director; Mrs. Margie Freeman, assistant secretary). Mr. John Cullen held the newly created position of tenant chaplain.[62] Another change in the tenant association structure was the introduction of two-year terms for tenant association officers, which allowed for long-term projects and initiatives. With such a large residential population, tenant association officers were tasked with large-scale projects and often worked with local community groups to achieve project goals.

The first project of note was the construction of the Perry Homes Community Center, which was not completed at the time of the opening. As described in chapter 2 and throughout this chapter, public space was sorely needed in the Black community, as the majority of Black land use was dedicated to residential construction. Floyd A. Hunter describes in detail the segregated spaces of power for Black and white leaders: while white leaders met in private homes and hotels, Black leaders of equal socioeconomic status were typically confined to the basements of Black churches and the Butler Street YMCA.[63] In spite of the significant gains in political economic power after 1946, Atlanta's Black community remained spatially marginalized in the postwar city. Upon the 1955 completion of Perry Homes, families moved into a development that was sited in an undeveloped neighborhood. On a positive note, this allowed residents, and by extension the tenant association, to take an active role in shaping the community around them.

Unlike the auditorium at University Homes that was planned and constructed as a political space, the AHA's intent for this multipurpose space was decidedly social. There is something to be said about the shift in prioritizing social space over political space, and I believe this relates directly to the increasing representation of women and children in the postwar public housing population. The programmatic initiatives of postwar public housing in Atlanta focus less on Americanizing residents into white, middle-class norms than the initiatives of those built by the PWA and AHA in the prewar era. During the 1958 dedication of the community center, AHA executive director M. B. Satterfield (a white male) noted that the event "marks the end of a period of delay and discouragement and the beginning of a period of pleasure of fulfillment in its use."[64]

Conversely, Black housing manager J. R. Henderson described the community center as a space of enrichment and social welfare: "we shall call upon all community resources in the fields of Education, Health, Religion, Welfare, and

Recreation to help us utilize this facility toward the building of better children, better parents, better homes, and a better City."[65] Thus, even as the AHA planned to provide for a play area for resident and neighborhood children, the tenants actively shaped the agenda for the community center to fit both their political and social needs. Here it is important to note the bottom-up sequencing of who the space serves and in what order—children, parents, homes, city—and how that relates to Black liberation as a decidedly social and communal project.

During the early years of Perry Homes, the tenant association worked with the Butler Street YMCA and the Board of Education to lobby for new school construction in the area.[66] What the residents lacked in economic power they made up for in sheer numbers, and it was through pressure on the city's electoral coalition that Perry Homes residents were able to advance their agenda. While city leaders constructed the northwest ghetto to isolate poor Black residents from their affluent white neighbors, they also indirectly created a powerful political base for poor, Black interests. Perry Homes alone housed five thousand residents in the development.[67] By 1958, residents had pushed for a shopping center, elementary school, and high school, which were all constructed within or adjacent to the Perry Homes development.[68]

The community center strengthened the development's ability to mobilize the resources of partners such as the Butler Street YMCA, but this partnership exposed a growing divide within the tenant population. The Atlanta Community Chest and Gate City Day Care Association provided funding and staff to open a branch of the Gate City Day Care in the Perry Homes community center, offering caretaking services to both residents and members of the surrounding community.[69] However, the recreational services the Butler Street YMCA provided were available only to those who had a membership at the YMCA. For many of the first families residing in Perry Homes, their working-class and middle-class salaries could bear the expense of a membership for childhood enrichment. However, a growing proportion of families in Perry Homes were not only receiving government subsidies but were also increasingly led by single women.[70] These demographic changes were not yet visible in the tenant association leadership until the early 1960s, when a number of officers are referred to as "Ms."[71]

This changing leadership focused much more on institutionalizing survival strategies than previous tenant associations. The AHA was openly hostile to working with these new tenant leaders—labeling the rise of single-woman households as proof of "the existence of serious family problems, some of them economic, and some social."[72] However, the Black women leadership were persistent in advocating for programs and facilities to accommodate the new lived realities in public housing.

When Archer High School attempted to solve its overcrowding problem by implementing double shifts, or two full school days in one, the Perry Homes tenant association and the local Community Relations Commission (CRC) protested.[73] The majority of Archer parents worked outside of the home (another recent demographic shift), and early dismissal of students without after-school activities or adequate recreational facilities would produce a deviant by-product of idle youth. The tenant association expanded its campaign for increased recreational opportunities and facilities by also mobilizing for more job opportunities near the development that matched the skills and needs of the unemployed resident population.[74]

Postwar public housing developments transformed as political opportunity structures by incorporating the interests and activism of women and women leaders. Tenant associations began advocating more directly for inclusion in urban planning and policymaking processes. The grievances of Black women on these changing tenant associations were intersectional, addressed the needs of working mothers and working caretakers, and understood the complexity of the extended family and queer family structures. This differs from earlier tenant association grievances that focused on Black male and traditional family structure needs and interests.

Between 1968 and 1969, Perry Homes residents were active through and against the tenant association. The most notable characteristic of the activity from Perry Homes tenants was the strong anti-management nature of the claims and grievances. Much of this anti-management political action stemmed from the age of the public housing developments. Aging developments had more maintenance issues that could not be addressed using the declining revenues from poorer households. A poorer and more militant tenant population received less AHA patronage, which had strengthened and empowered the pro-management leanings of earlier developments. Political organizations and spaces outside of the public housing development facilitated tenants' anti-management organizing.

In September 1966, the Atlanta Community Relations Commission moderated a series of community meetings immediately following the uprisings in Atlanta's Summerhill neighborhood.[75] The mayor appointed a committee that was authorized through an aldermanic ordinance to "work in the field of human relations, to foster understanding and education among different economic, social, and racial groups in the city."[76] The CRC remained instrumental in supporting the white supremacist spatial logics that prioritized the needs of all white residents over Black residents, up to and including the peaceful rearrangement of the racial geography of the city. In previous years, the group had worked in concert with tenant associations to force the school district to open up more high schools for Black students. The CRC addressed the needs of communities while procedurally continuing to marginalize Black residents in Atlanta. But the CRC did expand opportunities by bringing together multiple tenant associations residing in a particular area of the city. This is one of the first instances of gathering multiple tenant associations for the purpose of discussing citywide conditions.

Figure 3.5. CRC Exhibit in front of a public housing development, 1971.
Source: James G. Kenan Research Center, Atlanta History Center.

By January 1969, the AHA had taken the lead on these meetings and re-sorted to limiting them to specific developments. The AHA shifted the focus of the meetings to address the individual and development-level grievances of residents—those concerning maintenance, evictions, and changes in rent and rent collection. However, these meetings did little to change the conditions structuring daily life in Perry Homes, and tenants continued to organize around those conditions. The CRC was a space that allowed the initial exchange of grievances between public housing communities. By expanding the political geographies of public housing tenant associations—largely combining these disparate groups into common spaces over time to address spatial issues—these CRC community meetings formed the basis for new political opportunity structures that advocated for tenant procedural rights over space.

This era produced many alternative spaces for working-class politics that acted as both collaborators and foils to tenant associations, such as the local chapters of Tenants United for Fairness (TUFF). One of the earliest local chapters was founded by Ethel Mae Mathews at the Emmaus House, a community organization led by Catholic priest Father Austin Ford. Mathews was the first leader of Atlanta's chapter of the National Welfare Rights Organization, and she advocated through direct action protest and by running for the Board of Alderman in the 1970s (see figure 3.6).[77] TUFF's independence from the AHA, with its robust membership of both older and newer residents of subsidized housing, created a means of accountability for tenant associations. CRC, TUFF, and the Atlanta

Figure 3.6. Ethel Mae Mathews at an Atlanta Welfare Rights Organization protest, c. 1976. Source: James G. Kenan Research Center, Atlanta History Center, Boyd Lewis, photographer.

Figure 3.7. Protestors in front of AHA, 1969. Source: *Great Speckled Bird*, 2, no. 21 (August 4, 1969): 8. Courtesy of the Special Collections and Archives at Georgia State University Library, Atlanta Cooperative News Project, Richard Balugur, photographer.

Welfare Rights Organization were all critical spaces needed to expand and transform Atlanta's Black participatory geographies in the wake of the uneven gains from the civil rights movement. These spaces received external institutional support that was needed to mobilize broad structural change for tenant rights.

In 1970, Irene Martin, a tenant who supported the Perry Homes tenant association during the CRC meetings, sent a letter to Perry Homes housing manager Arthur Smith, AHA executive director Lester Persells, and AHA Board of Commissioners chair Edwin Sterne about the formation of a new chapter of TUFF. Martin writes, "It was necessary to become a stronger arm of the city-wide TUFF organization—because of the failure of the Atlanta Housing Authority to institute any meaningful changes in their rules and regulations and in their administrative policies, despite the Authority and the public's awareness of these problems for many months now."[78] Two months later on July 22, 1969, some three hundred public housing residents, TUFF members, and supporters marched and rallied on the AHA's front steps at the Hurt Building (see figure 3.7). Led by Reverend Ralph Abernathy, TUFF members led several days of protests around the issues of rent, grievances, and representation.

Abernathy and TUFF were pressing the AHA to adopt the Tenant's Bill of Rights that was released to the public in May 1969. At the protests, the conditions of the housing authority's properties that were becoming increasingly Black, led by women, and fiscally abandoned by federal authorities were outlined eloquently by Abernathy as women, children, and men held signs mocking the "pests" of the AHA.[79] The bill of rights included accommodations for nontraditional family structures and limited state surveillance during the application process: "questions concerning the legal standing or marital status of members of the family, the legitimacy of the children in the family, the police record of members of the family and other such information, including race or religion, shall not appear on the application form, or be asked by any Authority employee."[80] The bill of rights, the formation of TUFF, and the expansion of traditional Black participatory geographies such as the Black church to cover these deviant interests all suggest that public housing political opportunity structures were transforming to accommodate its new tenant majority: single Black women.

Conclusion

Public housing developments constructed in the postwar years were able to evolve as political opportunity structures following the exclusionary planning processes that produced spatial injustice within Atlanta's new metropolitan area. The Plan of Improvement in 1951 countered the political gains of the Black community following the 1946 *King v. Chapman* decision by increasing the white population relative to the Black population through annexation. The inclusion of more whites, and more residential area for whites to move to within Atlanta, weakened the new Black electorate. It also marked the beginning of the ghettoization of Black residents using the federal policies of urban redevelopment and urban renewal with the local prejudices and power of the AHA and CACUR. Although the segregation and concentration of Black residents was considered a potential exploitation of the Black vote or the cause of social unrest in Black communities, these excluded spaces also promoted political organizing and permitted the development of a spatial consciousness that served as a converging interest for the new tenant associations.[81]

The claims of the Perry Homes tenant association that focused not only on spatially just outcomes but also on spatially just processes mimic the shifts in Black organizing just before and immediately following the passage of the Civil Rights Act. In Atlanta, Black political organizing had been heavily influenced by the elite, and its leadership was dominated by socially advantaged men (and occasionally women). Black churches, historically Black colleges and universities, and Black social organizations were the traditional spaces of political organizing that promoted uplift ideology and accommodationist approaches to civil rights claims on the state. Thus, Perry Homes and other postwar developments expanded Black participatory geographies by institutionalizing political opportunity for those long ignored by elite Black political leadership.

The more adversarial, youth-oriented, and deviant-focused approaches to Black organizing that appeared on Black college campuses, segregated Black communities, and within the welfare rights movement demanded immediate attention to the social, economic, and political disparities between Black and white inhabitants in urban areas. As the demographics of public housing tenants transformed to younger, women-headed families, with increasing dependence on welfare subsidies, this bottom-up approach to Black political organizing appeared in tenant associations and produced new goals for the public housing development as a political opportunity structure. However, just as previous iterations of the political opportunity structure were limited, the focus on spatially just processes of inclusion for Perry Homes and other second-generation political opportunity structures did not foresee the structural shifts in urbanization. Although residents would soon gain greater control of spatial production, the city they controlled had a weakened urban tax base, fewer resources for public housing residents, and an increasing spatial mismatch for low-skill workers in the city as jobs moved to the northern suburbs.

Perry Homes residents, along with residents of other large developments in the northwest such as Bankhead Courts, continued to address this spatial mismatch and exclusionary planning logics. In 1979, Perry Homes tenant association president Mary Sanford, Oselka Stanfield, a blind resident residing in the nearby Hollywood neighborhood, and the NAACP filed a lawsuit against the Metropolitan Atlanta Regional Transit Authority (MARTA) for its failure to construct spa-

Figure 3.8. Mary Sanford speaking at a MARTA planning meeting, c. 1971.
Source: James G. Kenan Research Center, Atlanta History Center,
Boyd Lewis, photographer.

tially and procedurally equitable public transit in the metropolitan area (see figure 3.8).[82] Northwest residents had to take multiple buses to an east-west line, transfer downtown, and head north to go to work as domestics. Their children also had multimodal trips to get to their schools. In the long tradition of Black women organizers who united labor and community movements, Sanford and several others worked with the city, county, and MARTA to plan, advocate, and mobilize for a northwestern spur line connecting their community to downtown. In achieving this spatially just outcome—albeit thirteen years after the lawsuit was filed—Mary Sanford and the tenant association membership had demonstrated that Black women leadership had effectively shifted the political opportunity structure to capture a new form of deviance.[83]

The focus on spatial transformation and justice also marks a shift in tenant association activism, away from political equality and inclusion with whites and toward greater social and economic equity. Political inclusion in the regime was largely distributed to the elite, while these social and economic benefits of schools, sewage installations, and transit routes were redistributed more broadly. Although the Civil Rights Act and related legislation would provide a brief "new deal" for poor Black Americans to reclaim their political inclusion in state processes and institutions, the disparity between Black and white socioeconomic outcomes and opportunities continued to shape postwar tenant activism and grievances. This inequality was exacerbated with an economic downturn and political shift that reduced federal funding to cities (and housing authorities) as urban populations and tax bases declined. The next chapter discusses the institutional effects of this activism, and how these effects spurred another transformation of public housing developments as political opportunity structures.

Chapter 4

Grady Homes

Scaling Up Black Participatory Geographies

When Grady Homes held its first tenant association election on March 19, 1942, the coverage in the *Atlanta Daily World* underscored the community significance of the event. Calling the development "a hot bed of political activity for the past few weeks," the *ADW* highlights the importance of the tenant association, noting that candidates and their campaign managers mingled with "their supporters, and an air of suppressed excitement is felt throughout the project."[1] This civic engagement through tenant association participation was illustrated more clearly in the tenant association's constitution: "In order to insure equality of thought and action by each family residing in Henry Grady Homes, and to provide a fair and democratic form of tenant government, and to furnish a medium through which project club and activities may be supervised and integrated in the building of a more wholesome and better community life."[2]

Much like University and Perry Homes, the Grady Homes community amenities and community life were shaped by local resources and institutions in the 1940s. Grady Homes held a mass meeting in advance of its first tenant association elections, with guests Reverend B. L. Davis of Liberty Baptist Church and W. Y. Bell, executive secretary of the Atlanta Urban League. The two men spoke briefly on the importance of voting and political participation under the guise of the uplift ideology that pervaded the elite Black community at the time, stressing that such participation was an obligation for all to advance the race.

The tenant association candidates, all of whom were men, gave their stump speeches, focusing on community improvement such as streetlights and playground equipment. Turnout in the election was high: "the enthusiasm with which project residents approached the actual election was evident and was attributed to the fact that they have developed a community spirit through their living together in the project."[3] Early tenant association leadership and goals in Grady Homes were similar to those of the developments built in the first phase.

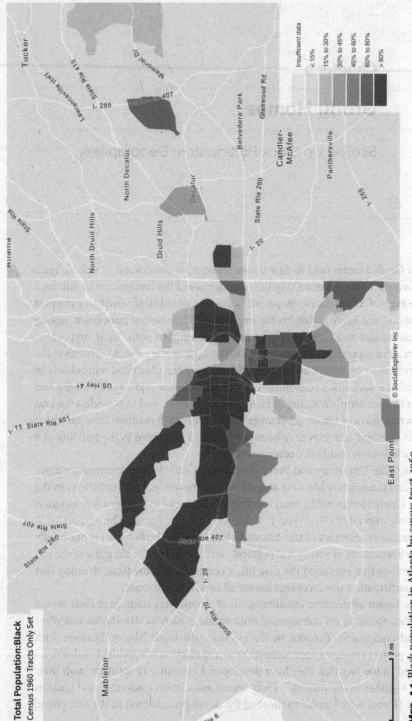

Total Population: Black
Census 1960 Tracts Only Set

Insufficient data
< 15%
15% to 30%
30% to 45%
45% to 60%
60% to 80%
> 80%

© SocialExplorer Inc

2 mi

Map. 4.1. Black population in Atlanta by census tract, 1960.
Source: U.S. Census Bureau, Social Explorer.

Yet Grady Homes would soon distinguish itself by hiring the first Black woman public housing manager, Miss Annie R. Hill, a graduate of the Atlanta University School of Social Work.[4] Hill's training encouraged uplift politics, but her gendered approach was more inclusive in providing political opportunity for girl and women tenants.

The development continued its political activism well into the 1960s, when fractures in the Black membership of the urban regime created opportunities for working-class advocacy.[5] The 1961 election of Mayor Ivan Allen Jr. marked the end of William Hartsfield's three-term reign and temporarily destabilized the order of the regime. Allen was a pro-business politician who was the son of an Atlanta businessman and a long-term member of the regime's governing coalition and old southern patrician legacy. To stimulate mobilization and engagement during his campaign, the women-led tenant association at Grady Homes created a "Voter Registration Badge of Honor" to award to voter registrants and place on their front door.[6] This "gimmick," as the local press referred to the effort, registered a new wave of low-income, working-class, migrant public housing tenants who could reap the benefits of a new administration.

The focus of this chapter is Grady Homes, a public housing development of approximately six hundred units located in Atlanta's Sweet Auburn neighborhood. Since the 1906 race riots, Sweet Auburn has functioned as an anchor for Atlanta's Black middle and upper classes, with Auburn Avenue serving as a vital economic, social, and civic space for upwardly mobile Black Atlantans. Home to headquarters of the Black-founded Atlanta Life Insurance Company, Citizens Trust Bank, Mutual Federal Savings & Loan, as well as the Black-owned Rucker Office Building and Savoy Hotel, Auburn Avenue provided a comprehensive, though segregated, space for Black life.

Since the *King v. Chapman* decision of 1946, the business, religious, and philanthropic leaders of Auburn Avenue were incorporated into Atlanta's urban regime, functioning as a crucial proportion of the city's electoral coalition. However, while elite Black Atlantans were granted patronage of municipal services and contracts for the Black vote, less affluent Black residents were marginalized in the political process and saw the fewest gains in the postwar city. The Grady Homes tenant association, in its close proximity to the actual Black spaces of power of Auburn Avenue, consistently pushed to expand the Black participatory geographies for more deviant political interests by engaging with, and redistributing from, these Black elites.

As noted in chapter 3, the political opportunities created by the Civil Rights Act and related legislation, along with the demographic transformation of public housing in the 1960s, produced a more inclusive politics for Black deviants living in public housing communities. These politics frequently clashed with the longstanding, and more accommodating, Black leadership in Atlanta. Not only were these radical politics inclusive of a more deviant set of interests, but they manifested into political expressions that diverged from the long-standing political actions, norms, and institutions of the "city too busy to hate."

Yet, the pace of this approach caused further marginalization. Black residents in overcrowded housing were forced to wait for whites in depopulating, segregated areas to move, causing more downward pressures on a too-tight Black housing market. During the late 1960s and early 1970s, tenant association members such as Grady Homes president Susie LaBord used their membership and legitimacy from national organizations to scale up the Black participatory geographies for public housing tenants. While the previous chapter noted the use of local organizations to expand these geographies, shifting political economic arrangements created more opportunities and resources for tenant organizing at the national level.

Just as they had done in the early years of public housing, tenants were again using resources from the national level to expand participation and inclusion at the local level. This produced new scales of public housing advocacy at the local level. In 1969, the Atlanta Housing Authority (AHA) established the Citywide Advisory Council on Public Housing (ACPH), with representatives from each tenant association board. The ACPH would oversee federally funded modernization projects and provide new opportunities and limitations for tenant participation and inclusion in Atlanta.

Susie LaBord and the Grady Homes' Tenant Association

The Grady Homes tenant association has planning and political roots that are quite similar to those of University and Perry Homes. Constructed in 1940, Grady Homes was one of the first developments built by the Atlanta Housing Authority, and its tenant association benefited from (and was limited by) the top-down leadership of its elite-trained housing managers. An analysis of early issues of the tenant newspaper *The Voice* and internal AHA documents shows male residents led the tenant association in the first decade of its existence.[7]

Many of the early tenant association events took advantage of the strong academic resources of local historically black colleges and universities (HBCUs) as well as the political and business connections from Auburn Avenue. The tenant association collected a one-dollar annual "Community Fee" from each household to fund its events that would provide social, academic, and economic development activities for tenants. One of the earliest endeavors of the tenant association was the organization and administration of "The People's College," an offering of seventy-five different topics (ranging from Salesmanship to the Southern Labor Problem) over ten weeks.[8] The courses required a fifty-cent registration fee and no other payment.

Atlanta University sponsored the courses and credited President Rufus E. Clement with conceiving the idea. Clement, an accommodationist who promoted uplift ideology for poor Black Atlantans, modeled the People's College off the successful "Citizenship Schools" the Atlanta NAACP offered in the 1930s to provide civic education to poor Black residents.[9] Here we see the similar attempt to acclimate the poor Black populace using social, economic, and political mores of the Black professional and upper classes, an approach that was also used in University Homes by Alonzo Moron and the influential and affluent advisory committee. Clement would later go on to become the first Black person elected to an Atlanta municipal office after the end of Reconstruction, when he was elected to the city's school board in 1953.[10]

Yet Grady Homes differed from University Homes in its spillover effects into the community. While University Homes served as a resource for local residents who were spatially and legally isolated from adequate public facilities, the Sweet Auburn neighborhood was affluent and established enough to not require such extensive resources from public housing developments. Grady Homes added to an already resource-rich community. Thus, Grady residents were able to benefit from the wealth of offerings for Atlanta's Black citizenry, such as the long-standing civic, religious, and philanthropic institutions of the Wheat Street Baptist Church, Big Bethel African Methodist Episcopal Church, and the Butler Street YMCA. The Auburn Avenue branch of the Carnegie Public Library offered the first books for Black Atlantans to check out in 1921, while the Atlanta Life Insurance Company issued some of the earliest life insurance policies for Black residents, when white insurers refused to cover them.

Many local branches of national organizations such as the NAACP and the Urban League were located on Auburn Avenue, and in the pivotal local elections of the 1960s, mayoral candidates shrewdly located campaign offices in Sweet Auburn.[11] In spite of this resource-rich setting, Grady Homes offered Sweet Auburn residents a benefit many developments continued to provide—publicly funded and maintained space for youth and adults. Local schools and youth-oriented groups used the playground and ballfields at Grady Homes, while the community center provided meeting space for adult activities.[12]

As urban renewal and open housing transformed the demographics of public housing developments from heteronormative nuclear families to single woman–headed households, the goals and composition of the tenant associations changed to reflect this transition. With a poorer public housing population, the relationship between public housing tenants and local residents became less communal and reflected the NIMBYism (not-in-my-backyard-ism, a common land use term for local resistance to new, often denser, development) frequently expressed toward contemporary public housing developments. A telling example of this NIMBYism is displayed toward Atlanta's ambitious highway program that encir-

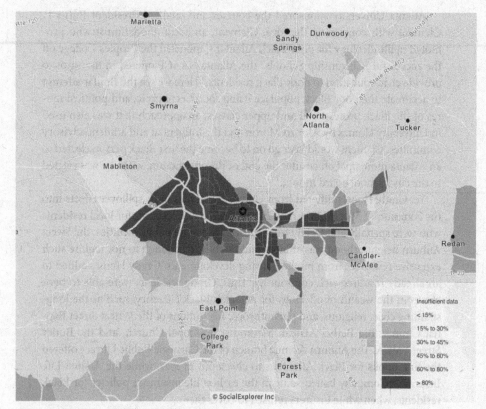

Map 4.2. Atlanta's major highways and percentage of census tract that is Black, 1970. Source: U.S. Census, Social Explorer.

cles and twice bisects the city's boundaries. Interstate 285 encircles the city, isolating the prestigious northern white suburbs from their less affluent neighbors. Interstates 75 and 85 bisect the city into eastern and western halves, while Interstate 20 bisects the city into northern and southern halves (see map 4.2).

Displacement for highway construction targeted the poor Black and white communities around the CBD, as Atlanta's business interests continued to dictate urban development policy.[13] Atlanta's highway planning and construction began in 1946 (well before the Federal Aid Highway Act of 1956), when the State Highway Department of Georgia commissioned a comprehensive highway and transportation plan from the H. W. Lochner Company of Chicago. The Lochner Report emphasized the necessity of highway construction and advocated for the clearance of substandard areas in order to rejuvenate the city. The report's arterial system of expressways that converged into the CBD facilitated the transformation of the downtown from a mix of commercial and residential land use to an area of private and public office buildings.

In 1955, the AHA sold land surrounding Grady Homes and the all-white Capitol Homes to the city of Atlanta for the construction of the Downtown Connector (the north-south highway, or Interstate 75/85). The Connector created a man-made buffer between the Sweet Auburn neighborhood and the CBD. An AHA Annual Report states:

> The downtown connector segment of the main Expressway, in its finally determined location, will pass through a portion of two low-rent housing projects, Grady Homes and Capitol Homes. The City of Atlanta desired to begin Clearance work in the Grady Homes section first. The Authority, recognizing the compelling area-wide need for completion of a North-South Expressway, agreed to transfer the necessary Grady Homes project land to the City for Expressway use. In return, the City furnished the Authority with additional land to compensate for that relinquished by the Authority and agreed to move the sixteen buildings standing in the Expressway path to other locations approved by the Authority. By June 30, this complicated move of sixteen large concrete buildings was well underway.[14]

The "compelling need" to complete the expressway was that of the powerful northern suburbs wanting an expedient mode of transport through Atlanta's less desirable areas during their commutes. Over the next three years, the city moved over twenty public housing buildings to accommodate highway construction, in addition to demolishing several hundred substandard homes in poor communities.[15] These moves were conducted largely without any public resistance from neighborhood advocates. In the quest to develop Atlanta as a regional transportation hub in the postwar era of automobiles, the political interests of the poor were frequently subordinated to those of the downtown business interests and their allies. The Lochner report's original plan for the east-west highway, Interstate 20, would have demolished Auburn Avenue had the *King v. Chapman* decision not increased the political power of the Black upper classes.

Just as elite Black leaders advocated for—and received—expanded and improved residential areas in the Plan of Improvement, they were also able to preserve Auburn Avenue by shifting the construction of the east-west highway just south of their neighborhood. The biracial coalition that served as a shining example of the power of the ballot in 1946 was beginning to lose its luster for poor Black Atlantans. They continued to have their electoral power exploited while their social, economic, and political gains remained stagnant relative to their elite leaders. Black businessowners, much like their white counterparts, continued to be overrepresented in the regime's membership.

One woman who attempted to rectify this disparity between Grady Homes and its wealthier neighbors was Susie LaBord. LaBord and her husband, Gus, operated a barbeque restaurant at Fourth and Cain Streets in the old fourth ward neighborhood for twenty-two years before their business was demolished for the

Figure 4.1. Downtown Connector construction, Grady Homes on right, 1962.
Source: James G. Kenan Research Center, Atlanta History Center.

construction of the Downtown Connector.[16] During the Great Depression, the LaBords created an alliance of small business owners in the old fourth ward to provide money and goods to poorer residents. The demise of these informal spatial networks of mutual aid were yet another casualty of the disruptive processes of urban renewal and redevelopment borne by poor Black Atlantans.

The LaBords moved into Grady Homes in the early 1950s following Gus's cancer diagnosis; he died a year later. Susie LaBord never remarried and instead devoted the remainder of her life to improving the Grady Homes community. As a single Black woman living in public housing, LaBord focused on childcare, public health, and educational programs for poor Black families. As a resident, LaBord both founded and volunteered at the Grady Homes day care center.[17] Using her previous experience as a mutual aid coordinator in the old fourth ward, she arranged for tenants to act as volunteers during the day until the program was able to obtain AHA funding for paid work.

This commitment to Grady Homes elevated LaBord to president of the tenant association, a position she held for over thirty years until her death. After Lyndon B. Johnson signed the Economic Opportunity Act in 1964 to conduct his War on Poverty, LaBord sent Johnson a handwritten letter asking for funding and support for a Grady Homes Head Start program.[18] LaBord frequently utilized her unofficial position as Grady Homes advocate to circumvent classist urban politics and gain political opportunities at the federal level, quite similar to the relationship between the early University Homes leadership and the progressive members of the Roosevelt administration.

The combination of LaBord's ability to mobilize resources, the Johnson administration's goal to create landmark legislation with the Great Society programs and civil rights acts, and Atlanta's legacy as a pilot for federal social welfare programs, created a new political opportunity structure within Atlanta's public housing developments in the 1960s and 1970s. The White House replied to LaBord's letter within two weeks of receipt and coordinated funding with Economic Opportunity Atlanta (EOA) to launch the East Central Neighborhood Economic Opportunity Atlanta Center. Susie LaBord was named as the East Central EOA founder and president. Through the East Central EOA, LaBord was able to host a variety of means-tested programs to benefit the Grady Homes community.[19]

Poor Peoples Movements: Grady Homes and the Fight for Inclusive Economic Opportunity

The East Central EOA, like all other EOA branches, used two complementary strategies to address community needs. At the director level, advisers (who were either elected by residents at their local EOA service center or appointed by local community leaders) identified community needs and possible programmatic solutions. At the service aide level—paid employees from the community who were hired to meet the maximum feasible participation requirements of the Economic Opportunity Act—service workers went into the communities to find marginalized individuals to match with available programs, funding, education, training, and employment.[20] This two-pronged approach of place- and people-based strategies for economic development provided a bottom-up approach to community development that was not previously available to the poorer residents of the Sweet Auburn neighborhood (see figures 4.2 and 4.3).

The launch of the East Central EOA suggests another transformation of the public housing development as a political opportunity structure. As resources for political opportunities bypassed urban governments and were directed to neighborhood groups and organizations (encapsulated by the Community Action Program with maximum feasible participation for disenfranchised populations), the urban poor were finally able to create political spaces with inclusive processes toward equitable outcomes for their own interests. The late 1960s and early 1970s allowed for more deviant interests to briefly have representation at the local level, which in Atlanta translated to the incorporation of the poor and working-class interests in the biracial regime.[21]

Figure 4.2. EOA fresh produce distribution, c. 1974. Source: James G. Kenan Research Center, Atlanta History Center, Boyd Lewis, photographer.

Figure 4.3. EOA drug rehabilitation house, undated. Source: James G. Kenan Research Center, Atlanta History Center, Boyd Lewis, photographer.

In 1972, LaBord was the first public housing tenant appointed as a voting member to the Atlanta Housing Authority Board of Commissioners. Under Mayor Ivan Allen Jr., two Black men had been appointed to the Board of Commissioners. Jesse B. Blayton, of the Perry Homes Advisory Committee and founder of the first Black-owned radio station in Atlanta, was appointed in 1964, and Dr. Rev. William H. Borders, pastor of the Wheat Street Baptist Church, was appointed in 1969.[22]

The Board of Commissioners set policies for the Atlanta Housing Authority, and previous commissioners had all been professional or academic males. Although the terms were five-year appointments, there had only been sixteen commissioners since 1938. The average tenure for a commissioner was ten years, with four commissioners serving over fifteen years.[23] LaBord had served previously as a resident commissioner, a nonvoting member of the board with a one-year term. Thus, the appointment of Susie LaBord following Borders's resignation is another indication of the shift toward a more inclusive and community-centric urban political process.

LaBord held her voting commissioner position until her death in 1991. During her tenure with the Board of Commissioners, the AHA launched a series of work training and development programs for residents. LaBord was a major proponent of lifting residents out of poverty through better training and expanding job opportunities in low-income neighborhoods. She insisted that the AHA staff more positions with residents and shunned welfare programs that "rewarded" women for having more children as job opportunities decreased in inner cities.[24]

Beginning with her 1973 reelection as president of the Grady Homes tenant association, LaBord envisioned herself as representing not only the interests of her own public housing development but also the interests of all public housing tenants in Atlanta: "[My goal is] to be a much better president in 1973. I want to make Grady Homes and all public housing in Atlanta the best in the nation."[25] At this point, LaBord was actively involved in citywide and national organizations to promote the interests of poor residents and community associations. Yet her representation of poor interests narrowed over time, as evidenced by her comments on tenants who receive welfare.

In 1974, LaBord was elected as second vice president of the National Association of Community Development (NACD) by a vote of 1,283 to 500. The NACD was a nationwide coalition of community organizations dedicated to advocating for and promoting social programs for the poor. At the time of her election and for her next two terms as second vice president of the NACD, LaBord's approach was lockstep with the individualistic theories of poverty: "Lots of poor people of all races get a chance to stand on their own feet, learn, earn, and carry their share of the load through programs of community action. We cannot let them go down the drain now."[26]

Figure 4.4. Susie LaBord, undated. Source: Atlanta Housing Authority Archives.

LaBord continued to spotlight Atlanta public housing at the national level in her many trips to Washington, D.C., by testifying on various subcommittees on issues of education, poverty, housing, and community economic development. LaBord frequently used examples from Grady Homes and her experience with poor Atlantans through the East Central EOA during her testimonies. Such examples likely contributed to the steady funding of poverty pilot programs that were sited within and around public housing developments in the early 1970s, such as day care centers, Job Corps training centers, nutritional and substance abuse treatment programs, and adult literacy facilities.

Nearly a decade after writing that first letter to President Johnson, LaBord was sought out as a speaker to community organizations and was a legitimate expert in her work advocating for the poor. Despite shrinking federal funding to support public housing, LaBord was integral in organizing the funding and construction of the Susie LaBord Community Center at Grady Homes in 1976. Keeping with LaBord's focus on expanding the rights of the poor, the community center functioned as a gathering space for tenant association and grievance committee meetings.

Susie LaBord's tireless advocacy on behalf of Grady Homes sustained this development as a political opportunity structure even as public housing funding continued to decline throughout the 1970s. Under LaBord's leadership, the Grady Homes tenant association mobilized resources from the federal level to improve their marginalized political legitimacy at the city level. LaBord also strengthened the political legitimacy of neighborhood and community organizations through her connections with the NACD, EOA, and United Way. Although LaBord remained dedicated to maintaining a social safety net for marginalized groups, poverty rates and welfare receipts continued to increase across Atlanta and within its public housing population. The political evolution of Atlanta's low-income housing organizations in the 1970s and the response at the city level are described in the next two sections.

LaBord's mode of leadership shaped the next two decades of public housing organizing, with many benefits and constraints for Black women. The Black feminist politics practiced in this period of tenant association organizing legitimated the lived experiences of a younger and more diverse leadership. Yet, LaBord's views on receiving welfare as a character flaw instead of a structural outcome were becoming more common across tenant association leadership, decreasing the types of programs offered, and the populations served, in developments. The irreplaceable personal connections LaBord developed over her lifetime further limited the incentive to develop new and more diverse leadership, as evidenced by LaBord's thirty-year term as tenant association president. These constraints created new cracks in tenant solidarity politics, revealed during a new public relations campaign in the 1970s.

Winning the Public Relations War on Public Housing: AHA and Helen Bullard

At the end of the 1960s, the reputation of the Atlanta Housing Authority was in the toilet following a decade of urban renewal, displacement, stalled desegregation and nonexistent integration, declining funding, and an increasing tenant population. Tenants and managers, who had worked cooperatively for the first three decades, were finding themselves at odds with one another at the start of the 1970s. Wanting to prevent any further tensions, Executive Director Lester Persells hired Helen Bullard of the public relations firm Helen Bullard Associates.

Helen Bullard founded her own public relations firm in 1967 and managed or served on the campaigns of Mayors Hartsfield, Allen, and Massell. As someone who had roles both in the governing and electoral coalitions of the urban regime, Bullard was a fairly understudied white, college-educated woman who dedicated her life to public service and politics. She served on the Citizens Advisory Community for Urban Development (CACUD), the Atlanta Community Relations

Commission (CRC), and the Atlanta Urban League. Her politics were not particularly progressive—in fact, her public service committee work did much to uphold the white supremacist classism that privileged the needs of Atlanta's white citizens over the Black ones, and its rich over its poor. Nonetheless, Bullard consistently served causes and campaigns that fought for constitutionally guaranteed Black civil rights.

The March 1, 1969, contract between the AHA and Helen Bullard Associates scoped out two primary tasks. The first task was a survey of tenants, managers, and agencies that serve tenants. Its purpose was to assess the AHA and its policies that could turn into "an action program designed to lessen the tensions of both residents and managers."[27] The second task was "an interpretive program [that] would include a better system of communication between residents, managers, the Housing Authority and the community at large."[28] Bullard's contract illustrates the core problem of externalizing race from urban planning processes—by failing to address the centrality of race in the geography of Atlanta and the politics of its land use, tensions between residents and managers, and the AHA and the communities surrounding their developments, became unmanageable after the federal mandates for public housing desegregation.[29]

Figure 4.5 is an undated list titled "Atlanta Housing Authority," itemizing what looks like notes from an executive or managerial listening session. This list identifies legitimate managerial priorities for an administrative agency facing social, political, and financial stress, but it also suggests the continuation of racial logics in shaping decision-making and policymaking processes. The top, or first interest, was hiring a new executive director, which was needed as Persells was clearly clashing too much with the new tenant leadership. The rent strikes and tensions around urban renewal and desegregation were happening on his watch, and it was clearly time for younger, fresher leadership.

Further down the list are more troublesome priorities. The third item, which states "Don't allow Tenant Commissioner to vote or limit his term," is in direct reference to the newly created state (and federal) regulations mandating tenant representation on housing authority boards.[30] In response to the urban rebellions, many federally funded state agencies mandated greater citizen participation in the local production and administration of government plans and programs. To counteract this power shift, the state limited voting tenant commissioners to one-year terms instead of the five-year terms of voting nontenant members. The law also ensured the number of resident members would never exceed nonresident members.[31]

Number eight on the list is "Evicting undesirables," pointing again to an individualistic approach of scapegoating the structural problems of public housing onto individual tenants. In the minds of housing managers—an ideology that long-term residents would later take up—public housing had an image problem, and this was largely caused by a few bad apples.[32] In labeling some residents

ATLANTA HOUSING AUTHORITY

1. Select New Director
2. Commissioners do serve legally until they or successor elected.
3. Don't allow Tenant Commissioner to vote or limit his term.
4. AHA's recommendations for implementing Task Force's suggestions.
5. Shelton matter
6. Nicole Harrison matter.
7. Lease
8. Evicting undesirables
9. Program to effectively reduce "vacated charge offs".
10. Problems involving West End PAC.
11. Is Candler Warehouse matter O.K.?
12. Antoinette Grayson's letter.
13. Park Central request for changes.
14. Quarterly Meeting of Tenant Association Pres.
15. Refresher Course and Public Relations for AHA Staff.
16. Complaint form for tenant use.
17. Fulton County Housing Authority.
18. City take over of Urban Redevelopment.
19. Progress on new locations
20. Report on M I P.
21. Equal Opportunity policy for Housing.
22. Liability Insurance for Commissioners.
23. Past dues too high.
24. Report on T P P.

Figure 4.5. Undated list in Helen Bullard Papers on the Atlanta Housing Authority. Source: Atlanta Housing Authority Ephemera, 1974–1979, Helen Bullard Papers, MSS 58, James G. Kenan Research Center, Atlanta History Center.

as undesirable, the housing authority elided its own responsibility, disinvesting from the initial goal of public housing to uplift the submerged working and middle classes through the provision of safe and affordable housing. In constructing the undesirable tenant as a problem, housing authorities solved this issue by adding behavioral requirements to tenant leases. Eviction was provided as a quick fix to the new crisis of public housing financial solvency.[33]

Results from the tenant survey are illuminative of structural and citywide tenant priorities that were not represented by individual tenant associations. The survey identifies the factors that prevented the public housing development from becoming a public housing community—lack of control over spacemaking for the equitable distribution of public goods and services. The top three grievances from the survey across eleven developments and nearly eight thousand respondents were the need for more recreation facilities, tile floors (instead of cement), and better lighting. The survey was administered door to door and listed thirty-five possible grievances, largely concerning the design of the individual unit and wider development ("more closets" "day care facilities"), as well as some behavioral issues ("have parents discipline their children").[34] Tenant grievances around recreation, floors, and lighting articulate the emerging concerns of Black women concerning the quality of their homes, the opportunities available to their children, and the safety, livability, and comfort of the surrounding community.

Bullard's role at the AHA was to continue to uphold Atlanta's race-friendly image in the wake of national urban unrest. Bullard did so through a series of compromises and messaging—she helped create bureaucracies around new tenant association formations (such as the Citywide Advisory Council on Public Housing), which facilitated folding these tenant representatives into the newer, more progressive housing authority. At the same time that some tenants were being empowered and folded into the political regime, others were systemically identified and evicted as undesirables. Bullard's time at AHA marks a significant period of change—where some tenants would be empowered and would gain more political opportunities within the structure, while others would be permanently disenfranchised, marginalized, and eventually removed from it.

Tenant Organization and Urban Bureaucracy: The Citywide Advisory Council on Public Housing

In 1969, tenant association leaders and the Atlanta Housing Authority formed the Citywide Advisory Council on Public Housing (ACPH), whose purpose was to formally bridge the gap between the Atlanta Housing Authority and the unique tenant associations. The 1965 Housing and Urban Development Act and the 1968 Housing Act authorized the construction of over six million public housing units over ten years. Between 1968 and 1973, the AHA constructed ten public housing developments with over five thousand new units of housing—over 30 percent of the total number of Atlanta's public housing units.[35] Within a decade, public housing would comprise nearly 10 percent of all Atlanta's housing stock, 15 percent of all Atlanta's rental housing stock, and house nearly 4 percent of all Atlanta's residents.[36]

Atlanta's population was becoming poorer and Blacker, and jobs were continuing to leave at a rapid rate. While organizations for tenant rights and poor advocacy truly flourished in the late 1960s, during the 1970s these associations grew bureaucratized as they were subsumed within Atlanta's urban regime. Simultaneously, tensions mounted between advocates over territory (the public housing development), resources (programmatic funding and staff), and the most effective solutions to poverty (individual versus structural).

By externalizing shared interests and pooling resources, the utility of public housing developments as political opportunity structures had declined during the 1970s. The ACPH tenant leadership was dominated by the larger public housing developments such as Perry and Carver Homes' residents. In addition, the tenant leadership was also predominantly Black and female, reflecting the majority populations in public housing. There were never any white tenants involved in the leadership of the ACPH. In spite of the tenant population changes, the head of the AHA was a white male until the 1977 appointment of Ernest C. Jackson as the first Black AHA executive director.[37]

The previous director, Lester H. Persells, was extremely reluctant to integrate public housing developments and equally resistant to the Black female leadership of the ACPH. Jackson had served for over a decade as the housing director of the AHA and was a frequent target of Atlanta's Black leadership for his complacency in AHA's deliberate (and possibly illegal) process of housing desegregation.[38] Although Jackson was much more responsive to tenant needs as the new executive director, the lack of funding limited his ability to effect change across public housing communities.

In its formative years, the ACPH was extremely effective in mobilizing new resources into public housing developments. The ACPH voiced the shared grievances of the city's public housing communities, maximizing the effectiveness of the organization as a new political opportunity structure for poor Black Atlantans. The ACPH was also more effective because during its early years, tenants worked *with* AHA executives and management staff instead of *against* them, particularly when it came to advocating for more federal funds. This cooperation led to the ACPH becoming a legitimate member of the regime.

One of the earlier efforts of the ACPH was to petition Governor Jimmy Carter, Senators Herman E. Talmaldge Sr. and Sam Nunn, and President Nixon to prevent budget cuts to dozens of public housing antipoverty programs and resident jobs within the housing authority.[39] The ACPH was frequently able to mobilize its population of nearly fifty thousand residents to support public housing programs and legitimize the political efficacy of poor Atlantans. These early mobilizations were often successful due to national support from the National Tenants Organization and other emergent tenant representation groups. The availability of these national resources helped facilitate the ACPH's incorporation into the regime.

However, by November 1972, the relationship between ACPH tenant members and the AHA board became decidedly antagonistic.[40] Louise Watley, president of the Carver Homes tenant association, emerged as the more radical tenant leader of the ACPH and was advocating for a citywide rent strike in response to poor housing conditions. Watley clashed frequently with the more accommodationist Susie LaBord, who had just resigned from the ACPH tenant chairmanship due to her appointment to the AHA Board of Commissioners. While only Ernest Jackson (then serving as director of housing) typically attended the ACPH meetings as the formal AHA representative, Executive Director Lester Persells, all five members of the AHA Board of Commissioners, and the Housing and Urban Development director of housing management and community services attended the November 1972 meeting. The gathering of such influential leaders increased the political visibility and efficacy of the public housing tenants and their interests through the ACPH.

Launching a citywide rent strike, however, did little to expedite the congressional authorization of HUD funds to local housing authorities, and AHA leaders and HUD representatives used this meeting to shift the blame from themselves to Congress.[41] In response, Watley attacked the political process and advocated for more transparency from the government, particularly the release of HUD and AHA budgets to the public. Watley stated that if tenants had an idea of the budget, they would temper their demands and champion cost-effective and resource-efficient solutions.

The two sides reached a compromise to streamline the maintenance process to prevent residential "favoritism" from maintenance workers, by centralizing maintenance requests in development management offices. Tenants who overburdened the maintenance system relative to the size or age of their unit would receive additional charges on their rent bill to cover the additional maintenance. Further, the AHA would begin providing classes to educate tenants on housing maintenance and upkeep, mimicking its managerial approach to acclimating tenants to middle-class values in the 1930s. However, implementation stalled on both the classes and the maintenance system, and the rent strike continued.[42]

In February 1973, Dennis Goldstein, the Atlanta Legal Aid representative to ACPH, provided an update on the rent strikes. Following nine months of rent payments into escrow accounts set up by the courts, the AHA retaliated by sending eviction notices and dispossessory warrants to striking tenants.[43] AHA and Legal Aid attorneys met to reach another compromise regarding the inefficient maintenance and grievance procedures that marginalized tenant needs and caused the current rent strike.

The new maintenance procedure included mandatory semiannual housing inspections for each unit, which would result in a maintenance needs card for each household. Maintenance workers would address each need from the inspection, and tenants would submit their satisfaction with the maintenance to the housing director, Ernest Jackson. If the maintenance provided was not satisfactory, AHA would send out a maintenance person from their centralized staff to address the issue. The rent strike ended after nine months, and the resources of the ACPH and its partners provided a progressive resolution to long-standing issues about grievance procedures and housing conditions.

The racial composition and size of the ACPH and public housing developments made it an electoral necessity for local candidates. The ACPH hosted a series of debates for the 1974 mayoral elections, using their significant voting power to make demands on municipal offices ranging from health programs to employment opportunities.[44] During this time, representatives from Congressman Andrew Young's office attended ACPH meetings and offered the office resources directly to public housing residents. Three members of his office were staffed exclusively for public housing casework and other social welfare programs for the poor.[45] Within five years of its creation, ACPH was using its monthly meetings to provide public housing tenants with access to local and national community organizations (from the EOA to the National Tenants Organization), legal and health entities (Legal Aid and the Fulton County Health Department), and local, state, and federal elected officials.[46]

Bolstered by the effectiveness of the rent strike on the maintenance process and the support of outside organizations and officials, the ACPH's next campaign was against the public housing recreation centers. In recent years, the AHA began leasing development recreation centers to local childcare organizations to provide day care services. Frequently, public housing tenants were employed in these centers. However, tenants lodged complaints with their ACPH representatives, as they were effectively barred from using the centers, even when the day cares were not operating. Meeting and gathering space served as an integral part of community development in public housing communities, and Louise Watley (elected as ACPH president earlier in the year) gave AHA one month to address this issue.[47] At the next monthly meeting, Ernest Jackson relayed that he and the tenant associations of the effected developments were meeting with local organizations to provide space for tenant meetings.[48] While holding tenant meetings off-site isolated tenant associations from the tenants, it also expanded the interests of the associations to include the needs and spaces of the surrounding community.

In the summer of 1973, ACPH leadership focused on tenant job training programs and improved security measures in public housing developments.[49] The Atlanta Housing Authority was one of the largest public housing agencies that did not have its own security force, and tenants were increasingly worried that "outside neighbors" were taking advantage of vacant units and undermaintained streetlights to conduct criminal activity. Representatives from the Atlanta Police Department spoke at the June 1973 meeting, offering a community policing program that would provide residents with security and negotiation training in addition to supplying electronic surveillance equipment for developments.[50] Police representatives promoted the latest advances in surveillance technology, including a new helicopter patrol that would necessitate that the AHA paint house numbers on the building roofs for easy identification. While tenant members of the ACPH were interested in curtailing crime through building a trusting relationship with police officers (e.g., encouraging residents to call the police when they witnessed a crime), the police favored a less personal approach that would do little to foster community trust.

The summer also sparked more grievances against the management regarding AHA's policies and processes. Louise Watley demanded the ACPH draw up a resolution (an oft-used method of formally registering grievances with the AHA Boards of Commissioners and Directors) to force the AHA to release their budgets, as well as the racial composition of their employees. Mary Sanford, president of the Perry Homes tenant association and an ACPH member who promoted tenant inclusion on most AHA policy and programmatic decision-making, suggested the resolution should also include a caveat for tenants to sit in on AHA budget hearings. Sanford had previously questioned the AHA's process for selecting tenant job training and youth recreation programs, stating that such programs were often "forced" on tenants regardless of the tenants' interests.[51]

Sanford advocated for more specialized programming, which was crafted from the suggestions of tenants and not from outside consultants, a move supported by the AHA director of the Management Improvement Program, Dwight Jackson. When polled by the ACPH training subcommittee, tenants requested courses in community organizing, group dynamics, and communication—indicating that tenants were interested in becoming more politically active. The outcomes of the summer of 1973 suggests that ACPH tenant leaders were focusing on transforming both the policy processes and outcomes of the Atlanta Housing Authority.

Although Executive Director Lester Persells was often the target of the more outspoken advocates of the ACPH, he rarely appeared at any of the meetings. His assistant, David Warner, often sat in on meetings, but not as an official representative of the executive director's staff.[52] Instead, Warner would take notes at each meeting and provide them as memos to Lester Persells, even as the ACPH distributed meeting minutes to the AHA leadership.

While some of Warner's notations highlighted issues that would be of interest to an executive director, such as requests for the progress of the modernization program, others include rather racist subtext that belittled tenant leadership. Warner often noted the "disorganization" of and "melees" at ACPH meetings and the loudness of its participants. Resolutions were frequently derided as being "illiterate" and containing the "nonsense language" favored by tenant leaders.[53] After Louise Watley and John Shabazz put forth a resolution to bar Lester Persells from anything related to tenant association elections, Warner's memo suggested the two residents were targeting Persells to maintain their leadership positions within the ACPH.[54]

Persells's response to the more confrontational ACPH leadership was to use legal maneuvers to stall or thwart negotiations and to address tenant grievances with bureaucratic solutions. After derailing previous rent strikes with eviction notices, Persells relied on the AHA's counsel to negotiate with ACPH, exhausting the group's legal aid resources in the process. ACPH members accused the AHA Board of Commissioners of not showing good faith by appearing at meetings to address tenant inclusion into policymaking matters. The group pursued legal action as a form of protest, suing the housing authority for failing to implement the federally mandated Model Lease and Grievance procedure.[55] However, concessions to the group's demands were frequently bureaucratized—mired in so many layers of procedure and legal language that changes in public housing policy and procedures were often slowly realized.

Figure 4.6. Maynard Jackson (tall man on far right) visits Bowen Homes, 1974.
Source: James G. Kenan Research Center, Atlanta History Center,
Boyd Lewis, photographer.

Maynard Jackson Jr. and Public Housing Communities

When Maynard Jackson Jr. was elected as Atlanta's first Black mayor in the 1974 election, his longstanding relationship with public housing groups, including ACPH, made him popular with tenant leaders. At a January 1974 meeting, Louise Watley suggested that AHA commissioners should respond a bit more quickly to their demands or they would "march to City Hall" with a powerful delegation to get new commissioners appointed.[56] Susie LaBord quickly interjected that Maynard Jackson would act as a mayor to "all people" and not just public housing tenants.[57]

Maynard Jackson Jr.'s first term as mayor of Atlanta was a radical departure from the Massell, Allen, and Hartsfield regimes that preceded it. During his term as vice-mayor, Jackson began implementing the initial components of his lifelong campaign for Black representation in Atlanta's municipal workforce and budgets. Jackson's three mayoral administrations (consecutive terms from 1974 to 1982,

and then a third term from 1990 to 1994) reflect the will of a man who was determined to gain political reparations for the Black communities of Atlanta. His internal notes and memoranda reflect that these reparations would come at the direct expense of the white political and business elites that had long dominated the
city's power structure, as well as from Black political elites whom he perceived as
undermining him.[58]

Jackson also enlisted the assistance of academics, civil rights leaders, bureaucrats, state senators, and a loyal inner circle to amass data, public support, and
political buy-in for overhauling Atlanta's municipal workforce and city contracts.
Jackson used investment into large infrastructure projects for MARTA and the
airport to better channel resources from the Black power structure to an emergent Black professional class.[59] He also transformed the bureaucracy and procedures for municipal governance with the creation of the Neighborhood Planning
Unit (NPU) system.[60]

The NPU system initially created twenty-four units within Atlanta, each covering a set of neighborhoods, which allowed citizens to make very local decisions
on land use and development. NPU members worked with planners to develop
neighborhood plans, which were later compiled into the city's comprehensive
plan. These planning processes took place either annually, every five years, or every fifteen years, depending on mayoral discretion. NPU representation and by-
laws were all determined by NPU constituents, with minimal fiscal support and
oversight by the city. To support and legitimate the NPU system, Jackson linked
the approval of NPU neighborhood and citywide comprehensive plans into the
municipal budgetary approval process, creating a joint Department of Budget
and Planning.[61]

Jackson approached urban governance from an urban planning advocacy and
participatory budgeting perspective. He implemented targeted poverty and social
welfare programs in high-need neighborhoods. These neighborhoods were prioritized using census and other planning data. In a turn away from the biracial
urban regime that privileged the policymaking needs of the business-led governing coalition, Jackson used racial and economic household data and community
input from the electoral coalition to shape and prioritize budgetary needs.[62]

Jackson's first term was shaped by a confluence of political, economic, and social shifts in the city. In 1971, Grace Towns Hamilton, the former head of the Atlanta Urban League and the first Black woman elected to the Georgia Senate,
sponsored a bill to revise Atlanta's charter. The purpose of the bill was to create
a city government more representative of the growing and diverse Black population.[63] Atlanta's government was also in need of modernization and reform, away
from its post-Reconstruction Democratic machine politics and patronage. Black
and white elite interests converged again as charter reform would expand Black
political opportunity with more descriptive representation but would be limited
by reforms to patronage and municipal employment.

The Georgia state legislature authorized and selected the Atlanta Charter Commission (ACC) to recommend the size and apportionment of Atlanta's Boards of Aldermen and Education, the reallocation of powers between the legislative and executive branches, and the overall restructuring of the city's administration and departments. Ten of the ACC's members, or a third of the group, were Black legislators or activists, and all thirty members were Atlanta residents. In spite of Senator Hamilton's sponsorship of the bill, there were few Black women and hardly any representation from the formally or informally organized labor unions. Of this strategic selection and avoidance, historian David A. Harmon writes:

> The two major aims of the Charter Commission were to balance racially and politically the government and alleviate white fears of Black political control. The Charter Commission reached important compromises on such issues as the size and procedure for electing new members to the council. Ward elections, for example, assured that various white viewpoints would be represented. African American leaders successfully fought against proposals which they perceived as reducing the political influence of Black voters. The separation of powers between the legislative and executive branches and the creation of the president of the council position were proposed by the Commission in part to alleviate white fears that African Americans would control all of the city's political structures. The Charter Commission did not, however, directly address highly emotional issues such as new sources of revenue for the city and the meaningful desegregation of the public school system.[64]

The redistribution of electoral power was in response to a growing Black population and the increasing likelihood that Atlanta's next mayor would be Black. As the Black population increased, so too did Atlanta's Black public housing population. The AHA's racist site selection structured by segregation and containment had created political wards dominated by all-Black public housing developments. The AHA had constructed nearly fourteen thousand public housing units by 1970, and wards three, four, and nine contained about ten thousand of these units.

Alderman Marvin Arrington, a former Grady Homes resident and current representative for ward nine (which included Techwood/Clark Howell, University/John Hope, Herndon Homes, and Palmer House), had begun applying pressure to Executive Director Lester Persells on behalf of public housing tenants outside of his district.[65] The political opportunity structure that was built through individual public housing tenant associations and institutionalized through the Advisory Council on Public Housing was an untapped source of mobilization for the urban regime. Jackson and Arrington both realized the election of Atlanta's next mayor could depend on an electoral coalition that used the political opportunity structure developed by public housing tenants.

Tenants were incorporated into the electoral coalition when elected officials took a greater interest in public housing affairs. Tenants had complained to individual housing managers, tenant association presidents, and the ACPH about possible eviction from overdue utility bills. These excess utility bills were the result of heating and cooling homes with warped doors and faulty weather stripping. Arrington forced Persells's hand to eliminate or reduce debts incurred by tenants for their excess utility allowance.[66]

Instead of the traditional governing coalition of white downtown business interests and Black Auburn Avenue interests, Jackson's regime used a community-based, small-scale approach that focused on economic development for Black people and neighborhoods. It was not corporate growth that drove the machine, nor was it aiming for equitable growth, as often favored by progressives. Instead, Jackson's urban governance plan was for reparative growth that specifically sought to empower and grow the most marginalized and distressed communities. As the first Black vice-mayor in Atlanta under Mayor Sam Massell, Jackson distanced himself from the traditional urban regime by assembling a coalition of neighborhood interests during his tenure.

Jackson managed to align himself with neighborhood groups across the racial and economic geography of Atlanta. His advocacy for the preservation of peripheral downtown neighborhoods against highway construction aligned him with working-class white residents who could not afford to abandon their intown neighborhoods. His support for extending the MARTA rail system to Perry Homes and Proctor Creek also garnered him votes in the public service–deficient Black communities of northwest Atlanta. Jackson's political capital increased at a time when Atlanta's population had a sustained Black majority, and the necessity of placating white business interests within the urban regime faded ever so slightly for Black leaders in the 1970s.[67]

One of the first ways in which Jackson distanced himself from Mayor Sam Massell during his vice-mayoral term was by supporting the nine-month rent strike organized by the Advisory Council on Public Housing. Jackson met with tenants and heard their demands. Massell took the politically judicious approach of staying out of the dispute.

After his election in November 1974, Jackson appeared at a special ACPH meeting to discuss his plan for public housing in Atlanta, using the case of Bankhead Courts as an example. Built during the public housing construction boom from the 1968 Housing Act, Bankhead Court was a 550-unit complex in northwest Atlanta that was cheaply constructed and severely underserved by public services and private businesses. Crime rates soared due to the lack of recreational facilities and employment opportunities for young residents, and Jackson approached the ACPH with solutions to improve not only Bankhead Courts but also the surrounding neighborhood. He stated that "95 percent of the problems we have are not the fault of tenants. These problems are the result of the lack of proper environment for tenants of public housing."[68]

City councilman and former AHA director of family services Carl Ware announced a council task force to examine the improvement of quality of life in public housing, the improvement of rehabilitated housing, and the amount of housing produced. Jackson asked that tenant association presidents submit comments about the state of their individual housing projects. His office also convened a task force of students from Emory University, Georgia State University, Georgia Tech, and the colleges of the Atlanta University Center Consortium to address these issues and draw up salient solutions.

Suburbanization of both Atlanta's Black and white middle-class residents and its downtown economic engine harmed not only the mayor's image but also his ability to stimulate the local economy. His failure to secure relationships with downtown business interests—Jackson claimed that he ran on the "issues"—subsequently isolated him from the influential media powerhouses, the *Atlanta Journal* and *Atlanta Constitution*. Since the Hartsfield regime, the two daily newspapers worked closely with downtown business leaders to promote Atlanta and protect the urban regime from any press that could detract from its progressive and business-friendly image.

The decline in business activity shaped Jackson's more conservative governance approach by the end of his first term. This conservative turn would have an impact on the political opportunities available for public housing tenants. On March 28, 1977, shortly before the city's primary, the nine hundred members of the American Federation of State, County, and Municipal Employees (AFSCME) Local 1644, representing Atlanta's predominantly Black sanitation workers, went on strike. Four days later, these workers were fired by Mayor Jackson. Three days after that—on the ninth anniversary of the assassination of Martin Luther King Jr. during his Memphis visit to support striking AFSCME Local 1733 sanitation workers—Jackson hired new, nonunion employees.

Even at the time, it was noted that Jackson was "the first Black mayor to break a strike by the mostly Black, mostly low-income city workers who overwhelmingly supported his election."[69] The headline above this statement noted that the strike was, in fact, "full of ironies."[70] Jackson had famously supported the same local seven years prior when he was vice-mayor, and Mayor Sam Massell had called to terminate their contracts. Now, after switching sides, he had few public detractors—Jackson's strikebreaking supporters included the Atlanta Urban League, the president of the Southern Christian Leadership Conference, and the Atlanta Baptist Minister's Union, including Rev. Martin Luther King Sr.[71]

Following the terminations and new hires, the Atlanta Chamber of Commerce issued a press release in support of the mayor's actions, listing the ACPH as a signatory among other organizations. At an April 20 meeting, the members of the ACPH commenced a vigorous discussion about who and what constitutes "support" from the citywide organization, while ACPH president Rebecca English was in the hospital. In response, the group formed the Mass Communications Committee and immediately released a statement through member-at-large and Legal Aid attorney Dennis Goldstein to "refute any alleged statements of support" for the mayor concerning his response to the strike.[72] The group's statement went on to say that "any statements to the contrary are inaccurate and misleading," suggesting they would get in front of any opportunistic individuals who would speak on behalf of the group in the future.[73]

The caveat didn't dissuade President Rebecca English of Bankhead Courts, who got out of the hospital and gave a fiery speech condemning the reversal: "I want to know why they WOULD NOT support him. I still say if I had been the Mayor, I would have fired the hell out of them."[74] As if signaling her allegiance to the Jackson regime, English used the exact same phrase King Sr. used in his support of Mayor Jackson a few weeks prior—"If you do everything you can and don't get satisfaction, then fire the hell out of them."[75] A month later, after winning the mayoral primary, Jackson appointed English to one of the two nonvoting, one-year term, resident commissioner positions for the AHA board.

English's support of Jackson—both initially and in the reversal—was a demonstration of her power within the ACPH, despite the fact that she had served as president for less than a year. Per the *Tenants News*, during the May 18 ACPH meeting, English "strongly affirmed her position as the dedicated leader of the group, challenged anyone present to stand up and express any criticism they might have of her presidency, and was backed up unanimously by the membership's resounding voice vote."[76] While some could interpret English's actions as passionate, her need to reassert her control and authority over the ACPH could also imply a dangerous suppression of debate and discord under her leadership.

Shifting almost into a caretaking, patronizing leadership style, English suggested her support of the mayor on *behalf* of the ACPH was the "sort of thing [a chairperson has to do] from time to time because of the urgency of matters that arise suddenly, without allowing time to get the Council together first."[77] She reminded the members that they had elected her, vested trust in her, and should either give her credit for doing her best to make decisions on behalf of, and in the interest of, all council members—or else they should "remove her from office."[78] These tyrannical comments demonstrate how the power of citywide leadership had begun to corrupt some of the more democratic principles and structures of the tenant association.

These conversations and disputes, and Mayor Jackson's response of installing Rebecca English as the tenant representative on the AHA's Board of Commissioners, suggests that the ACPH was both recognizing and institutionally reorganizing itself to be a more integral player in Atlanta politics. Similarly, the Atlanta urban regime was recognizing and reorganizing itself to accommodate the loyal interests within the ACPH. It also revealed some serious schisms within the ACPH, the weakening of the tenant coalition, and the possibility that dominant regime interests could co-opt and demobilize the more radical interests of the council. English continued to advocate for more anti-tenant and pro-management positions through the ACPH, such as when she called for cleaning up public housing to clear the area of disruptive and illegal activities. "It is time for us to start making some examples [through evictions], and if we do, we are going to clean up public housing," English said during the July 1977 ACPH meeting, sounding like any tough-on-crime urban police commissioner during the 1970s.

The English-Watley schism became an official split with the founding and incorporation of the United Tenants Council, Inc. (UTC) in 1979 by Rebecca English and fifteen others. The UTC was founded to, among other things, "be a leading champion and keeper of human rights for all tenants in public housing" and "promote tenants unity and encourage collective participation in the decision-making in the Atlanta Housing Authority."[79] The UTC was also founded to address the more practical needs of AHA tenants such as "to seek help for those who are in dire need of social services that are not being provided for by the Atlanta Housing Authority" and "to provide a continual communication network between the tenants, city government, and the Atlanta Housing Authority for planning and implementation of tenant services."

Abandoning the community control, empowerment, and deviant spatial divergence that characterized tenant needs at the beginning of the decade, the UTC was repositioning itself as a social service provider for the AHA. The organization was providing individual-level social services when community organization and mobilization were needed to address the impact of Atlanta's economic restructuring. The growth in tenant organization and representation did not necessarily translate to more political mobilization and tenant power.

The sixteen individuals incorporating the UTC Board of Directors lived across eight developments, including Techwood, Perry Homes, Capitol Homes, Carver Homes, McDaniel-Glen, and Kimberly Courts, and it also included community representatives, such as Reverend John H. Cross, associate pastor of the Oakhurst Baptist Church. Cross moved to Decatur from Birmingham, Alabama, in 1972. He served for a decade as the pastor of the city's 16th Street Baptist Church and was there that September morning when a white supremacist bombed the church basement and assassinated four young girls. Before the bombing Cross took no leadership roles in the growing civil rights movement, but after he would dedicate the rest of his life to racial reconciliation through his ministry and community work.[80]

Cross was a noted conservative throughout his life, which is unsurprising considering the violent and traumatic event that shaped his political mobilizing. Nonetheless, he would have fit under the accommodationist community power structure of prewar Atlanta. Overall, the members of UTC were representative of the more socially conservative branch of the ACPH that preserved uplift ideology, supported traditional heteronormative family structures and gender roles, and centered the Black church in its political organizing and ideology. Married couples, former and current male tenant association leaders, and church leaders attended their meetings and supported their resolutions.[81] This conservative tenant movement, which excluded deviant interests, capitulated to the emerging Black urban regime and wanted to control public housing spaces. These interests would be afforded a wealth of political opportunities during the conservative alignment of the consecutive terms of the Reagan presidential and Young mayoral administrations in the 1980s.

Conclusion

At the end of Jackson's first term as mayor, many Black residents realized significant economic, social, and political gains. The $400 million expansion of Atlanta's airport required 25 percent of all contracts go to minority businesses. In 1974, minority businesses received 1 percent of all city contracts; by 1976, minority businesses received nearly 25 percent of contracts and received nearly 40 percent in 1978.[82] Although Jackson received strong resistance from both white contractors (who would resist partnering with minority contractors until the city threatened to sue for damages) and white voters (who rejected a bond referendum in 1975 as a rejection of the increased Black political and economic visibility in Atlanta), he was reelected in 1977 with no opposition.

Jackson continued to be a champion of public housing residents and their active tenant associations and citywide committees. Of greatest significance for all poor Black residents were the neighborhood planning units in the city that promoted an inclusive planning process, using a bottom-up approach to neighborhood planning. By institutionalizing the small-scale approach to political processes encapsulated by the public housing development as a political opportunity structure, the Jackson administration finally lent these political spaces legitimacy. Yet growing tensions between local needs and public funding caused Jackson to shift away from his bottom-up approach to governance in his subsequent mayoral terms.

The cases of Grady Homes and the Advisory Council on Public Housing describe the final transformation of public housing as a political opportunity structure in Atlanta. The case of Grady Homes describes the structural limitations of the development for sustaining political opportunity, particularly as the city's proportion of public housing tenants increased while federal subsidies and local rent receipts decreased. However, it also provides an example of a tenant successfully using the organizational capacity and political legitimacy of the structure to transcend political scales for justice through space, using the resources of both new federal programs and local organizations.

Using the political acumen of Susie LaBord and her ability to acquire and effectively mobilize resources for Grady Homes' residents, the public housing development was able to weather the structural issues of the declining urban tax base, decreasing rental receipts, and increasing poverty rates among public housing residents. The Grady Homes Head Start program provided both jobs and childcare for a population of single-woman-headed households that were facing increasing employment discrimination and limited job opportunities in the postwar city. The 1969 Brooke Amendment that capped tenant rent at 25 percent of their incomes, in addition to the consistent influx of urban renewal displacees, decreased the working-class and middle-class population in public housing that had allowed local housing authorities to remain solvent.

While the racialization of poverty had long undermined the political legitimacy (yet increased the political necessity) of the public housing development as political opportunity structure, the subsequent intersection of the feminization of poverty further reduced the legitimacy of public housing tenants and their advocates. Although poor Black women were marginalized and generally excluded from participating in mainstream civic, social, and economic life, public housing tenant associations provided opportunities for these women to engage and express their interests to the state using the political opportunity structure. Thus, an individual such as Susie LaBord was able to transcend this local discrimination and advocate for tenant rights effectively at the federal level, benefiting the residents and the city through increased federal attention and funds.

Susie LaBord's resource mobilization came with its costs and constraints. LaBord acted as president of the Grady Homes tenant association from the late 1950s until her death in 1991. Her accomplishments during this tenure are numerous and effectively helped achieve the goals of its residents, but the structural limitations of a tenant association without the solidary incentives for deviant membership restricted the inclusiveness. LaBord's individualistic approach to poverty continued a decades-long obsession of social welfare policies cream skimming for the deserving poor, while excluding the most vulnerable of the poor population. While LaBord helped address the lack of job training and employment opportunities in the city using her resources at Economic Opportunity Atlanta, this did little to address the increasing number of jobs that were relocating to the northern suburbs and the increasing obsolescence of government job training and opportunities.

The ACPH helped overcome the structural limitations of the individual public housing development as political opportunity structure by realizing and institutionalizing the linked political interests of Atlanta's public housing population in the 1970s. It also reflects the growing tenant movement that emerged out of the civil rights and welfare rights movements of the 1960s.[83] Due to declining urban resources and the political success of the Community Action Programs that required maximum feasible participation of community residents, local housing authorities were piloting tenant management programs to address the growing antagonism between tenants and management.[84] This antagonism developed after decades of fairly amiable and cooperative relations between the Atlanta Housing Authority management and its tenants.

The ACPH directly addressed these structural limitations by creating a supra-tenant association that increased tenant representation, visibility, and political legitimacy, particularly in its founding years. The election of Maynard Jackson Jr. and his neighborhood-centric administration helped integrate the ACPH into the new urban regime, thus institutionalizing it as a new political opportunity structure for poor Black residents in Atlanta. However, new types of deviants—from child abductors to welfare queens—would soon destabilize the ACPH's effectiveness in the 1980s.

Chapter 5

"What Are We Doing to Help Ourselves?"

Atlanta's Black Urban Regime and the Limits to Tenant Activism

I think I profited a lot by what I think were Maynard's mistakes. . . . What Blacks need to do is be a part of the mainstream of the American economic and political life, and in Atlanta, they are having that opportunity.

> —Mayor Andrew Young, quoted in the *Washington Post*, October 8, 1985

We believe in unity, and we believe a strong tenant group is one of the answers to building strength and adding power to "Helping People Help Themselves"

> —Atlanta Housing Authority executive director Samuel A. Hider at the installation ceremony for tenant association presidents

So we are saying, give us a choice . . . give us that right. . . . We know that they are not going to give it to us, we are going to have to take it.

> —Citywide Advisory Council on Public Housing president Louise Watley at the Heritage Foundation Forum, "How Business Leaders Can Save Education," September 2, 1992, speaking in support of school vouchers

After the growth and consolidation of tenant association power in the 1970s with the establishment of both the Citywide Advisory Council on Public Housing (ACPH) in 1969 and the Neighborhood Planning Unit (NPU) system in 1974, the 1980s is a decade of significant change in local, state, and national public housing politics. At the national level, social welfare policies were devolving administrative, fiscal, and policymaking responsibilities from federal to state agencies. At the state level, this newfound responsibility would create different fractures and alliances in a Georgia legislature that had only recently stabilized following the shock of suburbanization and growing Black representation. The

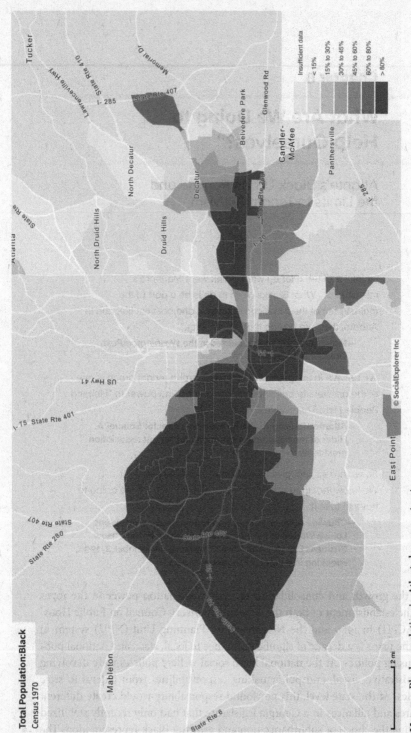

Map 5.1. Black population in Atlanta by census tract, 1970.
Source: U.S. Census Bureau, Social Explorer.

suburban-and-rural alliance took aggressive stances against funding Georgia's predominantly Black urban centers that were constructed as absorbing social welfare spending while contributing little in the way of state tax revenues.

In Atlanta, Maynard Jackson's historic two-term administration transitioned into Andrew Young's back-to-back terms. The emergence of the Black urban regime—Adolph Reed Jr.'s racialized synthesis of Clarence Stone's regime theory—strengthened by a growing Black middle class, made Atlanta the new "Black Mecca."[1] Atlanta's Black urban regime differed slightly from those established in Newark, New Orleans, Detroit, and Washington, D.C., due to this sizable Black middle class that remained in the central city.

However, this group's historical predilection toward conservative and respectability politics yielded limited political opportunities for residents with radical politics in tenant associations. For residents with more conservative approaches to political inclusion—particularly those who parroted the "choice" talking points of the neoliberal urban entrepreneur—a plethora of political opportunities was available. The politics of choice invoked the rhetoric of resident empowerment while simultaneously acting as a means of resident demobilization, such as the spatial deconcentration of public housing residents in the Housing Choice Voucher Program (formerly, the Section 8 Voucher Program).

At the national level, the War on Poverty was turning into the War on the Poor. The conservative backlash to the United States' relative decline in political and economic stature following the economic downturn of the 1970s facilitated an aggressive retrenchment of the welfare state. This retrenchment deepened spatial inequalities between suburban areas and cities, as well as between the deindustrializing Rust Belt of the Northeast and suburbanizing Sun Belt.

The chapter epigraphs capture some of these shifts in the political opportunity structure and the conservative turn in urban politics. Mayor Young's vocal opposition to his predecessor was a signal that Atlanta's urban regime had returned to "business" as usual. AHA executive director Samuel A. Hider repackaged uplift ideology as tenant empowerment, predicating unity for an economically divided Black Atlanta on the socioeconomic betterment of public housing residents. Finally, Louise Watley, the strong-willed tenant leader from Carver Homes and president of the Citywide Advisory Council on Public Housing, gave a twenty-minute speech at the Heritage Foundation in September 1992. She advocated for school vouchers at the conservative think tank as a way to sustain Atlanta's underfunded public schools, paving the ideological way for tenant association support of housing choice vouchers over the next decade.

The 1980s also mark a shift in the construction of deviance in public housing, one that would divide residents along age and marital status lines, weakening the membership incentives and resource mobilization capabilities of the tenant association. The decade began with the disappearance and murder of thirty Black Atlantans, nearly a third of whom were public housing residents. The abduction of children was foregrounded in the dropping employment rates and rising welfare use of public housing residents, prompting widespread criticism of the mothers of the victims at the local level. At the national level, Reagan's racialized and gendered construction of welfare recipients facilitated the rolling back of the managerial welfare city-state and the rolling out of the entrepreneurial workfare city-state.

These multiscalar forms of deviance rhetoric and social construction emerged just as Black women were finally able to benefit from the racially gendered welfare state that had long excluded them as a deserving population. Welfare recipient rates were less than 10 percent of the U.S. population in 1978, yet Black women head of households, households in urban areas, and households in the South were overrepresented in this population. While a select few tenant leaders maintained power and legitimacy over the decade, the use of the tenant association as a mobilizer for deviant Black political interests diminished substantially under this form of deviance construction.

Spatially, the city of Atlanta was undergoing the revitalization and revalorization processes that accompanied second-stage gentrification.[2] Under Mayor Andrew Young's administration, the city returned to its business-friendly corporate urban regime that was both in response to and facilitated by Reagan's reduced support of municipal budgets. Research Atlanta, the city's urban policy think tank, released a damning report in 1983 on the state of the city's public housing, advocating for the demolition and sale of downtown public housing lands.[3] Commenting on the finding that 10 percent of the city's population resided in public housing, the report linked the waning city revenues, growing poverty rates, and stagnant public housing population to the spatial footprint of nontaxable land occupied by the aging and sprawling public housing developments.

The Black participatory geographies of Atlanta's public housing developments in the desegregated era shifted in ways that made the production of space increasingly difficult to retain under the control of its more marginalized tenants. Reagan's aggressive domestic war against urban crime broke down the trust, bonds, and organizational resources that supported the public housing political opportunity structure. With less opportunity and access to state and federal funding, tenant associations were forced to compete for limited resources and began to take on more conservative viewpoints to maintain political power and legitimacy.

These initiatives increased the isolation of the public housing development in the depopulating city. The participatory geographies of Atlanta's Black public housing developments, which once afforded political opportunities to deviant residents within and outside of these developments, rapidly shrank due to this conservative turn. This chapter traces the history of these shrinking geographies in the 1980s.

Constructing Deviants at the Local Scale:
STOP, Bat Patrol, and the Atlanta Child Murders

The election of President Ronald Reagan marked a new era in social welfare policy, and thus in the social construction of these policy targets.[4] Reagan's 1981 Omnibus Budget and Reconciliation Act (OBRA) was a direct response to the U.S. economy that had significantly slowed its growth over the past decade. OBRA was Reagan's means of implementing his governing logic of New Federalism, which shifted federal responsibilities for social policies, in both funding and design, to state and local governments, as well as the private/nonprofit sector.

In the same month that Congress passed OBRA, residents in Techwood and Capitol Homes were beginning to respond in new ways to government disinvestment and neglect. Techwood and Capitol Homes were constructed in 1936 and 1942, respectively, as all-white housing developments and were adjacent to two major public institutions: the former next to the Georgia Institute of Technology (Georgia Tech) and the latter next to the state Capitol. When these two developments were all white, both the tenants and tenant associations benefited from the segregated programming offered by these local institutions to enhance tenant home life. Following AHA's reluctant desegregation in 1969, a series of urban renewal projects surrounding these housing developments left newly arrived Black residents with few points of access to the downtown institutions that had supported white tenants before them. The two urban renewal projects that isolated Georgia Tech from Techwood Homes in an expansive modernist campus design included a four-lane highway, ten years of construction, and the addition of over 450 acres to the centrally located campus (see map 5.2).[5]

The targeted investment of urban renewal funds into areas surrounding public housing developments (but specifically, not *in* public housing developments) is a phenomenon also described by Irene V. Holliman in her analysis of Atlanta's program from 1963 to 1966. These investments serve to buffer downtown property from the blight of public housing developments and other slum properties that serviced the city's low-income populations.[6] While these investments were meant to create stronger civic institutions and stimulate private development, they were also intended to physically protect these potentially profitable spaces from documented blight. Holliman writes that redevelopment projects like the downtown Civic Center would "serve a mostly white population" and that local residents noted the process "had unilaterally emphasized white downtown business expansion even as white tourists and shoppers alike continued to abandon downtown."[7] Thus, this spatially disparate allocation of federal funding created a racially uneven landscape in the city, producing a central business district that is an overinvested, fortressed white area surrounded by isolated, disinvested Black areas.

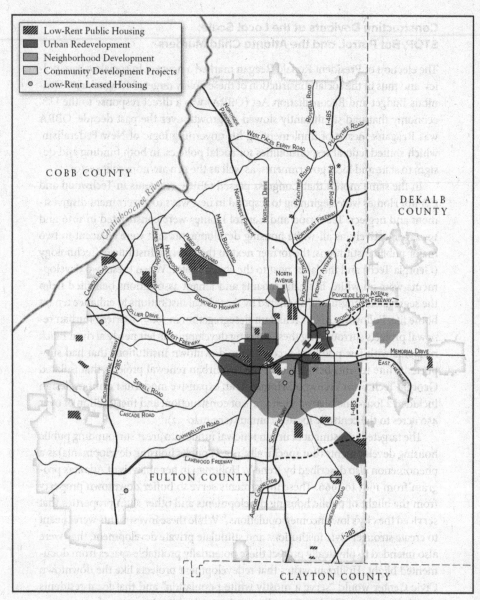

Map 5.2. Atlanta's low-rent housing and urban renewal program, Atlanta Housing Authority. Source: Redrawn from Planning Atlanta City Planning Maps Collection, Georgia State University.

This isolation, disinvestment, and lagging economy drove up the city's crime rates in the 1970s. Between 1970 and 1979, the homicide rate for Black Atlantans was nearly twice that of white Atlantans (89 murders for every 100,000 Black Atlantans compared to 46 murders for every 100,000 white Atlantans). The sharp uptick in violence was especially profound in the contiguous, concentrated census tracts of majority-Black neighborhoods that contained public housing developments.

Political and media elites were increasingly linking the risk of Black homicide to public housing's developments, blowing that old dog whistle of race, place, and crime, while carefully eliding any blame for their role in the racially disparate homicide rates. Katie Marages Schank writes that within a year of its 1971 opening, the East Lake Meadows public housing development was dubbed "Little Vietnam."[8] This moniker was from a 1972 *Atlanta Constitution* article claiming that the number of American fatalities in the fall of 1971 was identical for the city of Atlanta and the Vietnam War.[9]

East Lake was more susceptible to these racially disproportionate crime rates due to its siting on the DeKalb County line, which discouraged both Atlanta City police and DeKalb County police from entering and arresting criminals in the development. This avoidance approach was replicated across other isolated and self-contained public housing developments and exacerbated the city and housing authority's disinvestment in the communities surrounding public housing developments. The increasing Black homicide rates in majority Black neighborhoods were a result of the local state's condemnation, avoidance, and neglect.

It is in this inner-city environment of state isolation and neglect that a series of homicides collectively known as the "Atlanta Child Murders" occurred between 1979 and 1981. Of the twenty-nine documented victims, more than a third were current or former residents of Atlanta's public housing developments at the time of their abduction. Many of those who did not live in public housing frequented the recreational centers or attended the public schools that served its residents. The majority of the victims were found in the woods east of downtown Atlanta, in the Chattahoochee River to the west, or in abandoned houses and schools. They were found, on average, a month after they were first reported missing or last seen.

Initial reports compiled during the FBI's investigation show that Atlanta's police officers often attributed the crimes to drug revenge killings or suicides, in spite of the evidence linking a common perpetrator across many victims.[10] Many of the later victims (post-1980) were both aware of and cautious against the serial killer, even going so far as to carry weapons, walk in groups, or avoid the areas where bodies were found.[11] It was not until July 1980, nearly twelve months after the disappearance of the first found victim, that the city of Atlanta (represented by Mayor Jackson, Chief of Police George Napper, and Public Safety Commissioner Lee Brown) even acknowledged that the twenty-nine missing and murdered cases were related. In February 1982, Wayne Betram Williams, a Black man from a middle-class family, was convicted of two of the homicides and sentenced to two consecutive life terms.

One of the first organizational responses to the Atlanta Child Murders (ACM) was the Committee to Stop Children's Murders (known as STOP), founded by a McDaniel–Glenn Homes resident. Camille Bell, the mother of the fourth identified victim, Yusuf Bell, formed the group in response to her son's abduction and murder in October 1979. Bell's body was found in a nearby abandoned school, and he had disappeared during a routine run to the local store to purchase chewing tobacco for an elderly neighbor. The common patterns linking Bell and the other ACM victims explains the lack of police involvement or interest in the cases: the disappearance of Black youth, occasionally truant, lacking recreational, educational, and employment opportunities, supporting themselves by running errands and performing household labor for community residents.

Camille Bell worked tirelessly with other parents to push city, state, and federal officials to open an investigation into these serial killings. In July 1980, the city of Atlanta and the Atlanta Police Department created a thirty-five-member special task force to solve the abductions and murders, and in November 1980 the FBI officially opened its own investigation in cooperation with the GBI (Georgia Bureau of Investigation). This yearlong gap between the first abductions and murders and the acknowledgment of the state made STOP and other organizations a necessity for deviant spaces and populations. Their interests were ignored by the state; their pleas were dismissed or belittled.[12]

STOP's founding was in the Black feminist political tradition of community liberation as justice. In May 1980, Bell reached out to the other mothers (and othermothers) of the victims, and through exchanging information and experiences (sometimes at kitchen tables, sometimes over the phone), they discovered the common neglect and suspicious responses families received from the police. At first, many mothers and tenant associations had called for citywide curfews to protect children from abduction. These curfews were slowly dissolved, particularly as the mothers began to recognize that most children were abducted during the day.

The women continued to talk and began institutionalizing that information exchange into the organization's mobilizing praxis. Bell says, "We were encouraging people to get to know their neighbors. . . . We were encouraging the busybodies to go back to dipping into everybody's business. We were saying that if you tolerated crime in your neighborhood you were asking for trouble."[13] STOP was mimicking the informal survey practices that tenant association presidents and community leaders had long practiced as needs assessment tools.

The primary organizing goal of STOP was to bring justice to the families of those affected by the Atlanta Child Murders. And the methods and framework in which the group articulated that mobilization toward community justice evolved as it gained legitimacy over time. From the start, Bell and the othermothers put forth an intersectional argument about race and class within Atlanta's political economy as the reason why the state refused to dedicate resources to the investigation. As Toni Cade Bambara writes in her posthumously published work, *Those Bones Are Not My Child*, at STOP's inaugural press conference, "they charged that authorities were dragging their feet because of race; because of class; because the city, the country's third-busiest convention center, was trying to protect its image and was trying to mask a crisis that might threaten Atlanta's convention trade dollars."[14]

Camille Bell was born in Philadelphia and moved to Atlanta to work with the Student National Coordinating Committee in 1967 after attending Morristown College in Tennessee. Bell was divorced and had quit her job at an employment agency to stay at home with her youngest daughter, who she claimed "was suffering from institutionalization at daycare centers. . . . I decided to do something about it."[15] Bell's decreased household income and single marital status made her eligible for public housing, and the mother of four moved into McDaniel–Glenn Homes in 1978. Her path into public housing was not unconventional in a time when divorce was becoming a more socially acceptable option for women. While at the national level, policymakers and the conservative Reagan administration were maligning the moral character of the single Black mother living in public housing receiving welfare benefits ("The Welfare Queen"), at the local level these women were constructing inclusive spaces for their families and household needs using the political opportunity structure of the public housing development.

Most of the ACM victims lived with one caregiver. After reporting the abduction, families claimed police investigations were minimal due to the victims' perceived deviant attachment to the community and households. STOP countered this deviance, first by naming and claiming these deviants as "children" in the organization's name, and then by mobilizing to keep constant pressure on Mayor Jackson, Chief Napper, Public Safety Officer Eldrin Bell, Governor George Busbee, the GBI, and the FBI.[16]

STOP members noted that before their organization, there was little contact between caretakers of abducted or murdered victims and the police.[17] As Eddie George of Bowen Homes put it, "Nobody understands what's going on. It just hurts. I guess Maynard Jackson is a good mayor; he tries to do what he can do. But they don't care. The mayor, the police chief and all, they don't really care."[18] During a visit to New York City in March 1981, Bell and other STOP members continued to criticize Mayor Jackson for "what they called 'silly press statements' that gave the impression that all of the murdered and missing children were street urchins who come from broken homes and families on welfare."

Over time, STOP used its growing profile to devote resources to the needs of nontraditional low-income and public housing families across the country. During that same visit to New York, STOP met with Rev. Calvin Butts of Abyssinian Baptist Church and city officials to discuss ways to increase child safety in the city. Earlier that day, another mother (Venus Taylor, mother to victim Angel Lanier) met with corporate sponsors at Harvard Law School, where she solicited enough funding to send a thousand Atlanta children to Disney World that summer. Despite STOP's engagement with corporate sponsors, whose one-time philanthropy would not address the root causes of Black childhood trauma in Atlanta, Bell was committed to the following: "What we really want is to free our children."[19]

Another response to the police department's perceived inaction toward the Atlanta Child Murders was the Bat Patrol, a resident-led group that guarded some of the public housing developments. Techwood Homes tenant association president Israel Green and former Perry Homes tenant association president Reverend C. A. Samples acted as spokesmen for the group, which was loosely organized across a few developments.[20] These two men represented one of the last cohorts of male tenant association presidents in Atlanta's public housing. Both men were retired from Black middle-class jobs (head of a church for Samples and postal worker for Green), who may not have appreciated the new leadership by working-class women tenants in recent years.

Photos of the Bat Patrol show women and young boys with bats, and adult men with handguns and rifles, demonstrating the divide between women and men in public housing affairs.[21] The politics of women and children holding bats next to men holding guns not only serves to infantilize the women tenant leaders but also reasserts patriarchal norms and family structures in the public housing community. Yet, the legacy of community policing in Black neighborhoods as a performative indictment of state failure and state crisis is well documented in the Black liberation literature.[22] As Reverend Samples lamented: "Our community is, in a sense, isolated from the mainstream of the Atlanta community. However, it is one of the larger public housing projects in the city. We have to constantly struggle for any kind of public safety."[23]

Nonetheless, the gendered performative nature of the Bat Patrol is an example of one of the fractures that was weakening the public housing tenant association as a site for radical politics in the 1980s. In comparison to Camille Bell's Black feminist approach to community organizing and political mobilizing with STOP, the Bat Patrol was largely absent of policy goals and resident development that addressed intersectional disparities. The Bat Patrol's leadership and mobilization strategies focused instead on asserting male dominance in the space of public housing developments and, by extension, public housing politics.

The Bat Patrol's performative strategies also attracted (or relied on) police surveillance and occupation, which would have a disproportionate effect on the lives of the women who headed most of the developments' households. I consider the Bat Patrol to be a performative act as the group provided no systemic training or organized self-defense courses, and the guns volunteers carried were not loaded,

Figure 5.1. Chimurenga Jenga (looking at camera) and other Bat Patrol members following his arrest, Saturday, May 21, 1981. Source: AJCP312-005a, *Atlanta Journal Constitution* Photographic Archives. Special Collections and Archives, Georgia State University Library, copyright held by *Atlanta Journal Constitution*, George A. Clark, photographer.

so as to not commit a felony. The group's first patrol was announced a week in advance, and residents, police officers, and members of the press were all at Techwood to document the event (see figure 5.1).

Although the Bat Patrol and its male leadership wanted to shift spatial production and community control from Black women to Black men, these men also faced systemic racism and targeting through hyper-surveillance from the increasingly present police state. Green, in an interview from the day the patrols commenced, stated, "They say we're vigilantes, but we're not. . . . We're only here to protect our community."[24] Green faced both resistance and support from within the development. Margie Smith, who would later go on to lead the Techwood tenant association after Green, stated, "I'm against them. . . . Some of the ones with the baseball bats are the same ones you see every night around here trying to rape and mug people."[25] Another spectator (unnamed in the article) states, "I don't blame them. I know its white people that's doing all this. I know it." Green also spoke of protecting residents from a "crazed racist killer."[26]

The underlying threat of white supremacy was also a target of STOP's organizing. The group's commitment to using knowledge produced from below—or from the actual community—to disrupt dominant knowledge produced for and by the state is another reason it endured as a radical political organization. Public housing residents, and Atlanta's Black community more broadly, were suspicious of the rash of deaths, which were not just limited to Black boys, and which took place beyond the "spree" committed by Williams from 1980 to 1982. Allegations of sex cults, of the revival of the Ku Klux Klan, of human, drug, and sex trafficking were quickly dismissed by police and the task force but were given serious consideration in the Black community and its collective knowledge archive.

Toni Cade Bambara and James Baldwin both write at length about the collective folk knowledge that grounded alternative theories to the serial killings.[27] The community was convinced there was more than one killer, with rumors hypothesizing that the crimes were more likely committed by a network. What is important to note is that the rumored threat was systemic and faceless, and it kept with the pattern of ongoing and occluded racial terror and violence in Atlanta. In short, white supremacy was to blame for the death of Atlanta's Black children, and the community's political response needed to reflect this.

On the first day of the patrols in Techwood Homes, Chimurenga Jenga and Gene Ferguson were arrested for carrying a firearm at a public gathering. While Ferguson offered no resistance to the arrest, Jenga was "dragged from the scene by the police . . . arrested as [he] emerged from the community center with an M1 rifle."[28] Deputy Police Chief Eldrin Bell met with the group prior to the arrests, while Public Safety Commissioner Lee P. Brown stated unequivocally to the press that "there will only be one police force in Atlanta. . . . We will not be placed in an adversary relationship with our citizens."[29] Jenga was not a resident of Techwood Homes, and his presence as an "outsider" was met with suspicion, particularly by women tenant leaders. Camille Bell said of him and other outsiders, "Those leeches follow us around and talk about 'the racist murders' when we don't even know what the motivation is."[30]

Although some tenants were against the Bat Patrol and the outside attention it drew, forty-four volunteers (double from the previous day) showed up for the second evening of patrols. That night police served warrants and arrested tenants who were alleged to have carried firearms at the first patrol. During the conflict, residents laid in front of police cars to prevent police from leaving the development—yet another bodily performance condemning the racially disparate response of the state. Two of the protesters, Modibe Kadalie (Edward Cooper) and Jerome Gibbs, were arrested that night and charged with assaulting a police officer.

When asked to comment on the case, Deputy Police Chief Bell restated what was now becoming the city's position: "Police will not tolerate any vigilante-type activity. . . . What these outsiders want is totally different from what the majority of Techwood residents want from the police. . . . We want to work with the residents." However, in a show of solidarity, protestors marched to the police department's headquarters that Sunday chanting, "Lock us all up, lock us all up," in protest of Kadalie's arrest. The gathering of people and the occupation of public streets and spaces—all for the release of a person who was not a Techwood Homes resident—act as brief articulations of the expansive definitions and geographies of Black public housing politics in Atlanta.

The use of these spaces in public housing—both as a site of the armed patrol guards and as a site of the protest against Kadalie's arrest—reveal new spatial tensions in public housing politics. These spatial tensions emerge around how tenants incorporate (or not) "outsiders" or "newcomers" into public housing politics. What was the role of the wider Black community in public housing affairs, particularly as the Black middle class gained growing power in Andrew Young's Black urban regime? And how could tenant associations mobilize when the fractures between long-term public housing residents and newer residents weakened citywide organizations and alliances formed during the previous decade?

To answer these questions, I turn to geographer James A. Tyner's analysis of the spatial-political evolution of the Black Panther Party (BPP). Using the BPP's spaces of dependency and spaces of engagement, to borrow from Kevin Cox's analysis of territorial conflict in the city, Tyner shows how the rescaling of community is reflected in the BPP's transitions to Black nationalism, revolutionary nationalism, revolutionary internationalism, and intercommunalism. These ideological shifts are best understood through the leaderships' intentional divergence of spaces of dependency into spaces of engagement.

The BPP exposed, through performance, the problems of the Black community: state-deprived and -controlled spaces of dependency. The group articulated the solutions to these issues by diverging spaces of dependency into spaces of engagement open to the broader community. So, the problem of police brutality by Oakland's majority-white police force in Black communities was opened up to critique and engagement through the BPP's Police-Alert Patrol. BPP leader Huey Newton said, "We hoped that by raising encounters to a higher level, by patrolling the police with arms, we would see a change in their behavior."[31] In Atlanta, the Bat Patrol was demonstrating to both police and the broader Black community that the failure to protect public housing residents required a change in the status quo.

In Judith Butler's *Notes toward a Performative Theory of Assembly*, the author situates the vulnerability—what I consider here to be analogous with precarity and disposability—of a body into the larger context of the people, places, and inanimate objects (such as the built environment) that contribute to that body's vulnerability. Tracing the path of the police's capture of Kadalie, the placing of bodies in front of the police cars to protest his arrest, the march that began in Techwood Homes and ended at the Atlanta Police Department's headquarters—one can map the web of vulnerability around the children, caregivers, and "outsiders" that make up the public housing community. This vulnerability extends to the physical form of the public housing development.

Butler notes that vulnerability is a "political effect . . . unequally distributed effects of a field of power that acts on and through bodies."[32] Although gendered in ways that did not center the plight and vulnerability of public housing's women and children tenants, the Bat Patrol, and its performative politics, demonstrate how the state's indifference to public housing and its residents was having a disparate effect on the larger Black community. The Bat Patrol, and responses to it, expanded Black participatory geographies in the increasingly conservative Black urban regime.

The effects of the Atlanta Child Murders on the Black Atlanta community, particularly the community of mothers and othermothers that led Atlanta's public housing developments, lasted long after the conviction of Wayne Bertram Williams in February 1982. STOP continued to press for more answers and greater accountability from the city and the police department, as Williams was convicted of only two murders and linked to twenty-two of the twenty-nine missing victims. Yet the efforts of these women were largely in vain, as the city responded to both the murders and public housing's defunding with increased police surveillance and aggressive anti-crime tactics.

Literary scholar Eric Gary Anderson analyzes media's role in driving narratives comparing the disposability of the victims to the disposability (and subsequent renewal) of the urban core. The article notes the bodies were recovered from rivers, woods, abandoned lots, and other sites of urban disposal, and how this linked the declining urban built environment to the discarded bodies of the "urban underclass." Anderson describes this relationship using *Those Bones Are Not My Child*:

> Bambara . . . sees the dumping of bodies in the Chattahoochee as one part of a longer history of race crimes that has everything to do with the disposal of black people's bodies. Equated with garbage, these bodies are both dehumanized and dehumanizing; presented as a type of urban pollution, they haunt and horrify Bambara, prompting her to raise tough questions about the causes and the consequences of the murders. What sort of home place is Atlanta? How habitable is it? What exactly are the relations among new construction, urban renewal, fractured natural environments, and the murders? Why did the Atlanta mayor, Maynard Jackson, equate the crimes to natural disasters (Headley 101)? And what happens when interrelatedness, an ecological principle capable of speaking powerfully to multiethnic constructions of community, is threatened or lost or twisted into unfathomable horrors such as a river washing over dead black children and, until the killings accelerated to nearly epidemic status, a far reaching official indifference to black Atlanta's troubles and to black Atlanta's vital place in a larger urban system?[33]

The dehumanization, disposability, and deviance construction of the victims extended to their mothers as well. When asked to comment about the murders,

Perry Homes tenant association president Mary Sanford claimed that in public housing, it was not unusual for welfare mothers to sit at home all day and then send their young children out alone at night on shopping errands.[34] Sanford called for increased day care capacity to enable welfare mothers to work—a move that would increase her resources and power as head of the tenant association, while failing to address the lack of employment opportunities for public housing residents and educational opportunities for children.

The need to control resources, particularly as the tenant association structure was weakening and fracturing due to changes in federal community development and subsidized housing policy, drove Sanford to promote more conservative policy solutions. These conservative solutions were politically feasible through the social construction of a deviant parent, which was supported by the pervasive welfare queen rhetoric that dominated public housing and social policy discussions. This turn toward targeting behaviors to address poverty is how the War on Poverty was transforming into the War on the Poor.

The spectacle of the Atlanta Child Murders, the responses to them, and the impact on tenant association political organizing (or the lack thereof) have long-term impacts on the efficacy and legitimacy of the tenant association as a space for radical politics. The ACPH and long-term tenant association presidents did little to support STOP, even as this group continued to advocate at the local, state, and national levels for child safety measures and youth rights. The ACPH appeared to show only public support for the New York City–based group, The Guardian Angels.

The Guardian Angels are a group founded by Curtis Silwa in 1979. The predominantly white and male group wore red berets and black jackets, and they patrolled New York City subway stations in performative protest to its own local state's failure to protect citizens from robberies and assaults. Widely criticized for patrolling stations that served businesses instead of residential districts, the group was supported by a New York businessman to go down to Atlanta, and was hosted by the ACPH and other local community groups. Louise Watley even went so far as to send an open letter to Public Safety Commissioner Lee P. Brown, reprimanding him for failing to support a local chapter of the group. The letter completely omits any acknowledgment of the role of either STOP or the Bat Patrol in mobilizing and advocating for public safety in public housing communities.

What's more, the Atlanta Housing Authority, with legislative capacity from the Young administration, the Georgia state legislature, and HUD, implemented policies and practices that both mitigated the causes of, while also suppressing the responses to, the Atlanta Child Murders. State legislation and local partnerships with the police expanded the reach and authority of the Atlanta Police Department over public housing residents and within public housing spaces. Policy from the AHA Board of Commissioners put clearer definitions on which tenant associations "counted," and discouraged outsider influence from shaping public housing tenant affairs.

State Legislation and Public Housing Political Opportunities

In April 1989, the Georgia state legislature passed a statute that "redefine[d] the offense of fraudulently obtaining or attempting to obtain public housing." This new legislation made the reporting, or the assistance in the reporting, of fraudulent income or eligibility requirements for a public housing program a misdemeanor instead of a noncriminal (civil) offense.[35] This criminalization of public housing took on a distinctively spatial aspect in the same month, when the legislature also approved a statute allowing municipalities and housing authorities to demolish buildings that were housing "nuisances, generally," but particularly the site of "drug crimes."[36] The revised legislation stated:

> Power is conferred upon such county or municipality to exercise its police power to repair, close, or demolish the aforesaid dwellings, buildings, or structure . . . to provide for the determination by public officers that a dwelling, building, or structure is being used in connection with the commission of drug crimes; to provide for powers of public officers in regard to certain buildings or structures in which drug crimes are being committed. . . . In no event shall the governing authority of any such county or municipality require removal or demolition of any dwelling, building, or structure except upon a finding that the cost of repair, alteration, or improvement thereof exceeds one-half the value such dwelling, building, or structure will have when repaired to satisfy the minimum requirements of this law.[37]

While the use of government police powers to transfer land and property from private to public ownership was not unheard of—it is the foundation of slum clearance, urban renewal, and virtually all large-scale public works projects—this expansion of land use police powers was supported by the nation's increasingly aggressive War on Drugs. This manipulation of the urban landscape and the built environment directly links the construction of deviance at the local scale to the revalorization of the space housing these deviants.

Urban planning with police dollars was a seemingly rational response for states that were struggling with a federal government that increasingly subsidized this category of municipal expenditure. In Robert Vargas and Philip McHarris's analysis of police expenditures and racial threat in the United States between 1980 and 2010, the authors found that cities with increasing Black populations also had increasing police expenditures between 1980 and 1990, and those with increasing Latino populations had increasing police expenditures between 2000 and 2010. Since 1980, the nationwide average police expenditure has increased by

$4,760 per thousand residents each decade, controlling for violent crime rates, poverty and unemployment rates, and population size. The authors conclude that "federal aid has played an important role in financing city police departments (Koper, Moore, and Roth 2003; Roth et al. 2000). Our results suggest that racial threat operates not only through how local governments socially control racial minorities but also through relationships between local and federal government[s] that help cities afford such social control efforts."[38]

In this same April 1989 legislative session, Black state representative Gloria Taylor sponsored an amendment to strengthen tenant representation in housing authority policymaking manners. Taylor's legislation changed language relating to the appointment, qualifications, and tenure of housing authority commissioners to read:

> the mayor shall appoint, in addition to the other commissioners authorized under paragraph (1) of this subsection, two commissioners to be known as resident commissioners who shall be residents of a housing project in said city. These resident commissioners shall be appointed for a term of office of one year. The two resident commissioners shall be voting members and four commissioners shall constitute a quorum of such authority for the purpose of conducting its business and exercising its powers and for all other purposes. In the event any person serving as a resident commissioner ceases to be a resident of a housing project in said city, then such person shall cease to be a resident commissioner and a vacancy shall result. Vacancies in the office of resident commissioner shall be filled for the unexpired term by appointment by the mayor of said city.[39]

The expansion of tenant voting powers and the concomitant criminalization of certain populations of tenants suggests the political opportunity structure was starting to shrink Black participatory geographies. The expansion of political opportunities on the board of commissioners was possibly a strategy of the AHA and elected leaders to limit the influence of outsiders, such as Kadalie and Jenga of the Bat Patrol, in public housing affairs. The state was actively working to transform spaces of engagement back into spaces of dependency, so that tenant politics could remain within the regime.

Atlanta's Black Urban Regime Shifts the Local Political Opportunity Structure

The 1982 election of former UN ambassador and civil rights movement leader Andrew Young as Atlanta's second Black mayor solidified the city's emerging Black urban regime. Young's election, in opposition to Maynard Jackson's electoral success, relied heavily on Atlanta's predominantly white downtown business community and white northern neighborhoods. However, Young captured the election by maintaining, and at times strengthening, ties with Atlanta's Black elite political community and the growing public housing tenant organizations. At the time, Young was critiqued by Black community organizers and political scholars that he capitulated too often to his white business regime interests. But the growth of Atlanta's Black middle class, Black public sector employment rates, and Black municipal contract participation rates indicates that Young's entrepreneurial approach was necessary to stabilize the core of the Black urban regime.

Young's election also marked an end to the neighborhood-driven caretaker regime of Maynard Jackson and the beginning of a racialized corporate urban regime. In 1983, the Georgia state legislature, under the recommendation of an Atlanta City Council resolution and vote to amend the City Charter, officially separated the Department of Planning from the Department of Budget. This severance ended the brief period of accountability by the regime's governing coalition—in the city's budget—to the electoral coalition—in their NPU plans. In 1983, the city created the Department of Community Development (DCD) to house the Bureau of Buildings, Planning, Housing and Physical Development, Comprehensive Employment and Training, and Office of Redevelopment. Budgeting responsibilities were placed within the Department of the Mayor, in the Office of Budget, Audit, and Management.

Young's acceptance by and support from Atlanta's white business community was noted after he passed a one percent sales tax increase in his first year in office. In a 1983 *Washington Post* article, Thomas R. Williams, the white president of the First National Bank of Atlanta, commented: "On the whole, the business community is quite impressed with the job Andy Young is doing. . . . He's provided excellent leadership to move the city forward."[40] These white business leaders were relieved after they had "blanched at the prospect of another confrontational mayor such as Young's predecessor, Maynard Jackson."[41]

Young's entrepreneurial approach to urban governance was often couched in language that mimicked the conservative respectability embraced by the Atlanta Negro Voters League and other early Black political elites. As a result, his policies were critiqued by more radical Black residents who worried about Young's capitulations to white business and residential communities. Charles King, president of the EOA-funded Urban Crisis Center, said Young's proposed sales tax increase was "regressive" and that Young was "operating under Reagan's 'trickle-down' theory, which doesn't work for Black people. But Andy is faced with a dilemma. He must balance."[42] Michael Lomax, the Black chairman of the Fulton County Commission who would later run in the 1990 Atlanta mayoral election with endorsements from tenant leaders, supported Young's decision wholeheartedly: "Andy understands that a vital and growing economy is the best protection for poor and Black people in a Reagan America. . . . Progressive Black officials need to learn from Andy Young if they don't want to preside over Harlems, Detroits, or Newarks. He's prepared to broker with the establishment."[43]

The responses by King and Lomax represent the changing attitudes among the Black working class and working poor who were facing decreasing resources and political power in "Reagan's America." King's pragmatic response empathizes with Young's inability to continue to fund community and neighborhood groups under the municipal budgeting crisis produced by federal devolution. Lomax, on the other hand, sees the problem as less of a structural issue and more of a cultural issue. His reference to places that have either established Black urban regimes (Newark, New Jersey, which had a Black mayor since 1970 and a majority-Black city council since 1978) or established Black majorities (Detroit, with a population that was 63.1 percent Black in 1980, for example) are indicative of the shifting tide in Black political efficacy for places with Black descriptive representation.

The divides in the Black urban regime's electoral coalition—stemming from growing inequality within Black Atlanta—required the regime to expand its white electoral coalition. There was an explicitly racialized and spatialized approach to doing this. It centered around the demolition of Black public housing developments downtown and the construction of middle-class housing for white residents to replace them. In a February 1987 speech to the "virtually all-white" Rotary Club, Andrew Young was quoted as saying: "I don't think anybody is anxious to see a city become 70 percent black anymore . . . there's kind of a tipping point."[44]

In defense of these comments to nearly 250 white elites—a throwback to the racialized political spaces of Atlanta's community power structure—Young claimed that it was not racist but economic "facts of life," since cities with populations that are 60 percent Black were "flirting with losing . . . economic interest."[45] To address the Atlanta Housing Authority's annual funding crises, Young proposed setting aside $4 million to provide incentives for private development of middle-class homes downtown. This blatant attempt to attract not just middle-class, but white middle-class, residents into Atlanta runs counter to Young's early history as a radical organizer for Black liberation.

Helping Tenants Help Themselves: Rolling Back the Welfare State

Between 1979 and 1989, the logo, mission, and vision statement of the Atlanta Housing Authority underwent substantial changes to reflect the shifting priorities, funding structure, and programming that affected all local housing agencies during this decade. The 1979–80 Atlanta Housing Authority Activities report describes the goals of the authority, including pushing families toward self-sufficiency and using state resources to address crime, often through an increased police presence.

The AHA also reached out to local partners to help support the underfunded entity. In a return to the housing authority's origins under Charles Palmer, Executive Director Tyrone Hinton emphasized the economic and civic obligation of Atlanta's elite to support AHA's mission. During a speech to the interracial corporate philanthropy organization Resurgens in August 1979, Hinton urged the business and civic leadership of Atlanta to "help out in dealing with this problem of urban decay in public housing."[46]

On March 24, 1986, at the Dallas meeting of the Public Housing Authorities Directors Association, the Atlanta Housing Authority's executive director Samuel A. Hider delivered a speech that would encapsulate his technocratic, performance-management-driven approach to running the AHA. The speech, titled "What Are We Doing to Help Ourselves?," was intended to provide examples of how the beleaguered authority, which once faced a deficit and reduced federal and state subsidies, turned itself around to have both an operating surplus and reduced vacancy rate.

In 1981, Hider began developing the "Partnering for Progress" program for the AHA, marking yet another step toward a housing authority that was focused more on its bottom line than tenant outcomes. Per the AHA newsletter, the program "was developed and implemented . . . as AHA officials began anticipating sweeping changes likely to take place in federal funding for housing and social programs."[47] Much like its own tenants, the Atlanta Housing Authority was adapting in response to shifts in expected income, creating survival strategies that relied on partnerships with businesses, faith-based institutions, and nonprofits.

The program began with a partnership with Emory University's School of Business, which provided training to AHA management and staff on managerial best practices. This session signaled to both AHA residents and HUD officials Hider's aggressive approach to end the authority's reckless spending and management practices. In a summary report, Hider states: "Many times AHA's Accounts Receivable reflect retroactive rent which is back rent charged [to] tenants who get a job or another new source of income but fail to report this information to the manager. In projects where there is high retroactive rent, it indicates the manager is doing a good job of finding tenants who have not reported additional income."[48]

This awards system that chases back rent at the expense of a tenant's increased disposable income is one of the earlier shifts privileging AHA's financial solvency over tenant well-being. It also suggests a changing relationship between housing managers and tenants, one that is less trusting, less cooperative, and dependent on increased surveillance of private tenant affairs. Without trust and cooperation, the political opportunity structure has fewer resources to mobilize and less attractive solidary incentives.

The relationship between the Atlanta Housing Authority and local businesses became increasingly unbalanced as the private sector became the major funder and initiator of public-private partnerships. From the 1950s to the 1970s, downtown Atlanta's corporate real estate, legal, and banking interests were heavily involved in AHA policymaking, as evidenced by their leadership on the board of commissioners and the contracts awarded to their firms for urban renewal and urban redevelopment projects. As federal subsidies and political support for these large-scale, publicly subsidized, privately controlled projects declined during the Nixon, Ford, and Reagan administrations, private cooperation with housing authorities weakened. Contracts and partnerships were not renewed, and programmatic initiatives were short-term and superficial in their ability to effect social change.

Diluting Community Power:
The Interagency Council and University/
John Hope Homes Tenant Association

In February 1989, the Interagency Council (IAC) of the Atlanta Housing Authority for John Hope and University Homes began their meetings in earnest. This working group of local community organizations was tasked with pooling resources and leveraging existing assets for the betterment of the community. Analysis of meeting minutes from the IAC's first year demonstrates the waning role of tenant associations and their long-time Black women leaders, in both the meetings and the decision-making. In April 1989, Verna Mobley of University Homes presented the results of a survey conducted by the tenant association concerning the use of drugs in the community, police response, maintenance response, and garbage control.

The IAC included representatives from three distinct (albeit overlapping) units of Atlanta's regime: the state (including the housing authority, police department, Fulton County Department of Family and Child Services, and the Metropolitan Atlanta Regional Transit Authority), the civic-religious sector (including Providence Baptist Church, Church of the Perfect Gospel, a local boys club, and the Literacy Volunteers of America), and the landed interests (such as Morehouse and Clark Atlanta Universities, the AHA, the Bureau of Recreation, and MARTA). Working in concert, these units sought to enact Research Atlanta's plan of extracting value from the land under and around public housing developments. Operating as town halls and planning meetings, the IAC followed a fairly informal agenda in contrast to the more formal meetings run by local Black organizers.

The tenant association survey provides a means of entry for each tenant into the political process of planning and community resource allocation. Focusing on everyday issues such as garbage pickup and the response rate of police officers was a way of gauging resident needs while also educating residents on the state mechanisms that determine garbage pickup and police patrol frequencies. The ability to do community-wide surveys that were both tools of education and methods of community assessment and capacity were key Black feminist methods that politicized community development. The micro-geographies, centralized gathering spaces, and circuitous design of the public housing development are ideal conditions to facilitate this sort of face-to-face interaction. Surveys as civic engagement also help shape the conceptualization of community, creating one that extends beyond the formal site of the public housing development. The scale of the tenant survey demonstrates that Black women leaders understood the need to expand the assessment (and political opportunity) to the wider neighborhood.

However, the dominant role of the Interagency Council in designing both the survey and the responses to community needs largely excluded marginalized community interests. Thus, "substance abusers" were considered a problem, and "increasing the presence of the police" was put forward as the solution. The problem of youth truancy was solved by new recreational facilities, and high unemployment rates would end with the provision of quality day care options. While recreational and day care facilities were certainly needed in the community, an underfunded education system and a low-quality and low-wage local job market were the true culprits of declining socioeconomic conditions.

Reverend Dr. Gerald Durley, the chairperson of the IAC, often supported policies and programs that would "increase resident pride"—just like the early language of public housing managers in the 1930s who were attempting to Americanize and uplift the first public housing tenants. Durley received a PhD in urban education and psychology from the University of Massachusetts and later obtained his master of divinity from Howard University because he observed the "decaying moral, social, and family value systems throughout the nation."[49] In keeping with the political opportunities afforded by the punitive and profit-seeking AHA, Durley advocated for policies that would promote an ideal tenant and set of tenant behaviors and would penalize and marginalize tenants who acted otherwise. These deviant tenants could then be evicted from the community.

In the minutes of the IAC planning meetings, Elizabeth Webb, vice president of the University/John Hope Homes tenant association, noted the problem of unemployment was that the minimum wage was too low to provide any incentive for young mothers to leave the house. She put forth an idea to encourage increasing educational attainment to increase the earning potential for these young women. Webb's idea was immediately dismissed, as Mr. Aggarwal of the AHA suggested that tenants look for construction work with the housing authority under the Modernization Program.

Then another tenant, Mr. Whatley, advocated for tenant interests by suggesting the Modernization Program provide an opportunity to train tenants in both construction and management. This idea was shut down by the aptly named Mr. Profit, who suggested that, due to time constraints, the contractor was in no position to become a "training organization." While tenants in the IAC continued to advocate for improved and sustainable socioeconomic outcomes for their constituents, the diluted role of the tenant association in the IAC provided few opportunities to advance these interests.[50]

In addition to displacing deviant tenant interests from internal meetings, the Interagency Council was also displacing the tenant association as the primary community stakeholder in citywide decision-making. As a "partner" in the community, pro-business and pro-development interests that were represented in the council began to advocate on behalf of the community. Nonprofit developers were allowed to make presentations to "the community" during the IAC meetings. However, due to the declining role of the tenant association, this audience usually consisted of AHA employees, private realtors, and nonprofit operators who explicitly benefited from, and supported, this type of development.

In April 1989, Charles Walker of Providence Baptist Church presented the Neighborhood Plaza plan to the IAC. Through the acquisition of "abandoned" and "run down" businesses in the area, Walker planned to create a thirty-five-thousand-square-foot, mixed-use development with student and faculty housing along with private and nonprofit enterprises. In addition to market-rate rental housing, the Neighborhood Plaza was an attempt to create new neighborhood spaces between University and John Hope Homes and the colleges and universities of the Atlanta University Center Consortium (AUC).[51]

Durley also pushed for increased cooperation between the AHA, the Atlanta Police Department, and the private security forces of the members of the AUC. Durley and Profit, as members of the IAC's Public Safety Committee, put forth a slate of suggestions to address public safety needs. The following were intended to minimize intrusion from outsiders: ID badges for tenants, decals for tenant and visitor vehicles, roadblocks, street closings, and traffic redirected into a series of one-way streets through an established police presence within and around the public housing developments. "The purpose, as viewed by the committee, is that if you keep out those you don't want in, then you have corrected half of the problem."[52] Following months of lobbying by Profit and others on the Public Safety Committee, the Atlanta City Council authorized the Atlanta Police Department to enter into an agreement with the Atlanta Housing Authority to act as its agent. This designation allowed the police greater flexibility to arrest and prosecute unlawful individuals on AHA properties.

In the first year of IAC meetings, no more than 10 percent of the monthly meeting attendees were tenants. Out of eighty-nine total meeting participants, only twelve were public housing residents. Tenants were rarely asked to present ideas or plans, nor did their dissent ever override the affirmative votes of the other IAC leadership. Further, the IAC made decisions impacting residents surrounding John Hope and University Homes without any representation of those residents in meetings. The lack of resident diversity at the meetings—particularly against the overwhelming pro-capital alliance of housing nonprofit and for-profit interests—demonstrates how Black participatory geographies in public housing continued to shrink.

There were occasions when Durley advocated for deviant populations such as truant teenagers and residents with substance abuse issues. Durley often inquired of the state and private developers if there were employment opportunities, internships, or apprenticeships available for Black youth experiencing record unemployment rates in 1989. State programs and agencies such as the Violence Prevention Task Force and the Fulton County Alcohol Treatment Center provided representation for deviant interests in the community, only so far as they were able to attach public dollars to these interests. Durley wanted to install an alcohol treatment center on-site in the development, a move immediately supported by Mr. Maxam of the AHA, who volunteered to seek state funding for it.

In July 1989, AHA representatives Mr. Agarwal and Mr. Maxam presented the modernization plans to the IAC. These plans minimized or outright ignored tenant concerns about the modernization and demolition applications submitted to HUD that year. Modernization concerns, much like in the ACPH's meetings in the prior decade, dominated these pseudo-planning meetings. However, modernization had evolved beyond retrofitting units for electric stoves and gas radiators. Maxam and Agarwal were pushing for demolition, converting efficiency units into larger units accessible to residents with wheelchairs. In response to Durley's concern over the loss of 175 housing units following the demolition, Agarwal assured Durley that "through conversion they are only losing 68 units."[53] Agarwal downplayed the reduction of public housing units from 675 to 500 by emphasizing the increase in bedroom sizes and new availability of accessible units.

When Verna Mobley, tenant association president and member of the modernization committee, commented that she wanted to see a difference in the units, Agarwal noted she would, particularly in the doors and windows. Durley did not miss an opportunity to chastise tenants: "we should focus on keeping the community clean once it has been modernized."[54] Maxam also noted how there was not enough money for the planned day care center. Modernization was therefore doing double duty: transforming the development into a leaner, more profitable space (by reducing the overall number of units and non-revenue-generating communal spaces), while creating an opportunity to screen and evict deviant tenants through the relocation and readmission process. The AHA would pay for tenant relocation and moving in, but those who did not want to return would receive a one-time payment of fifty dollars (worth about ninety-seven dollars in 2020). The AHA also committed to screening tenants who displayed undesirable behavior in the past.[55]

During a September 1989 IAC meeting, Executive Director Samuel Hider was on the agenda to address tenant concerns about relocation and return during and after the modernization of University Homes. The meeting's discussion shows the decreasing control and inclusion tenants had in public housing affairs. Hider began and ended the meeting by advocating for increased attention and resources to the war on drugs. Hider situated the war in the context of the Black community's survival, insisting that winning the battle would preserve future generations. He stated his commitment to use the funds allocated by HUD secretary Jack Kemp to evict both drug traffickers *and* drug users from public housing.

Although tenants in previous meetings voiced concerns about the loss of units and the preservation of community life and communal spaces, there was no mention of these issues during the open meeting with Hider. The only tenant concern came from Durley, who again inquired about the "problem of moving undesirable tenants back into the project after modernization, thereby increasing the possibility that the newly remodeled units become damaged again."[56] Helen Jackson of AHA clarified the authority's readmission policy: tenants would be screened, counseled, and monitored monthly for good housekeeping and conduct. The notes from this meeting go on to state: "It was also emphasized that the tenant association leadership must work with management in a cooperative effort to ensure that the dwelling lease is understood and enforced."[57]

The shift to targeting deviant tenant behaviors, the exclusionary or occluded role of tenants in public housing affairs, and the expected cooperation between management and the tenant association in times of fiscal austerity all facilitated the growing conservatism of the public housing political opportunity structure.[58] The following month, the council approved two youth programs, a drug-free basketball league and a summer camp, funded through a federal grant led by the Morehouse School of Medicine and the statewide Minority Advocacy Group for Alcohol and Drug Prevention. In addition to school attendance and behavioral requirements, participating youth, and their parents, would be subject to drug testing.

Drug testing mandates for youth leagues and camps geared toward children aged nine to eighteen are vulgar policies that pervert the function and purpose of public housing and community development programs. However, these policies were openly supported by tenants who had no other options to address youth drug addiction. During a November 1989 meeting, Weyuca Johnson from Fulton County Alcohol and Drug Services noted there were no drug and alcohol rehabilitation services for youth who *were outside of the criminal justice system*. Referrals through the drug-free camp and basketball league would circumvent the need to arrest drug-addicted children, keeping them out of the criminal justice system.

Resource scarcity in the late 1980s prompted difficult decisions over using federal funding to address short-term community needs that could produce long-term community fractures. So, while children and parents got drug rehabilitation resources outside of the criminal justice system, Secretary Kemp's directive to evict substance abusers from public housing still punished this population.[59]

This criminalization and literal eviction of deviant behavior excludes a vital population from public housing affairs, yet with no resources to properly serve this population, the public housing community had little choice.

The community-wide impact of illicit substance use and addiction continued to plague University Homes even during the modernization process, which relocated at least one hundred households at a time. During a January 1990 IAC meeting, AHA representatives noted that the vandalism of renovated units for the theft of copper and aluminum had cost the housing authority $500,000. This particular type of property vandalism is a low-risk means for accruing metals to exchange for a few dollars at a metal scrap yard, and is often employed by vulnerable groups such as substance abusers.[60] Thus, even when the problematic elements—substance abusers—who lived in public housing are removed during the modernization process, the problems or issues of those deviants remain in the larger community.

Evicting these individual deviant residents will not remove the problem from the wider community. Yet the shrinking concept of community and dispersed public housing geographies would only exacerbate the divide between deviants and model tenants and limit their inclusion in tenant association politics. The IAC proposed a protective fence for approval by the tenant association, which agreed that such security measures were necessary to protect public housing (property) from outsiders. The AHA also approved undercover police patrols to protect the property on weekends, another extension of the state's surveillance of public housing communities.

Other parts of the modernization process furthered divisions between residents inside and outside of the public housing development. Dr. Charles Whatley of Providence Baptist Church asked during a modernization status meeting why so few tenants were employed on the modernization renovation project. An AHA representative replied that most of the applicants were from outside of the project and were thus not eligible for the tenant employment set-asides.[61] Excluding nearby residents from the opportunities afforded by the public housing program is another means of redefining the once-expansive participatory geographies of Atlanta's public housing developments.

Tenant attendance at IAC meetings decreased during the modernization period, and the meetings during the first quarter of 1990 were little more than updates from the many civic-religious and landed interests represented on the council. During a March 1990 meeting, Verna Mobley briefly introduced the prospect of tenant management and ownership, but there is no indication this idea was acknowledged by the larger council. The meeting ends with Durley noting a potential partnership between Clark Atlanta University (CAU), his employer at the time, and University and John Hope Homes (UJH). AHA would lease units to CAU students to live in and have them provide social services to public housing residents.[62]

During the reading of minutes for the April 1990 meeting, Verna Mobley and Elizabeth Webb both noted their objections to the CAU/UJH partnership. Mobley stated, "we do not want students in our community," and made a broader claim that through this partnership and the modernization renovation, units were being *taken from* residents.[63] Mobley articulated that the spatial struggles between residents and AHA, CAU, HUD, and others over housing units were political struggles over who got to determine what was done within the space of these developments. Now that the land beneath the public housing development was valuable, these spatial struggles took on increasing importance for the landed interests, and they increased their representation in the IAC as a result.

Reverend Durley and Carolyn Diamond of AHA downplayed the costs of these unit conversions as losses to the public housing community. Durley stressed that CAU students would move in to improve the overall community; here, community meant University and John Hope Homes as well as the broader Atlanta University Center Consortium campuses surrounding the development. Carolyn Diamond noted the demolition of four buildings in University Homes would create a more pleasant environment and atmosphere for returning residents. The IAC continued to determine the "best interests" of the public housing tenants, even when residents made countering claims.[64] For unknown reasons during the May 1990 meeting, Verna Mobley apologized for her comments and stressed the need to cooperate with Durley and others on the Interagency Council.[65]

What were the other reasons the tenant association leadership did not do more to advocate for tenant interests? Why were the tenant representatives so quick to capitulate to outside interests that subverted tenant needs to those of the "broader" community? While the representative power of tenants decreased during the modernization process, the tenant association leadership was explicitly co-opted through the funding and administrative mechanisms of federal grants that mandated tenant participation.

Project SUCCESS, the $500,000 federal grant administered by the Morehouse School of Medicine and the statewide Minority Advocacy Group for Alcohol and Drug Prevention, was headed by an IAC-approved board. Verna Mobley and Elizabeth Webb served as president and vice-president, respectively, of this board, and 70 percent of the board were public housing tenants. Board control over the Project SUCCESS grant was one of the few resources for the public housing political opportunity structure. The announcement of these board positions and responsibilities was made during the contentious April 1990 meeting where Mobley and Webb challenged Durley over the CAU/UJH partnership. Just as the state did in the 1970s, awarding more power to select tenants made it increasingly difficult to sustain a radical tenant politics within the political opportunity structure. The capitulation of the tenant association to conservative, profit-driven interests seemed inevitable.

Conclusion:
Expanding Police Powers
and Excising Deviant Perspectives

On December 15, 1989, tenant association presidents testified before Governor Joe Harris and the Georgia legislature about the rising violent crime rate and its proximity to public housing developments. In 1988, Atlanta had the nation's third highest murder rate of 48.8 per 100,000 people, or 217 of its 431,900 residents.[66] Limited economic opportunity, negligible social services, and outdated and overpopulated recreational facilities exacerbated the rise in crime and drove new partnerships and political alliances with the underresourced tenant associations. Similar to the spike in violence at the beginning of the decade that precipitated the Atlanta Child Murders, these crimes impacted young, Black, and predominantly male residents.

Louise Watley noted in a 1989 interview: "The missing and murdered children situation was horrible, but these drugs aren't costing us 30 children. They're costing us a whole generation."[67] State representative "Able" Mable Thomas also noted the parallels: "In both cases the children are victims, helpless to defend themselves. And in both cases, it just kept going on and on, no end or relief. The kids who should be living are dying too young, and we are helpless to stop it."[68] These honest assessments about the limits of the tenant association to work in its current fractured form to address community issues forced tenants to turn outward for solutions. In response to tenant testimony (and the negative national media coverage), Mayor Jackson placed two hundred police officers in forty-two public housing developments for a sixty-day crackdown beginning on January 1, 1990.

The partnership between the Atlanta Police Department and the Atlanta Housing Authority was requested by tenant association presidents but was not accountable to, nor cooperating with, the tenant population. During the sixty-day occupation, the Atlanta Police Department (APD) made 6,918 arrests and incarcerated 2,005 people. Per the APD, most of the arrests were of people who lived outside of the developments.[69]

In 1991, residents of Techwood and Clark Howell Homes protested the housing manager's—and by extension the AHA's—compliance in providing the APD with a master key to the units.[70] The purpose of the master key was to allow police to investigate vacant units where people were suspected of storing or using drugs. Here, the police were acting as agents of the Atlanta Housing Authority to enforce its strict trespassing policy. The police also requested the use of the key to "gain entry into units for which they had obtained 'no knock' warrants."[71] The police were acting as agents of the state in the latter use, but with the assistance of management and the housing authority. This shift in the use of the APD by the

AHA marks the beginning of a relationship that was cooperative between the two agencies and increasingly hostile to public housing residents.

The antagonistic shift in the APD's and AHA's relationship with tenants evicted deviant perspectives from public housing and limited the ability of the tenant association to diverge participatory geographies under this new arrangement. The 1980s was indeed a pivotal decade in public housing policy and the public housing development as a political opportunity structure. The political opportunities were increasingly hoarded by conservative and accommodationist interests within and surrounding the public housing development. Political opportunity for deviants was limited and outright eliminated during this period, and the spatial justice and divergence for these interests began to wane by the early 1990s.

At its best, this decade produced collective governance and solidarity around spatially just mobilizations that sprang from its developments. From STOP to Granny's House, a program that provided temporary foster care services for children whose primary caregivers were seeking emergency substance abuse treatment, Black women took initiatives to reclaim Black children and mothers from the deviance construction of those in power. They challenged these narratives by diverging disinvested spaces for deviant residents.

At its worst, the austere municipal budgets of this decade facilitated partnerships between the AHA and interests that demanded accommodation to the urban growth machine. The police, the nonprofit complex, and universities became willing partners in this regime shift to evict deviant perspectives from newly revalorized land occupied by downtown public housing developments. The space of public housing soon became too valuable to diverge for deviant purposes. Just as it happened to Indigenous peoples, slum dwellers, and residents in blighted communities over the last two centuries, public housing residents in the 1990s were legislatively othered, politically excluded, and forcibly displaced. Those who supported and conformed to white supremacist spatial logics profited.

Chapter 6

Deviancy, Demolition, and Demobilization

The End of Atlanta's Public Housing

Unfortunately, the bright promises of many public housing developments have been broken as physical deterioration and social disintegration have transformed these developments into housing of last resort where the American Dream for most residents is a dream of a chance of escape.

> —**Prepared statement of Senator Alphonse D'Amato at Hearing on the National Commission of Distressed Public Housing**

What I'm saying is, is that the resident as a result of living in public housing and surviving (as best one can in this challenging environment), knows more about their needs than the most well-intentioned outsider who occasionally visits a public housing development only to return to his/her safe, sanitary, and decent home in a more desirable part of town.

> —**Prepared statement of Irene Johnson, resident manager of LeClair Court in Chicago, at the Hearing on the National Commission of Distressed Public Housing**

The New Landlords in the Shadow State: Resident Management Corporations

Beginning in 1989, Housing and Urban Development secretary Jack Kemp pushed an agenda of resident empowerment through resident management. Under a broader mission of deregulation, Kemp saw an opportunity to address both tenant grievances with management and the untenable financial structure of traditional public housing ownership and operation. The predecessor to resident management, the National Tenant Management Demonstration program, ran from 1976 to 1979 yet was not recommended for expansion due to the minimal (if any) cost savings and the varying support of the project by housing authori-

Total Population:Black
Census 1980

Insufficient data
<15%
15% to 30%
30% to 45%
45% to 60%
60% to 80%
> 80%

Lawre

Redan

Tucker

Dunwoody

North
Atlanta

Sandy
Springs

Forest
Park

Atlanta

East Point

College
Park

Smyrna

Mableton

Marietta

Douglasville

© SocialExplorer Inc

2 mi

Map 6.1. Black population in Atlanta by census tract, 1980.
Source: U.S. Census Bureau, Social Explorer.

ties.[1] Resident managers were unable to improve on rent collection, vacancies, and maintenance response times, yet tenants were still more satisfied with tenant management than housing authority management.[2]

In spite of the mixed results of the demonstration program, the Housing and Community Development Act of 1987 provided funding of up to $100,000 to formally train and develop resident management corporations. Resident empowerment through resident management is a type of compassionate conservatism. It allows the state to provide compassion (here, as resident empowerment) without actually providing the services (fiscal conservatism, here as resident-provided management). It complies with devolution, allowing the federal government to provide technical assistance and management trainings instead of capital improvements under federal management and oversight. These underlying conservative principals, cloaked in the community control rhetoric of Black self-help and empowerment (modern uplift politics), helped shift the tenant association into an integral part of Atlanta's increasingly conservative Black urban regime during this decade.

In December 1991, Kemp released his "Perestroika: A Choice Plan for Public Housing Tenants," a three-pronged attempt to rescue the twenty-four failing public housing authorities that were at risk of federal (or resident) takeover due to delinquent rent collection and high vacancy rates. *Perestroika*, the Russian word for political economic restructuring, was the reorganizing logic of Mikhail Gorbachev in 1980s Russia. Deploying this term allowed Kemp to invoke imagery of the U.S. public housing system as corrupt and dysfunctional from bureaucracy and government waste.

Kemp proposed an authorization of nearly $400 million in the FY 1993 budget from other HUD programs to train resident managers. The resident management program was to work in concert with Kemp's affordable homeownership policy, HOPE I (Housing Opportunities for People Everywhere). The revamped resident management program offered tenants three choices (which he termed as "rights") in the restructuring: choice in management (the right for tenants to choose their management), choice in ownership (the right for tenants to choose new owners: themselves, a nonprofit, or another public agency), and the choice to remove the boards (the right to transfer ownership of vacant housing authority properties to themselves, a nonprofit, or public agency).[3] Omitted from these choices or rights was the ability to fully fund and restructure the existing housing authority model where the federal government supported local authorities.[4]

Kemp sold the idea of this plan directly to residents through his twenty-four-city tour of the most troubled public housing authorities in 1989. Kemp fashioned himself as an "activist," visiting Atlanta two days after he was sworn into office to tour disinvested communities and speak with tenant leaders and low-income housing organizers.[5] Eager for the listening session, tenants and organizers spoke with Kemp about the mismanagement and turmoil at the Atlanta Housing Authority, issues within housing developments and communities, and the physical condition of the buildings and facilities.

The many years of serving on modernization committees had amplified tensions between tenants who authorized and planned the improvements and the housing management that struggled to implement these plans. The prospect of resident takeover appealed to tenants who, in the wake of management scandals such as the fraud that occurred during the Grady Homes modernization, were increasingly distrustful of the AHA's leadership.[6] Tenants were eager for choice, or control, of the spatial logics that structured their everyday lives.

Daphne Spain, in her gendered analysis of policies that contributed to the feminization of poverty and the prevalence of women-headed households in public housing, suggests that the combination of tenant management and cooperative ownership appeals to poor women excluded from the private housing market. The transfer of ownership from the housing authority to individual tenants, she notes, would only serve to strengthen gender and marital status disparities in homeownership. These transfer programs target the most socioeconomically mobile tenants, placing them into newer, scattered-site public housing developments, while further isolating the poor households that are "left behind" in public ownership.[7]

In June 1992, the University/John Hope Homes tenant association reorganized itself into the University/John Hope Homes Resident Management Corporation (UJHHRMC, hereafter known as UJH). The reorganization was in name only, as the tenant association was not officially incorporated until 1994. Yet the board, led by a majority of Black women, was quite eager to begin to reclaim the community using the new housing legislation that funded resident management corporations.

The UJH board was chaired by tenant association president Verna Mobley. Women occupied five of the six positions on the executive board and five of the six positions on the grievance committee. The organization viewed itself as a throwback to the early spatial uplift days of the public housing development, as evidenced by their motto: "A Mecca for Home, A Haven for Hope, A Source of Pride, a Role Model for All."[8] Demographically, the leadership skewed older than its average resident and was composed of women who had longstanding leadership positions in public housing politics.

By the end of 1994, Mobley was the elected president of the UJH, the elected president of the University/John Hope tenant association, and also a member of the grievance committee. Mobley's leadership in all three groups was both typical of other tenant associations and resident management corporations (RMC)s and emblematic of why tenant participation was rapidly shrinking and demobilized. Occupying all three of these positions (which did not contain term limits) only served to further marginalize minority tenant interests; while ideally the resident management and the tenant association should agree, the leadership should be diverse enough to accommodate differing tenant perspectives.

As Kemp intended, the UJH served to increase (some) resident empowerment while also serving as a model for privatizing public housing developments. One means of furthering privatization interests was through the transfer of responsibility from the state to private citizens—in this case, transferring the deferred maintenance and disinvestment from the housing authority to public housing residents. Politically, this shifts the target of public housing mobilization from the state to other tenants, creating tensions and instability within the political opportunity structure.

In March 1993, Verna Mobley sent a letter to AHA executive director Earl Phillips. Mobley asked for the AHA to cede administrative and operational responsibilities for the following services: grounds maintenance, lawn cutting, moving services for relocating residents, laundry, preparation of vacant units, construction debris removal, and custodial services. These low-skill, low-wage, often temporary jobs were "inclusive of the RMC's strategic economic development/self-sufficiency plans."[9] This request shows the limits of the RMC and its quest to manage communities better than the AHA.

The jobs were similar to the quality of job that housing authorities offered to residents with past self-sufficiency programs. But unlike the state-designed and state-administered initiatives of the past, these jobs did not provide clear paths of advancement within the housing authority bureaucracy. In fact, deregulations in the 1992 Housing and Community Development Act allowed the secretary of HUD to waive fair wage requirements for RMCs that housing authorities were mandated to follow.[10]

The HUD secretary had the sole authority to waive any requirements established by its own office "that the Secretary determines to unnecessarily increase the costs or restrict the income of a public housing project."[11] The UJH's contracting request was rejected since the UJH had no legal authority to enter into an agreement with the AHA. Nonetheless, Phillips met with the residents and began the initial steps to incorporate the RMC, whose members were anxious to begin their takeover of the development.

The resident management corporation model also served to transform the organizing goals and political interests of its resident leadership. The profit-seeking logics that transformed public housing authority management in the 1980s were soon taken on by the RMCs in the early 1990s. RMCs followed the goals, objectives, and metrics of the Public Housing Management Assessment Program (PHMAP), often pitting managers against friends and neighbors. As managers of public housing developments, the RMCs were forced to abide by eviction policies and grievance procedures that were bureaucratic and antagonistic to residents. The RMCs were at risk of losing their contracts with the housing authorities if

PHMAP scores were too low. Tactics to maximize profit did not just include leasing vacant units and reducing operating costs but also included the administration of cost-effective social programs that relied on surveilling and monitoring tenant behavior and occupancy. RMCs were responsible for both management duties and social service provision, and the contract terms were written to maximize the overlap between the two.

An example of this overlap is the administration of drug elimination programs (DEP)s. If housing authorities received DEP grants, RMCs were required to offer drug elimination services, which included reporting suspected drug use and activity to the cooperating police department or to external rehabilitation programs. Drug use and trafficking were also grounds for lease termination; as managers, tenants were put in difficult situations of evicting friends who needed or sought treatment. These tensions stand in sharp contrast to the creative use of vacant apartments to foster the children of parents in treatment through the Granny's House program.

An interesting note about the RMC model is the illusion of control provided by the policy, when, in practice, the RMC had very little autonomy to effect larger changes in the community. Two examples of this weak autonomy present themselves in the standard RMC contract. The first is around leasing—which includes the separate functions of who is admitted, what are the conditions required to stay, and what constitutes grounds to terminate the lease. While RMCs may *add* to the screening criteria and admission requirements or make it more difficult to move into public housing developments, the housing authority has the final say in what constitutes grounds for lease termination and eviction.

Further, the RMC was tasked with carrying out the entire eviction process, with the housing authority providing legal assistance if necessary. The RMC contract positioned the RMC as the face of public housing's increasingly strict admission, occupancy, and lease termination policies, even as these residents did not control the design of these policies. When residents were tasked with evicting other residents, it became challenging to build community norms and trust that sustained the mobilization component of the political opportunity structure.

The second example of weak RMC autonomy involved contracting and capital improvements. While RMCs had control over operational and administrative contracts, such as for landscaping and accounting services, they were still bound to share control with the housing authority over the more significant modernization funding. Building condition and modernization remained high priorities for Atlanta's public housing tenants in the early 1990s, and slow or nonexistent responses to these grievances would be blamed on the RMC.[12] Blame for grievances was in fact a stipulation in the RMC contract with AHA: "Providing an outlet for resident complaints, requests, and other suggestions concerning RMC management of the development. Any comments received by the HA[housing authority] will be referred to the RMC."[13]

During this period, tenant associations aligned their politics with a suite of federal programs offering homeownership options for public housing tenants. This was done through a partnership with a new community development corporation (CDC) run by the former executive director of Economic Opportunity Atlanta, Bill Allison. In July 1993, HUD approved a University Community Development Corporation (UCDC) request from the AHA, allocating two vacant housing units as office space for the group to operate and administer HOPE I.[14]

HOPE I provided funding to expand ownership options as empowerment for disinvested communities, including the option to purchase public housing developments, foreclosed multifamily buildings, or single-family homes.[15] The UJH, UCDC, and AHA continued to establish relationships throughout the early 1990s that were central to ceding control of University and John Hope Homes from the public housing authority to private nonprofit corporations.[16] In addition to lessening the budgetary burdens of these housing authorities, these contracts served to further estrange and isolate tenants from the city's bureaucracy that served as a space of engagement for public housing residents.

Nonprofit contracts also removed the housing authority as the target for tenant resistance, replacing it with the nonprofit-RMC. The emergence of a shadow state in the post–civil rights era, according to Kathe Newman and Robert W. Lake, "transform[ed] community-based organizations . . . relegated to providing a rudimentary level of social welfare or directly participating in the developmental activities of the local urban regime."[17] This transformation of community organizations—from political advocates and resource mobilizers to service providers—is necessary to roll back the national welfare state and roll out privatization on the urban scale. UCDC was instrumental in helping the city secure $400,000 of federal funding to implement Atlanta's first HOPE I program through the UJH.

Successful RMCs depend on cooperative relationships with the housing authority, strong site leadership, resource mobilizing capacity, and ties to community institutions.[18] Nonprofits play a key role in all four of these determinants, particularly if they have undergone the transformation from community-based organization to appendage of the shadow state. Nonprofits also have an important role both in the stabilization of the Black urban regime and in the boosterism of what Preston Smith calls the "new Black privatism."[19]

In John Arena's study of the New Orleans housing authority's privatization of public housing after Hurricane Katrina, he notes that nonprofits' "isolat[ion of] residents from their indigenous sources of power and other working-class allies in exchange for an alliance with regime elites did not gain residents increased protection. Indeed, it increased vulnerability."[20] This alliance with regime elites promotes a rationalization of neoliberal solutions as common sense. Urban disinvestment further contributes to the standardization and acceptability of nonprofit shadow state service provision by residents, in lieu of community organizing.[21]

In 1991, the city, Atlanta Chamber of Commerce, and the Atlanta Economic Development Corporation (EDC) established the Atlanta Neighborhood Development Partnership (ANDP). The ANDP provided financial and technical assistance to neighborhood CDCs to implement and administer homeownership programs. The ANDP increased the capacity to promote homeownership as a spatial fix to disinvested communities. Public housing and local community politics were moving toward privatized place-based investment and individualized people-based strategies.

The transformation of organizations into service providers for the University/John Hope Homes community was accelerated due to the sharp cuts in federal aid in the 1980s. In an interview, EOA and UCDC executive director Bill Allison spoke freely about the need to "pivot" tenant association organizing goals toward the goals of means-tested social policy programs.[22] HOPE I was just another resource for the political opportunity structure to mobilize on behalf of tenant interests. However, this created new conflicts.

For the political opportunity structure of the public housing development to be effective, it needed to have membership incentives, including political efficacy. The Citywide Advisory Council on Public Housing had the most influence across all developments, particularly over the modernization planning and funds. The "pivots" of modernization committee members toward private homeownership, privatization, and other forms of public housing disposition limited the efficacy of the citywide council to advocate for capital improvements and accountability from housing authorities. A faction of tenant leaders who were antagonistic toward the housing authority emerged in opposition to tenant leaders of RMCs that had more cooperative (and contractual) agreements with the state.[23]

Political conservatism continued to provide political opportunity to the resource-depleted RMC. Verna Mobley sent an invitation to Newt Gingrich, Republican congressman from Georgia, around 1994. The letter immediately lent support to Gingrich's campaign for a "Contract with America":

> The residents of University/John Hope Homes are excited about the the the [sic] Republican Contract with America. We look forward to the implementation of many of the items you have outlined in the contract. We are particularly supportive of welfare reform that emphasizes work and family, an effective anti-violent crime bill, economic growth and the pro-family legislation that you will introduce and support during this session of congress.
>
> As public housing residents, we share the belief that people who are down on their luck need a hand, not a handout. We need short term federal programs that allow us to become more self-reliant than those that force us to become more dependent upon public assistance. We live by the adage that "If you give a man a fish, he'll eat for a day. However, if you teach him to fish, he'll eat for a lifetime." That is true empowerment and the goal of our initiatives in the University/John Hope Homes community.[24]

Mobley's deduction that long-term government assistance is harmful to the Black community, more broadly, and the Black family, specifically, captures two important threads of Black politics at the time. The first is the conflation of the interests of the Black elite and the Black working poor and working class. Political scientist Preston Smith notes that Black conservatives "think that a hidden organic Black hand will magically guide the various private interests of black business people and property owners to realize the common interests of the Black community."[25] This fallacious approach has stymied progressive Black politics in favor of electoral politics since the 1970s.[26]

The second thread is the continuation of the sexist problematizing of the Black family structure that pathologizes single-parent, queer, and multigenerational households. As Patricia Hill Collins writes, "the conservative right and African American nationalists both invoke the language of family in advancing their political agendas."[27] This rhetoric perpetuates racist, patriarchal, heterosexist narratives of ideal household formation and private, single-family homeownership, and limits deviant alternatives to these politics in the tenant associations.

The UJH incorporated many aspects of early welfare reform into their lease agreements, which helped shape their 1994 community empowerment plan. The plan subtly shifts the organizing logics of the tenant association/resident management corporation from one of intra- and intercommunity development and improvement to one of individual training, improvement, and "escape." Escape is an important aspect of the neoliberal project for public housing.[28]

The tenant association, as a centralized space for addressing community-wide grievances for the improvement of both the public housing development and the wider community, lost its Black radical tradition toward a social, or communal, liberation. While early public housing tenant associations advocated for more communal spaces that improved the development and surrounding Black neighborhoods, tenant associations in the modern era had largely abandoned this spatial justice as community liberation logic. Instead, the individuated profit-driven organizing logics of RMCs, in the context of decaying trust networks within and around the public housing development, created a renewed focus on self-improvement to escape public tenancy for private ownership.

Homeownership is the goal of the UJH plan, but its achievement is impossible: the development's low-income tenant population could not afford to own and maintain a private, single-family housing unit. The plan is wholly devoid of any community development activities. The sparsely worded "Economic Empowerment" section is a plan to survey tenants, match existing skills to possible jobs within the development, and match small business ideas to microloans or other funding streams. The plan allocated no support for any cooperative or existing tenant-led businesses in its stated goals.[29]

Mobilizing resources across the tenant associations was a major source of political power and legitimacy in previous decades. The inability for the UJH to diversify its leadership, particularly to lessen the control of Verna Mobley and UCDC over resident affairs and interests, led to new tenant organizations. In 1996 an informally organized group, Tenants for Justice, retained the law firm of Troutman Saunders to investigate the RMC over five allegations.

The allegations concerned procedural and incorporation inconsistencies that called into question the process by which Verna Mobley and the RMC board were elected. Allegations against tenant association presidents were not wholly uncommon. In 1979 the East Lake Meadows tenant association accused the association's president, Eva Bell Davis, of election misconduct and was unsuccessful in its attempts to recall her. Tenants for Justice collected signatures from residents calling for the resignation of Verna Mobley and treasurer Annie Tighe, alleging improper use of funds and improper nomination and election procedures.

The Office of the Inspector General for the regional HUD office conducted an investigation and found no improprieties with the nominating committee or the loan to an RMC board member. An erroneously filed set of bylaws during the incorporation of the RMC in 1994 was the only finding against the UJH. The most interesting aspect of these accusations is the disparity in the mobilization against the election and the participation rate in that election. The RMC board election that was open to all dues-paying members had only 27 total votes, 25 in favor of the candidates and 2 abstaining. Conversely, the petition to investigate this election had 77 tenant signatures.[30]

Mobley was also accused of exploiting the control over Project SUCCESS funds to push out a competing nonprofit—the Community Connection Program (CCP)—that was also offering substance abuse and counseling services in the development. A letter from the law firm representing CCP claimed Mobley and other members of the tenant association were threatening to report CCP's participants for substance use. As the face of the state, the RMC used the AHA's policy to evict tenants who use illegal substances, just to maintain control over the limited resources.[31] The CCP eventually was evicted from the University Homes development, although the program continued to serve in the same capacity at Bowen Homes.

Mobley's control over the tenant association, the RMC, and the grievance committee allowed her to have unchecked power that not only limited the ability to accommodate differing interests but also eroded the trust networks that sustained the political opportunities afforded to public housing tenants. By 1998, the UJH had largely disbanded as RMC funding declined and John Hope Homes was approved for demolition and redevelopment under the HOPE VI program. There was minimal to no resistance to either the demolition or the dissolution of the joint RMC.

The RMC, like other forms of empowerment and citizen participation mandated for post-1960s urban policies, was limited in the ability to transform social relations in the 1990s. Empowerment in the 1990s specifically targeted certain groups to empower and provided the terms by which they could gain access to that power. The empowerment project thus constructs categories of powerless deviants and the pathways to empower these deviants. These pathways transform deviants into active citizens by allowing them to take on the failures of those in power—in the case of the RMC, the ownership or management of a disinvested public asset.[32]

The scale of citizen participation in federal programs shifted between the 1960s and the 1990s. Citizens went from participating and controlling funds at the neighborhood level with the 1960s EOA to controlling smaller spaces, such as the individual public housing development RMC, in the 1990s. This scalar shift limited both who controlled funds and who benefited from the resources. As Kim McKee's study of the transfer of ownership from the state to local housing organizations in Glasgow, Scotland, shows, "while empowering citizens may have the effect of maximizing control, its prime function is the shaping of individuals towards desired ends."[33]

Finally, the rise of the nonprofit and the shadow state as a mediator between the Black urban regime and the conservative RMCs created yet another barrier to mobilizing the more deviant interests within public housing developments. The increasing spatial control of the RMCs did not translate into stronger Black participatory geographies but instead limited the political opportunities to those who accommodated the conservative regime. These tensions in the public housing development's political opportunity structure contributed to the demobilized resistance to public housing demolition and the subsequent redevelopment of downtown Atlanta for the 1996 Summer Olympics.

The Problem of Severely Distressed Public Housing and HOPE VI as the Solution

In 1991, Congress passed legislation authorizing the formation of the National Commission of Severely Distressed Public Housing. The findings from the commission shifted how public housing was conceptualized, funded, and operated in the United States. The Urban Revitalization Demonstration Program would become the model for the HOPE VI legislation and was the leading recommendation in this commission's final report. The federal Urban Revitalization Demonstration Program would fund Atlanta's local Olympic Legacy Program. Between March 1992 and May 1993, AHA executive director Earl Phillips and deputy executive director Rod Solomon both testified at two separate subcommittee hearings about the causes and responses to severely distressed public housing. Other housing authority leaders, housing academics and bureaucrats, as well as former or current resident managers, testified at these hearings.

Solomon, like Phillips, was a lifelong housing and community development professional. He was at the Boston Housing Authority when it was under receivership in the 1980s.[34] Although the presidential administration and the HUD secretary changed between the two hearings, the recommendations remained about the same: increased funding for demolition, modernization, and revitalization; greater autonomy for local housing authorities (and residents) to implement programs that were successful; and increased social services to address tenant needs. These hearings provided the language and rhetoric that justified the HOPE VI program. Testimony from these hearings is instrumental to understanding how legislators addressed the many tensions within the program.

During the subcommittee hearings, Nicholas Lemann, author of *The Promised Land: The Great Black Migration and How It Changed America*, provided expert testimony based on his investigations of public housing in Chicago. Lemann advocated for two simple solutions: increased property security and more stringent tenant screenings. The first solution would allow the housing authorities to continue to provide safe housing, a cornerstone of the original act. The second was meant to restore public housing to the days "when it worked," which meant an intensive application and screening process that would admit more socioeconomically mobile families. These families could again benefit from the space as a stepping stone into the private housing market. Senator Alan Cranston of California and Senator Christopher S. Bond of Missouri immediately interjected:

SENATOR BOND: Well, Mr. Lemann, to follow up on that, really, when you're talking about screening, you're talking about keeping out undesirables. You're talking about throwing out people, as you termed, who screw up. You are really making the tough decision to make them homeless. You're putting them back out. And this is one of the basic dilemmas because you throw them out of public housing and, ipso facto, you have homeless people.

MR. LEMANN: You can handle a set percent of homeless and problem families and whatever, in public housing, as long as it's not the whole project. And there's a kind of tipping point where the crime gets to a certain level and people really leave. Also, as a general proposition—

SENATOR CRANSTON: What should be done with the people that are turned out? What happens to them? What is our responsibility to them?

MR. LEMANN: Well, some of them—I mean, the most common cases, at least in this building where I spent a lot of time, they're dope dealers and they should be in jail, probably. And there's a whole variety of supportive, quasi-supportive environments and there's a variety of human problems. There's a lot of people who can keep living in the building. But the person who takes over an apartment in a high-rise and turns it into a place to deal drugs, and there's zillions of those apartments in high-rise public housing, they should go to jail, I think."[35]

AHA executive director Earl Phillips testified immediately after this exchange:

MR. PHILLIPS: But I think the one thing that I'd like to say as a public housing professional, is that I don't think public housing ought to be seen as the housing of last resort. Public housing is the housing of choice. And there's more than enough poor people to go around that are going to be able to follow the rules and regulations and to follow these guidelines spelled out by the lease requirements, and if we make it very clear that if you don't pay your rent, that if you are a person with negative behavior, we put you out.[36]

In addition to this individuated argument, Phillips also addressed the structural issues of public housing, particularly the tensions in funding programs that both tenants and housing authorities regarded as essential, such as security. "The dollars are not there coming though the operating program of our budget. And so, we then have to make due and we have to rely on various kinds of programs that perhaps may in fact give us dollars for security for a year, possibly a year and a half or two years max, and then you've got to go scratching for those dollars in order to maintain that security program."[37] Phillips followed up later with the position of the housing authority within the city, state, and federal governments, and how devolution and the push toward privatization and public-private partnerships was eroding the core mission of housing authorities:

One of the big problems you have in public housing is that you don't have monies for social services, you don't have monies for security. And that is a major fact. And the thing that we try to do, what I've done in all my experiences [as head of the Newark, New Jersey; Wilmington, Delaware; Houston; and Miami housing authorities] is try to develop partnerships in that community, partnerships with the city government, partnerships with the Federal Government, partnerships with our residents, partnerships with the business community. But I have to say to you, Senators, that that partnership does not continue to go on and on and on. After a while, you'll find that the business community wants to move to another sector. They want to put monies into other kinds of things that become more visible and are more glitzy, and so they'll move away. So you then have to try to create other kinds of partnerships. . . . Problems that we've had really stem from the leadership in the local community where the mayors and city councilmen will, in fact, appoint people to those boards who may not have the kind of concern or interest or even knowledge about public housing operation, and really don't have that kind of enthusiasm to make things happen. . . . The social services piece becomes really critical, and what you have to do in order to get these social services is that you've got to go out and you've got to become a grants person . . . you've got to try to get foundations to come in . . . the private sector. . . . But then the question becomes, Senator, how long can you continue that kind of movement on a volunteer basis.[38]

In the context of waning federal subsidies, negative operating revenues, and growing tenant needs, Phillips laid out a reasonable logic for the endurance of housing authorities on HUD "troubled PHA lists." In his testimony, Phillips contextualized how the success and failure of public housing authorities depends not only on federal funding and adequate revenues to cover operating expenses, but also on intentional and stable partnerships between the city, public housing authority (including tenants), local businesses, civic associations, and nonprofits.

The idea of government interference that facilitates these partnerships for the benefit of sustaining public housing authorities and their units was becoming deviant in an era of devolution. Phillips was advocating for a regime model that would support a progressive habitus that worked toward public housing preservation. This stood in sharp contrast to the emerging Atlanta regime that worked in favor of private property appreciation and accumulation. He testified:

> I really do see U.S. HUD playing a stronger role in the public housing areas. I think it's important that they do it, but I see them playing a stronger role with the local government entities, making sure that those governmental entities on a local basis are in fact doing the kinds of things that are going to be supportive of a public housing agency. I have no problems if a public housing director is not performing, that that individual needs to be removed from the job. But I think that there has to be that kind of relationship . . . [and congressmen] coming to the public housing meetings and participating in those communities and . . . coming back to Washington and then implementing some of those things that the residents want to have you support, those make a difference in communities.[39]

The testimony of the housing authority directors and resident managers who were under significant pressure to save public housing with no funding, along with that of leaders of depopulated cities with reduced tax bases, and an increasingly low-income and high-need tenant population shaped HOPE VI. The resultant austere goals of the HOPE VI program are to improve the living environment of public housing residents; to revitalize public housing sites through physical construction aimed at creating neighborhoods and not projects; to lessen the isolation and reduce the concentration of low-income families; to build sustainable and mixed-income communities; and to provide coordinated community and supportive service programs that help residents achieve self-sufficiency.[40] In spite of the testimony of Phillips and others on the structural causes of severely distressed housing, only the more punitive, behavioral-driven recommendations for tenant screening were adapted for the final legislation.

The goals suggest a reconceptualization of public housing, as it was understood in the original 1937 Housing Act. In the first public housing act, housing authorities were creating and maintaining public housing developments with the goal of addressing the affordable housing crisis produced by an industrializing and urbanizing nation. Public housing functioned as a pass-through for the submerged white middle class, but it also had a fundamental obligation to provide housing for those who could never afford it through private financing and private provision. HOPE VI appeared to be breaking down that distinction.

The first stated goal of HOPE VI was to improve the living environment of public housing residents. Most HOPE VI developments set aside housing for 20 to 40 percent of the original public housing population—it was assumed they would benefit both from new units and proximity to households with more affluent socioeconomic status ("role-modeling").[41] The remaining 60 to 80 percent of residents who were issued Section 8 vouchers were assumed to achieve the goal of improved living environments by moving off-site from disinvested public housing developments into privately managed rental housing. Yet research on HOPE VI relocation demonstrates the fallacy of this assumption. Those who stay in revitalized communities may have an improved *built* environment, but some residents also talk about social isolation and loss of community attachment, key components of a more holistic living environment.[42] The goals of HOPE VI were excellent at addressing the funding and administrative shortcomings of the public housing program created in the 1937 Housing Act. However, these goals did little to address the ongoing crises of capitalism that inspired the program: chronic poverty and the profit-driven housing markets that created the need for public housing in the first place.

The planning, implementation, and administration of HOPE VI differed both across and within public housing authorities. The spatial differentiation in successful HOPE VI programs within a housing authority's jurisdiction can depend on factors such as a site's proximity to valued neighborhood amenities. Time also plays a factor, both in increasing the experience of housing authorities to implement successful programs and in facilitating the depopulation and demobilization of public housing communities and tenant associations. In Atlanta, tenant demobilization was strengthened by reorienting the city's regime around the Olympics, HOPE VI, and the permanent spatial and political displacement of deviants from newly profitable lands in downtown.

Converging around Olympic Development: The Olympic Legacy Program and the Redevelopment Regime

The September 1990 announcement that Atlanta would host the 1996 Summer Olympics prompted a comprehensive planning process that recalibrated the feasibility of redeveloping downtown public housing developments. Since the late twentieth century, the Olympics have increasingly been viewed as "not merely an international sporting event but a vehicle for implementing the vision of a world-class city."[43] As Leon Eplan, Mayor Jackson's longtime city planner and neighborhood advocate, was quoted as saying, "Everything we do now has an Olympic focus. . . . The Olympics sets a common goal, gives us a timetable—it's a planner's delight."[44] The Olympics, and other mega-events more broadly, are welcome sources of revitalization for places forced to compete with each other to attract outside investment for the entrepreneurial city.

In Atlanta, this revitalization was spatialized into the "Olympic Ring," a two-mile radius around the central business district where the committee sited most of the event's stadiums and venues.[45] Atlanta's approach to planning and hosting the Olympics would provide the initial pedestrian infrastructure to make the downtown more walkable and accessible, a longtime criticism of the automobile-centric city. From the outset, the aging Techwood and Clark Howell Homes were singled out for being an "eyesore" that would confuse visitors for its proximity to the modern and newly constructed Olympic Village housing.[46]

Much like the regime convergence over urban redevelopment and urban renewal funds in postwar Atlanta, a new focus of the regime emerged to develop the Olympic Ring. This regime soon evolved to focus on the removal of deviants (e.g., poor Black women and children, people experiencing homelessness, people with mental and physical disabilities) from the Ring, and the regulation of where and how deviants could reenter the Ring. Although the object of convergence differed, the underlying spatial logics remained the same: clearing the downtown environs of deviant land uses to facilitate investment in land uses that would benefit the property owners. The only difference was that in this regime, many of the participants were Black, and some were even public housing residents.

The Atlanta Committee for the Olympic Games (ACOG), the group responsible for submitting the bid to the International Olympic Committee in 1989, fielded several proposals for the transformation of Techwood and Clark Howell Homes in preparation for the games. Chandra D. Ward notes that during the bid, ACOG described Atlanta as the "birthplace of the modern human rights movement" and how the group would ensure the benefits of hosting were "fairly and equitably apportioned among all the citizens of the community."[47] However, once the games were approved, ACOG quickly pivoted to using the business-friendly regime to advance the city's corporate and real estate interests above all else.

ACOG's initial offer to Techwood and Clark Howell residents was a redevelopment plan that would allocate only a tenth of all units to public housing residents, dispersing other residents into scattered site homeownership programs or other public housing units, and leaving others still unaccounted for.[48] During the Olympics, the committee proposed renting beds from the AHA for $5,000 each. AHA Board of Commissioners chair Jane Fortson met with Techwood and Clark Howell tenant association members, whose approval of the plan was mandatory for virtually all demolition and disposition grants submitted to HUD.

Tenants rejected the proposal, effectively stating they would not agree to any plan before the backlog of maintenance and renovation requests were complete.[49] They did, however, eventually agree to work with the housing authority and the mayor's office to select the plan to redevelop the units after the Olympics. They also contracted separately with the nonprofit Community Design Center of Atlanta, run by urban planner Maxwell Creighton and Georgia Tech urban planning professor Larry Keating, to conduct a survey of Techwood and Clark Howell residents about the redevelopment.

At least three proposals were submitted even before the AHA issued a request for proposals in June 1991. ACOG's preferred plan was for the AHA to sell 4.5 acres (114 units) of Techwood land for demolition and redevelopment into temporary Olympic housing and, later, into permanent housing for Georgia Tech students. Former Grady Homes resident and city council president Marvin Arrington was the most enthusiastic proponent of the plan, sending open letters to ACOG, Mayor Jackson, and the city council in support. The Techwood land was valued at $4 million, and ACOG initially proposed to purchase it from AHA for $2.7 million.[50] Although Arrington stated he wanted tenant approval before the plan moved forward, he also wanted to discourage those who were not "responsible and employed" from applying for the select number of units that would be available to low-income residents after the redevelopment.[51]

Conversely, Maynard Jackson was openly resistant to Arrington and ACOG's proposal, hoping to negotiate for redevelopment that minimized displacement and maximized benefits for the Black community, specifically for those residing in the targeted in-town neighborhoods hosting Olympic development. Jackson and Eplan convened a planning committee that would select a consultant to oversee a redevelopment plan to submit to ACOG by its October 4, 1991, deadline. That consultant was an organization named PATH, which would submit a $495,000 bid to ACOG to demolish and redevelop nearly 1,200 Techwood and Clark Howell units into 800 mixed-income units, with little detail on the breakdown of units across income groups.

PATH was an organization of four real estate companies with both Black and white ownership: Prentiss Properties, a national developer; Affordable Housing Partnership, Inc., a local company started by former Herman J. Russell employee Noel Khalil; Tyler/Yates Financial Group, a mortgage company; and Haseko of Georgia, a large national affiliate that specialized in student housing and worked with ACOG on its housing requirements. Jackson's support of PATH was interesting considering it was not the cheapest proposal (submitted by Bradfield Associates for $325,000), nor was it the proposal of a local Black business (submitted by HJ Russell and Turner Associates for $380,545).[52] It was later revealed that PATH's inflated bid included nearly $100,000 for external public relations as well as outreach efforts to address tenant concerns about revitalization.[53] Although tenants voted and narrowly approved the PATH plan 428-363, a number of improprieties in the voting process and circulation of the plan's components to tenants suggest that this vote was compromised.[54]

The fate of public housing was not a divisive issue for Atlanta's eighteen-member city council. Those in favor of public housing demolition in advance of the Olympics included white as well as Black city council members such as

Marvin Arrington, Bill Campbell, and Davetta Johnson. Following the Techwood vote in 1991, Johnson, who represented district five between 1989 and 1997, introduced a bill in the city council to dismantle the Atlanta Housing Authority and demolish all of its developments in favor of scattered site and private rentals. Johnson, a Black woman, grew up in and represented the narrow district that was anchored by three public housing communities—East Lake Meadows, Grady Homes, and Antoine Graves Homes (an elderly senior high-rise building)—which surrounded Black and white working-poor residential neighborhoods. Johnson's measure was supported internally, particularly by other council members who saw public housing as a blight on the city.[55]

When Jackson didn't seek a fourth term in office, the 1993 election of pro-demolition William (Bill) Campbell as mayor threatened the pro-revitalization plan supported by AHA director Earl Phillips. Soon after, Campbell appointed four new AHA board members to the five nonresidential positions. Without notice, Phillips "abruptly left" the housing authority.[56] The Atlanta Housing Authority board chair and former finance manager for Bill Campbell's campaign, Renee Glover, led the search for, and later served as, Phillips's replacement. Glover quickly pushed the Olympic Legacy Program as a feasible policy for public housing revitalization.

Alternative spaces for tenant resistance appeared now as they had with the political opportunities afforded in the late 1960s. Continuing her legacy of leadership with Tenants United for Fairness (TUFF), longtime organizer and welfare-rights advocate Ethel Mae Mathews founded Atlanta Neighborhoods United for Fairness (ANUFF) with advocate and frequent collaborator Columbus Ward. Based in Peoplestown but covering a number of Olympic Legacy neighborhoods, ANUFF began agitating through direct action protest and the construction of a "Resurrection City" of tents near a proposed stadium site.[57] The Resurrection City and tents were meant to harken back to the one constructed in Washington, D.C., for the 1968 Poor People's Campaign. To further this imagery of Olympic resistance as a civil rights issue, ANUFF collaborated with other groups such as the Concerned Black Clergy, the NPUs within the Olympic Ring, and labor unions to advocate for more community participation, jobs, and infrastructure to redistribute the event's economic benefits.[58] However, without consistent support of the public housing residents, concessions for poor Atlantans were few and far between.

The struggle over Olympic redevelopment, displacement, and relocation created new alliances and fractures between and within Atlanta's racialized regime. As this book shows, the struggles over space in Atlanta initially fell along racial lines. Legalized segregation and extralegal racial violence constricted the opportunity and mobility of all Black poor, working-poor, and middle-class households. The racist attacks on Black people and Black-owned property in 1906, the 1951 Plan of Improvement, and the use of urban renewal funds to remove Black homes from downtown to the west and northwestern areas of the city served to manipulate the city into its "too segregated to hate" racial geography. Residential segregation in the city increased *after* Black people were fully enfranchised in 1946—and "white flight" intensified after the desegregation of public spaces, goods, and services that were once forbidden to Black Atlantans.[59]

Yet, the redevelopment proposed by the ACOG regime was not about removing Black people, but poor people—specifically poor Black people—who lived in and around public housing developments. As Seth Gustafson states: "Olympics-related displacement worked to create a particular demographic image of the city, one without homeless, public housing residents, and other low-income Atlantans who were predominantly racial minorities. It was only by strategically displacing these residents . . . that Atlanta could create an image of itself as a prosperous, authentically global city."[60] It is not surprising that Atlanta's white business elite, or the traditional governing coalition, would be in favor of this racialized displacement; what is shocking is the support among Black council members, to the point of public disagreement with Mayor Jackson.

In the previous decade when Andrew Young made his comment about needing to attract white people into downtown Atlanta to prevent the city from becoming 70 percent Black, he was rebuked by Black civic and political leadership. That there was very little pushback from the elected Black urban regime over the disruption, disposition, and relocation of the all-Black public housing developments and in-town communities is a factor in the weak tenant mobilization against public housing demolition. The political opportunity structure of public housing was weakening, as neoliberal mega-event planning, deviant removal, and land speculation created a focus for a stable political environment. The role of Black women in this regime shift is discussed in the following section.

Black Women Leaders during the Neoliberal Turn

The tensions between Black urban regimes and their constituents, particularly the working-poor constituents who dominate the electoral coalition, have been well documented in the literature.[61] Yet, these analyses, while attentive to the class dynamics that exacerbate and sustain these tensions, do little justice to the gendered dynamics that contribute to deeper (and more discrete) oppression and inequality among the most marginalized populations. Working-class and working-poor Black women are disproportionately penalized by the centaurian characteristics of the neoliberal city—illustrated by its expanding penal state and its shrinking social welfare state.[62]

In Atlanta, this double-headed form of neoliberal urban policymaking invaded and transformed the space of public housing, as evidenced by the Partners in a Planned Community initiative. This program transferred public housing units from working-poor families in Atlanta to law enforcement officers, in the hopes of increasing the duration and reach of surveillance in public housing developments. This authoritarian and austere program was not designed by white heterosexual male landed interests, but instead by Black and white women. By the early 1990s, a Black woman (Renee Lewis Glover) headed the AHA, and a white woman (Jane Fortson) chaired the AHA's board of commissioners.

The increasing embeddedness of Atlanta's police officers in public housing continued even after a Black woman (Beverly Harvard) was appointed as chief of Atlanta's police department. What were the implications of the increasingly women-led Black urban regime on urban redevelopment in twenty-first-century Atlanta? Further, how do the logics of Black feminist identity politics obscure and further marginalize the deviant interests of working-poor Black women public housing tenants in the Black women urban regime?

Shirley Franklin, Atlanta's first woman (and first Black woman) mayor, was elected into office in November 2001 and was reelected in 2005. Mayor Franklin's inheritance at the turn of the century was a city with an unbalanced budget, retrenched federal funding for social welfare programs, increased federal funding for law enforcement programs, and a high (visible) profile following a successful stint hosting the Olympics. While Franklin implemented numerous progressive urban policies such as "greening" the city of Atlanta and increasing the transparency and efficiency of municipal hiring and management, she also oversaw major layoffs of Atlanta's predominantly Black municipal employees, and the demolition of over twenty-four public housing developments. Together, Franklin, Harvard, and Glover oversaw a period of economic development, public housing financial solubility, and reduced crime rates in Atlanta—a coup only strengthened by the fact that all three women were the first Black women to hold these positions in Atlanta's history.

Understanding the politics of Black women, as well as the leadership styles produced by these Black women politicians, requires an intersectional framework that centers Black women's knowledge, epistemologies, and practices.[63] The experience of Black women navigating the predominantly white, upper-class, male power structure as representatives for districts that are economically, socially, and politically less advantaged than those represented by their non-Black women counterparts is instrumental to understanding their politics and the policies for which they advocate.

While Black municipal empowerment via Black descriptive representation has surged since the 1972 National Black Political Convention in Gary, Indiana, the rise of the Black woman leader has been a more recent phenomenon.[64] In spite of the significant growth in Black woman descriptive representation at the local, state, and federal levels, Black women remain underrepresented at all levels compared to their proportion of the voting-age population.[65] Structural barriers of the political system constrain the political opportunities of Black congresswomen.

In the fourteen U.S. congressional districts Black women represented between 2013 and 2015, the proportion of the population that had a college degree was below that of districts non-Black women represented, and the median income of these fourteen districts was $13,612 less than median income of districts represented by non-Black women. In spite of Black women congressional candidates raising, on average, $234,058 less in campaign funds than their Black male counterparts in 2012, Black congresswomen obtained an average of 80 percent of the vote in the 2012 election compared to the 63 percent of the vote captured by the average non-Black congresswomen.[66] This overwhelming electoral support is certainly the result of housing segregation and discrimination that homogenizes Black-led congressional districts but also silences the interests of those excluded, discouraged, or distrustful of the electoral process. Troubling these deviant silences is also key to understanding Black women politics.

The structural deficiencies of having to represent poorer, more urban districts that are majority-Black residents are the cause of why Black women politicians have had to historically take a more conservative approach to legislative decision-making. As political scientist Nadia Brown notes, Black women politicians' "hypervisibility" in national political discourse heightens the circulation and critique of their images, opinions, and policies.[67]

This visibility limits the impact of the Black congressperson and the ability to advance more deviant interests. However, political opportunity is greater at the local level, particularly in large cities that have policymaking authority and autonomy from state legislatures. As such, the rise of the Black woman mayor (since 2002, there have been at least twenty Black women mayors to lead cities with populations over thirty thousand) creates greater political opportunity and efficacy for more marginalized Black women interests.[68]

A letter from Dr. Beverly Hall, the Black woman superintendent of Atlanta Public Schools (APS), to Renee Glover in support of a HOPE VI redevelopment project highlights the internal contradictions of the Black women regime. Hall mentions the strong partnership between AHA and APS, and its successful operation of traditional public schools such as M. Agnes Jones Elementary School, John Hope Elementary School, and Cook Elementary School. AHA and APS also partnered on "alternatives to traditional educational models," such as charter schools that have had a disproportionately negative impact on Black women labor force participation in publicly funded schools.[69]

Cooperation between the APS and the AHA was crucial in the urban redevelopment and revalorization regime. The failing state of APS was a major driver depressing prices in the single-family housing market, especially in areas surrounding public housing developments. If the city was going to center its land valorization efforts around public housing transformation, the institutions that supported public housing also had to be transformed toward the logic of valorization.

Just as the AHA needed to increase its PHMAP scores—through punitive de-sign and administration of lease policies—the APS also had to transform its wel-fare state responsibilities using more profit-driven logics. This process is known as the neoliberalization of education.[70] In partnership with the AHA, APS created Atlanta's first charter elementary school in the Villages of East Lake (formerly East Lake Meadows), as well as four specialized high school charters in Carver Village (formerly Carver Homes) and the STEM-focused elementary school in Centennial Place (formerly Techwood Homes).[71]

With the profit-driven missions that come with privatization, the costs of housing and educating those with higher social needs far outweigh the bene-fits that come from the per student/per unit public subsidy. Further, the resource scarcity within these transformed institutions mandates that some discrimina-tion within the institutions is necessary to stratify the distribution of benefits among participants. In public housing, this means that the best tenants—with the best credit—can access and succeed in homeownership programs, while oth-ers are trapped in the Sisyphean struggle of training for obsolete or precarious jobs, or taking on debt to fund for-profit college credits.[72] In public schools, the best students are recruited into charter schools that can implement exclusionary admission requirements while community schools take on the highest-need and highest-cost students.

Women who miss training classes because they lack childcare (only available to working mothers in most public housing self-sufficiency programs) are at risk of eviction from public housing for this lease violation. Schools that fail to meet standardized test minimums are at risk of closure for this performance failure. Yet the public housing residents who move into their homes and the all-Black male charter school that sends its entire senior class to a four-year college are held up as successes of a new Black political elite, furthering the privileging of their interests over the Black working poor.

The role of gender cannot be ignored in these dual processes. Black women are both the proponents of these urban policies and the heads of these civic associa-tions that advocate and implement them at the neighborhood level. In Black pub-lic housing and Black public schools, Black women are also leaders and heads—of the household and the classroom. When these two interests conflict in the public sphere, the limits to Black women representation are obvious through the privileging of the professional, middle-class, heteronormative, Christian woman interests over the interests of the working poor, nonworking, queer familial re-lationships, and disabled. These Black female representational limits create con-tradictory interpretations of the "community mother" that characterizes Black woman leadership.[73]

Elite Black women leaders are constructed through Black feminist theorist Michele Wallace's strong Black superwoman archetype.[74] This archetype balances a professional career and heteronormative family in ways that converge with Black middle-class norms. Conversely, advocates for and beneficiaries of the pre-transformed public housing and public schools often engaged in precarious work situations with queer family makeups that spanned multiple generations and households. The leadership style and voice of the former was privileged at the expense of the latter during the Black political urban transformation in the postindustrial city.

One factor that divided Atlanta's Black women in public housing politics was the death of eight-month-old Tameka Young. In May 1996, Tameka died of asphyxiation in her Perry Homes household that she shared with ten other family members in a five-bedroom unit.[75] The medical examiner determined the infant had inhaled a cockroach, setting off accusations between the AHA and the Young family about which party was responsible for the cockroaches in the apartment. While Glover openly stated that she, and the AHA, wept for Young, she also provided documentation of monthly extermination services for Young's household and failed housekeeping inspections at a press conference.[76] Glover positioned Young's death as an implication of the broader issues that plagued Perry Homes, which was too big and too old to transform into a habitable community. In June 1996, Glover and the AHA announced the commencement of "Operation: Clean Sweep" to address both development-wide and unit-specific issues in the maintenance of public housing communities.[77]

Black women tenants fought to resist these characterizations that relied on racist, gendered, and classed stereotypes about Black mothers, poor mothers, and public housing residents. Young's grandmother, Roynelle Young, articulated a number of arguments that resisted the notions of deviance that were attached to her granddaughter's unfortunate death. Young and her family had attempted to find larger accommodations for the multigenerational family, but the tight conditions that characterized the post-Olympic Atlanta metro housing market made that difficult. While she had at one point stated her complaints about pests in her apartment were not addressed by housing management, she later recanted and stated fumigators did spray the apartment, but these attempts did not address the pervasiveness of pests and vermin in the development.[78]

Pests and vermin were one of the longstanding grievances that tenants held against the housing authority. Three years before Young's death, ten Black women filed a class action suit through Atlanta Legal Aid against the AHA. Fulton County Superior Court judge Don Langham ordered AHA to move the women out of their units and address the infestations, leaks, and mold that caused "irreparable injury" to the tenants. Sylvia Peterson, of Techwood Homes, was quoted in the *Atlanta Journal* about how her housekeeping behavior was shaped by AHA's neglect: "That's the only thing I know—to keep a watch on them [her children]. My oldest son, he tries to play with the roaches and eat them."

Operation: Clean Sweep was an explicit attack on Black women, housekeeping, and deviant interests. In July 1996, the AHA began a thirty-day "sweep" of all apartments to conduct housekeeping inspections. Annual housekeeping inspections were already mandated by HUD for all PHA-managed units, but the practice lapsed at the AHA. Under Clean Sweep, if a tenant refused to allow AHA access to their unit for this inspection, it was considered a lease violation that could get the tenant evicted. Community cooperation with the inspectors and management was encouraged, and AHA would inspect every development each month. Households that failed the inspection would have two weeks to correct the issue; failure to do so would result in a five-day vacate (eviction) notice. This classist, ableist, and individuated approach to improving the public housing stock served to break down community trust. It also decreased acts of cooperative housekeeping between tenants and management that had previously sustained the public housing community when operating revenues were low.

A New Regime Forms:
HOPE VI Redevelopment

After the Olympics, HOPE VI provided federal funding to sustain the local regime's continued displacement of public housing residents as it demolished public buildings for private developments. The AHA's ability to attract federal funding increased its political power in setting local and state housing policy. In the "Capabilities" section of the first Perry Homes HOPE VI application submitted in 1996, the housing authority demonstrated its ability to achieve AHA and HUD objectives and priorities: "Successfully sponsored a bill through the Georgia state legislature to allow public housing units within mixed income developments to be operated by public housing even when the owner of the units was not a Public Housing Authority. This bill was signed into law in April 1996 and will allow ad valorem tax exemption of the public housing units, as required by HUD, despite inclusion in a leasehold."

This initial HOPE VI application also reveals a more insular, leaner redevelopment regime. Perhaps learning from partnerships with Legal Aid that supported the 1970s rent strikes, the AHA began creating their own nonprofit self-sufficiency community service organizations instead of contracting out these services. This protectionist approach limited the ability of the regime to redistribute political opportunities to the submerged working class, through the same patronage system that benefited the middle class in the 1980s.

AHA also included a local preference system in the proposed lease agreement, as encouraged by the HUD HOPE VI guidelines. The local preference system determined which displaced public housing residents were eligible to return to the redeveloped community. It would "extend housing opportunities to public housing eligible families in which one or more adult members are working full- or part-time or are participating in full-time training, education, or employment programs."[79] Across all developments, differentiated screening requirements implemented by private managers superseded the federal admissions requirements. New screening requirements were codified by the AHA's board of commissioners on September 4, 1996, through an amendment to the "Admissions and Continued Occupancy" policy and dwelling lease. Home visits, ceiling rents, and minimum rents were implemented as possible screening practices. The AHA also created a lottery from which to select tenants. It was a return to the PWA days of the program.

The Perry Homes application's managerial plan also described an improved relationship with the Atlanta police department (APD). The application emphasized the development's design: low-density buildings for improved sightlines between buildings and overall better property security, as well as the use of community and problem-oriented policing. The application suggests management will use "broken windows" approaches that criminalized minor offenses and ceded greater control and discretion to police on AHA properties.

The increased presence of the APD in AHA properties and communities made the likelihood of contact with police that much greater for its population. That the AHA would then screen residents before moving in, another act of surveillance, shows its transformation into an increasingly anti-tenant organization during this final phase of public housing construction. HUD's HOPE VI guidelines, however, used a point system for applications and rewarded housing authorities that implemented these punitive surveillance policies.

The relationship between the AHA and the police department was institutionalized beyond the HOPE VI application. In the 1980s, the AHA regularly contracted with the APD for the securitization and patrolling of AHA properties. These ad hoc contracts were legitimated through federal policy, the Public Housing Drug Elimination Program (PHDEP), which was authorized with HOPE I funding at the beginning of Kemp's HUD term. It was part of the package of solutions to prepare public housing developments for private reinvestment through deviant eviction. Unlike REDDOG (Run Every Drug Dealer Out of Georgia, a state program), the DEP was jointly run by the AHA and the APD.

In a July 31, 1997, letter to Renee Glover, police chief Beverly Harvard writes:

> "We are presently developing a new agreement that will redefine the role of the Atlanta Police Department and its relationship with the housing authority's public housing communities. This new agreement will seek to incorporate the following components of the AHA's 1997 Drug Elimination Plan, "Building Partnerships for a Safer Community:"
>
> 1. Establish a renewed collaboration with the housing authority and its residents to share information on crime incidents that specifically affect areas in and around public housing communities

2. Increased participation by law enforcement in policing strategies that include community-oriented policing tactics, and saturation/suppression of flagrant drug markets in and around public housing developments

3. Support enforcements of AHA's "One Strike and You're Out" policies, and participation in crime-prevention and educational tactics to reduce crime in and around public housing.[80]

The continued use of the APD by the AHA to manipulate the boundaries of the public housing community both contributed to and are the outcome of minimal tenant resistance. While earlier cooperation agreements between the AHA and APD were controversial enough to warrant protests and scandal, the APD framed its provision of additional support services as the "needed resources to bolster AHA's capability to provide healthy and safe housing that promotes the general well being of its residents."[81]

The supplementary law enforcement services above baseline patrolling duties are intended to assist in the AHA's strategic plan to "reclaim areas that have habitually been troubled by nuisance activity that increases crime opportunity."[82] "Nuisances" are the activities of deviants, the survival strategies of marginalized communities that thrive in informality and cooperation, the queer household formations that adopt children—and adults—into spaces that reject conventional heteronormative and patriarchal norms. The creative spatial reclamations of public housing tenants—such as appropriating an abandoned unit into a private play spaces for teens—are ripe for misinterpretation, and reappropriation, by a state using nuisance laws.

A week prior to writing a support letter for the Drug Elimination Plan, Chief Harvard sent an inquiry to Renee Glover. The letter concerned allegations of incentive payments to police officers who made arrests on AHA properties while employed with the private security contractor Interstate Protective Services (IPS). Arrests were cause for immediate eviction under the federal "one strike and you're out" policy, suggesting that the AHA was using the police as a workaround to evict problem tenants and households.[83] The letter was also sent to Deputy Chief B. J. Rocker, Major S. M. O'Brien, and John Spillers, director of protective services for the AHA. Spillers denied the use of bonuses for arrests on AHA property, and on August 19, 1997, Carl Bledsoe of IPS confirmed police officers were only paid for hours worked. However, Harvard did not receive the response to the accusation before submitting her letter of support for the DEP, or before signing and dating the DEP grant on August 1, 1997.[84]

The Final Phase:
Perry Homes' HOPE VI Redevelopment

The onerous, exclusionary, and drawn-out planning and redevelopment of some of the larger public housing developments served to further demobilize diverse tenant interests that were not compatible with the Atlanta redevelopment regime. The AHA submitted the first $25 million HOPE VI application for Perry Homes and Perry Homes Annex in 1996 and received a $20 million award in October of that year. It then submitted its first revitalization plan in September 1998. Following a site visit from HUD in December 1998 to address concerns with the plan, AHA withdrew its submission and revised its plan in December 1999. The latter redevelopment plan transformed Perry Homes into a mixed-income community with homeownership opportunities for low-income and market-rate residents. However, when this decision was made, residents were not included, and demolitions were nearly complete.

Demolition and remediation for Perry Homes closed out by 2001. Between 2000 and 2004, Perry Homes was redeveloped into West Highlands at Heman E. Perry Boulevard, a mixed-income, mixed-tenure, mixed-use community. During this eight-year process, the initial demolition was phased over three years; families were relocated, and homes were demolished in groups of roughly eighty housing units per quarter. Families were temporarily relocated in off-site public and private rental units and then later permanently displaced after the revitalization plan reduced the number of public rental units.

The redevelopment process at Perry Homes encapsulates the reasons why most tenant mobilization fell apart during this public housing transformation. First, the planning, demolition, and rebuilding processes lasted nearly a decade due to unrealistic federal assumptions about the local housing and real estate markets. Tenants originally supported and participated in plans for revitalizing Perry Homes, preserving it as a new, but smaller, public housing development. The regional HUD office rejected this proposal on the basis of the forecasted high operating costs for a public housing development. This revision process, and a weak housing market, slowed demolition and redevelopment at the turn of the century. Second, the authority began relying on new federal policies to surveil, silence, and evict more deviant interests during this prolonged redevelopment process.

The process at Perry Homes also illuminates some of the tensions between the Black urban regime, particularly the gendered tensions that emerge over redevelopment. Renee Glover and Mary Sanford, the appointed and elected representatives of the housing authority and tenant association, were both Black women who represented majority Black women–led households. From the outset, both women were heavily in favor of keeping the redeveloped Perry Homes exclusively for public housing residents. However, the design, marketing, and administration of the redevelopment were gendered in ways that perpetuated the construction of deviance and exclusion of single Black women–heads of household.

Perry Homes was also born out of the racist, sexist, and spatially discriminatory processes of the urban renewal program. From its isolated and disinvested site selection to its "containment and warehousing of the poor" admissions and leasing process, Perry Homes was not planned, designed, or operated to offer the same political opportunities as some of the earlier Black public housing developments. Without the citywide supports of the ACPH or a more mobilized national movement, Perry Homes tenants and community members were limited in their responses.

The first obstacle to a successful revitalization of Perry Homes was a reduced HOPE VI implementation grant for AHA. The housing authority received just $20 million of the requested $25 million, and this $5 million difference was deducted from the community empowerment and self-sufficiency programming and staffing.[85] The FY 1996 cycle was the first year that HOPE VI was available to all public housing authorities, and HUD awarded only twenty HOPE VI grants. In an effort to reduce the cost of the demolition and redevelopment, as well as increase the likelihood of receiving a grant award, the AHA did not even include the cost of community and resident services in the HOPE VI grant application.

Two years later, Perry Homes was awarded another $5.1 million HOPE VI grant for demolition; in addition, the Comprehensive Grant Program (CGP) provided annual funding from FY 1997 to FY 2002 to several AHA properties that were under demolition and redevelopment. In total, AHA received about $51 million in HOPE VI, CGP, Low-Income Housing Tax Credit (LIHTC), Section 202, Federal Home Loan Bank funding and $5.3 million in conventional debt to demolish and redevelop Perry Homes.[86] These increased public and private funds were only possible once the redevelopment plan included more market-rate housing and fewer public housing residents.

The second obstacle to the revitalization was this failure to keep the community exclusively for public housing residents. After accepting the HOPE VI award in 1996, AHA had to submit a revitalization plan (RP) detailing how the authority would spend the funds. The RP had to include a number of components that overwhelmingly favored housing authority applications that demolished, privatized, and otherwise removed public housing units from the Annual Contractual Contribution designation. Using a neighborhood analysis from the Land Interest Group as justification for why the redevelopment could not support market-rate units, the AHA instead submitted an initial RP that demolished 944 units in Perry Homes (827 of which were occupied) for 415 units of on-site public housing.

The neighborhood analysis—of census tracts 87.01 and 87.02—suggested that prospects for private commercial or residential development were limited due to the negative perceptions of the Perry Homes development.[87] After a HUD site visit to address the concerns of relocating 415 public housing units on a site described by the neighborhood analysis as "relatively isolated from other residential areas and employment centers,"[88] AHA was advised to resubmit its RP, which it did in December 1999. This revised revitalization plan (RRP) was actually a redevelopment plan, which called for 750 total units: 301 public housing (including elderly) rental units, 189 nonpublic housing LIHTC rental units, 80 HUD Section 202 (elderly non-income-restricted) rental units, 80 market-rate rental units, and 100 on-site homeownership units.[89]

The drafting of the Perry Homes RRP was led by the AHA's Resident Services and Economic Development (RSED) staff: Doug Faust, Dwan Packett, Renee Dixon, Dwayne Vaughn, and John Watson. The plan was to create two sets of occupancy standards: one for residents who were admitted through the AHA's new screening process with rigorous employment, criminal, and credit checks, and the other for those admitted into the Campus of Learners and Workers program, which would transition those unemployed, underemployed, and on welfare into economically self-sufficient workers.

The group immediately set about conducting a survey of resident needs, capabilities, and goals. Interviews with the Integral Group, another developer involved with other AHA mixed-income redevelopments, noted this was a process that was added after the contentious and divisive experience at Techwood Homes (now Centennial Place).[90] The failure to both survey tenants before relocation and establish a baseline made the program evaluation of HOPE VI at Centennial Place virtually impossible.

From a legislative perspective, tenant involvement in and approval of all redevelopment plans was required to receive HOPE VI awards. The RSED staff conducted 467 in-person surveys with the head of households in Perry Homes over a period of four weeks. From the initial survey, the RSED team estimated that only 50 percent of the relocated families would return. Initial residential preferences indicated that 35 percent of the households would either remain on-site during the redevelopment or go to other public housing developments, while 65 percent opted to use Section 8 vouchers to find private rental housing. During the time between the demolition application and the submission of the RRP, an additional 60 families left Perry Homes, reducing the total number of households to relocate to 762.[91] This level of attrition and rate of return was common across the other Atlanta redevelopments (see table 6.1).

These data suggest that HOPE VI, whether intentional or not, was successful in dispersing and deconcentrating public housing residents in public housing developments. The AHA's 1993 replacement housing policy was explicit in its goal of creating communities that were no more than 30 percent public housing.

During the master planning process, Black developer Noel Khalil, head of the newly formed Perry Homes Redevelopment LLC, wanted to create a legacy community, one that would inspire pride among residents for years. He implored residents to "dream big" and uphold the spirit and beauty of the commu-

Table 6.1. Relocation statistics for AHA developments, January 8, 1997

	Total number of units	Total number of vacant units	Total number of families to relocate	Number of families relocated	Total evictions or skips	Percent of families relocated with housing choice vouchers (%)	Percent of families relocated to public housing (%)	Percent of families relocated to homeownership (%)
John Eagan Homes	548	188	360	176	26	75.6	22.2	2.3
East Lake	650	267	383	181	25	63.0	37.0	0.0
Clark Howell	657	122	543	430	25	69.5	30.5	0.0

nity.[92] The language used in the planning sessions aligned well with the HOPE VI goal to mainstream public housing residents, while also serving to exclude the more deviant planning interests in the community. This was also reminiscent of PWA planning sessions and the uplift politics articulated by the housing advisory committee.

Tenant participation in the planning committee meetings varied across the three different phases of the full redevelopment process: (1) the development's master community plan, (2) the development's design, and (3) tenant relocation and social service provision. During the relocation phase when some tenants remained on-site, and others were searching for new Housing Choice Voucher units or waiting for reassignments to other AHA developments, the Perry Homes planning committee met monthly for about an hour. These convenings were sparsely attended compared to initial meetings around development design, when all tenants were still living on-site.

Even during these initial planning meetings, the tenant association president (Mary Sanford) was only allowed five minutes each for opening and closing remarks. The housing authority provided status updates and questions for the other fifty minutes of each meeting. The AHA led the question and answer segment and typically addressed questions posed by another AHA or community partner representative. Due to failing health, Mary Sanford missed several meetings in 1999, and there were no tenants who spoke in her stead. Perry Homes planning meetings during the final months of the development's existence had little to no tenant representation.

The Perry Homes Redevelopment LLC master plan included purchasing additional parcels surrounding Perry Homes. These parcels would be used to develop both the market-rate housing and the market-rate amenities needed to subsidize the cost of operating the public housing units. The master plan transformed the multifamily, low-rise buildings on the Perry Homes site into 700 multifamily units, 186 single-family units, and four holes of an eighteen-hole golf course. The adjacent Gun Club landfill would house eleven more holes of golf, a clubhouse, and a driving range. The group planned to site an additional 177 single-family homes in Gun Club Park, along with the final three holes of golf for the eighteen-hole course.[93]

Design-wise, Perry Homes Redevelopment LLC attempted to correct some of the mistakes of the AHA's earlier mixed-income redevelopments. It limited the height of the multifamily units to 2.5 stories and minimized the aesthetic distinction between multifamily and single-family households in the development.[94] The increase of single-family units, with private front yards and backyards, on the centrally located Gun Club Park, is a direct transfer of land from public to private hands. It also diluted the power of the subsidized renters, and the interests that inform their community needs and politics, in the Neighborhood Planning Unit. Although there were intentional design similarities between the subsi-

Figure 6.1. Columbia Parc Citi, mixed-use condominium. Source: Atlanta Housing Authority West Highlands at Perry Boulevard Records / JHP Architecture/Urban Design.

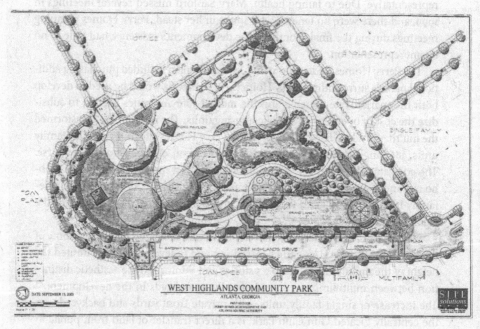

Figure 6.2. West Highlands Community Park. Source: Atlanta Housing Authority West Highlands at Perry Boulevard Records/Site Solutions LLC.

dized and market-rate housing, there was little thought put into designing shared spaces and amenities between the two types of households.

Renderings and descriptions of the proposed multifamily units show manor-style homes containing eight units in each building. The centrality of the golf course was a nod to the uplift opportunities promoted by golf course developers (see figures 6.1 and 6.2). Minutes from an August 1996 planning meeting suggest that the single most important element that the golf course would create for Perry Homes residents was employment opportunities.[95]

HUD advised housing authorities to include the following lease and admission requirements for units in the HOPE VI program: screening procedures, waiting list establishment and maintenance, local preference rules, unit transfer policies, maintenance procedures, positive incentives such as income disregards and ceiling rents, and other lease requirements that promote community service and transition from public housing.[96] These leasing and occupancy standards were foremost intended to "contribute to an overall objective of ending the social and economic isolation of low income people and promot[e] their economic independence."[97] The HUD regulations allowed for management to maintain separate admission and occupancy practices for each type of resident (public housing, tax credit, or market-rate), and AHA chose to only detail these practices for public housing tenants in the HOPE VI plans.

The shift to behavioral screening, criminalization, and occupancy standards created new mechanisms to exclude and regulate deviants in public housing redevelopments. The lease provisions for public housing in West Highlands, for example, required participation in the self-sufficiency program "designed to foster a sense of resident responsibility and . . . require[d] the residents to commit to self-improvement. Lease requirements include a commitment to 60 hours of community-service per year."[98]

Conclusion

After years in court, the golf course developers were countersued for failing to provide services, and the course was never constructed. The median income in the West Highlands community was approximately $26,000 as of 2015, and there was a 30 percent homeownership rate in a community that remained 90 percent Black. The grocery stores, restaurants, and retail opportunities did not come with the physical transformation of Perry Homes. The legacy of state disinvestment, the weakened community ties, and the protracted redevelopment process instead dissuaded investment in the community. However, construction is underway for new executive housing starting with townhomes priced at $400,000. Construction also continues for the expansion of the Atlanta Beltline, a citywide greenway that connects peripheral neighborhoods along the same expressway loop that separated the city from the suburbs. Early studies show neighborhoods adjacent to the Beltline have experienced displacement of renters, echoing some of the impacts of the Olympic Ring.[99]

The final decades of public housing tenant associations in Atlanta are a slow decline into political obsolescence, much like the eventual obsolesce and demolition of its buildings. The years of disinvestment and neglect that prompted resident management corporations were a means of co-opting and dividing public housing's greatest asset: its political opportunity derived from its tenant associations. The construction of a severely distressed public housing development and the deployment of HOPE VI programs created new opportunities for some tenants, often at the expense of others.

The spatial and political erasure of public housing developments from urban, state, and federal policies was not always as protracted as the Perry Homes example. Indeed, in New Orleans and Galveston, Texas, the processes were swift and without even the token inclusion of resident participation. The increasing proportion of public housing residents using housing vouchers created new, often concentrated, geographies of public housing. But without support from tenant associations, these spatial transformations actually shrank the city's Black participatory geographies.

Deviant interests, which suffered from the punitive neoliberal turn of HOPE VI, the Personal Responsibility and Work Opportunity Reconciliation Act (PRWORA), and the Quality Housing and Work Responsibility Act of 1998, faced limited political opportunity even under the gendered transformation of some parts of the Black urban regime. The tensions between Black women elites, tenant leaders, and tenants have their origins in the uplift politics proffered by club women in the 1930s, were refined during the Atlanta Child Murders, and came to a head with the passage of Operation: Clean Sweep. The permanent eviction of deviance from the public housing program facilitated the demobilized response to public housing demolition and privatization.

Public Housing Developments as Political Opportunity Structures

From its origins as New Deal spatial fixes and uplifts to its final gasps as warehouses for the poor, public housing developments have long served as structures of political opportunity for tenants and surrounding communities. The political opportunities afforded to these populations varied across time and space but largely reflect structural expansions and constraints set by federal policy, state intervention, and local planning and administration. Political opportunity theory assumes some level of political instability as a predicate for folding new interests into the political regime. In Atlanta, the instabilities of a changing economic, racial, and spatial order created political opportunities for many marginalized groups over time.

In its post-Depression origins, University Homes created unprecedented political opportunity at the local level for many Black residents. The ability to serve on advisory committees, the new priorities to employ and house Black residents, even the academic prospects for the emerging fields of urban sociology and the Atlanta School of Social Work's housing manager training program all created a wealth of opportunities for Black men and women in Atlanta. There were limits, of course, to this political opportunity. The residents of Beaver Slide—those whose homes were bought and razed by the government to construct over six hundred units of housing—were certainly poorly served by the elimination of their housing and subsequent displacement. With only five Black neighborhoods in an urbanizing and growing Atlanta, this displacement likely forced these residents into higher-cost and more substandard housing.

Although Atlanta had a history of radical labor organizing and interracial coalitions engaged in direct action for better working conditions, these political interests were not afforded many opportunities through the construction of public housing. Public housing developments, and the racialized compromises in New Deal policies, instead created new political opportunities structured around segregated labor unions that continued to perpetuate gendered exclusion in

Map C.1. Black population in Atlanta by census tract, 1990.
Source: U.S. Census Bureau, Social Explorer.

Persons:Black
Census 1990

Insufficient data

<15%
15% to 30%
30% to 45%
45% to 60%
60% to 80%
> 80%

© SocialExplorer Inc

2 mi

Lawre

Redan

Tucker

Candler-McAfee

Dunwoody

North
Atlanta

Sandy
Springs

Forest
Park

Atlanta

East
Point

College
Park

Smyrna

Marietta

Mableton

Douglasville

the building trades. Public housing policy created programmatic opportunities structured around raced, gendered, and heteronormative reifications of work, play, and family. The domination of uplift politics in Black elite circles, from Atlanta to Washington, D.C., ensured that the Black middle and submerged middle classes who conformed to these norms were able to directly benefit from the changing social order of New Deal Atlanta.

In this unstable political environment, Black elites structured local political opportunities through the spatial politics of land assembly. PWA public housing developments required the local state to cede control to federal authorities over land use, development, and maintenance. In the strategic siting of Black public housing developments, early elites expanded the Black residential and commercial footprints and the mobility of Black Atlantans. These spatial politics also laid the groundwork for concentrated Black areas that would become both spaces of exclusion and spaces of opportunity.

Postwar Black elites start to take advantage of these concentrations during the first transformation of public housing policy and the opportunity structure therein. Perry Homes, as one of the larger northwest public housing developments, became a fount of political action and mobilization as residents had to fight for the neighborhood amenities that were prioritized during the first wave of public housing sitings. The elite-led compromise of the 1951 Plan of Improvement created new neighborhoods for land-restricted Black Atlantans. Yet Black public housing residents, who were increasingly led by Black women tenant leaders, found that the benefit of more mobility and land for housing came with a lack of public investment and infrastructure. Without the privilege of federal "ownership" that early Black public housing residents leveraged to attract funding and support for neighborhood amenities, the postwar public housing political opportunity required direct engagement with local and state officials.

Yet the role of Black women also meant a new form of political opportunity that was more progressive than previous public housing politics. Fighting back against gendered and heteronormative assumptions of Black leadership, these postwar tenant leaders fought against an aggressive biracial urban regime focused on remaking the city through urban renewal funds. These women's efforts structured political opportunities for women like them—often single or the primary earner in the household who worked in isolating conditions and lived socially in communities not constructed for them. Public housing politics focused on new schools, better maintenance of the development, recreational spaces, and diversions for teen idleness.

These postwar Black women leaders transformed the political opportunity structure of public housing in a way that expanded Black participatory geographies. In laying the groundwork for effective political action at the local level, Black women were some of the first Black non-elites to gain concessions outside of the racialized spaces of power or at the ballot box. Atlanta's elite biracial regime

discouraged direct action from marginalized groups. In expanding these participatory geographies in the changing social order of post-1946 Black enfranchisement, the submerged Black working class was able to gain some power and representation in this period.

The tenant association at Grady Homes took advantage of this power and further transformed public housing political opportunity. Following three years of
rebellions in urban Black communities across the nation, there was renewed federal interest in and funding for urban areas. With an emphasis on the maximum
feasible participation of impoverished residents, tenant association leader Susie
LaBord was able to work directly with federal officials to craft an economic opportunity plan in Atlanta that served long-ignored Black populations—children,
single women caretakers, and the elderly. This federal support, along with the local regime change under Mayor Maynard Jackson, allowed LaBord and those she
represented to further expand Black participatory geographies.

Black participatory geographies during this period expanded up to a point.
Public housing operating policies changed once again with the Brooke Amendment of 1969, which capped all rents at 25 percent of tenant household income. As
urban employment, particularly Black urban employment, decreased in the deindustrializing city, urban infrastructure deteriorated with fewer revenue sources
to maintain it. Tenant political interests were shifting to work against the housing authority, taking on an increasingly contentious approach to a majority-white
management and board of commissioners. Tenant leaders like Susie LaBord had
narrow views of tenants and tenant needs and were therefore less likely to challenge the housing authority that often partnered with or employed them.

The federal support to cities did not last long. As public housing priorities
turned increasingly to austerity, the ACPH emerged as another transformation of
the political opportunity structure for disenfranchised residents. As a legitimate
council within the city's bureaucracy, the ACPH leadership leveraged its control
over the new modernization policy to demand greater control over space recon-
figurations in public housing developments. Similar to individual tenant associations, the ACPH worked to advocate for spaces, policies, and programs that reflected tenant and community needs.

But the ACPH suffered from its overreliance on traditional political structures that limited its ability to expand Black participatory geographies. The council's membership was tied to tenant associations' aging leadership, which was increasingly less representative of a changing, and younger, tenant population. The
ACPH was less likely to engage in some of the direct action that characterized the
more radical postwar tenant associations; instead of protests at the housing authority, it was more likely to release resolutions or press statements. Yet the visibility of the organization, especially at the local level, allowed it a great deal of
success in generating political opportunity.

Control over modernization funding and the incorporation into the regime was but a stopgap for the inevitable final transformation of public housing: into a severely distressed public asset in need of demolition and privatization. Resident management corporations provided the resource mobilization structure to complete this transformation. As residents took on the concerns and interests of the housing manager, public housing policies soon rolled back some of the progressive gains in grievance, admissions, and lease policies. Tenant interests, which began to divide in the late 1970s with the formation of new representative organizations such as TUFF and UTC, fractured even more as RMCs penalized tenants for late rent payments and lease violations.

The RMCs were provided political opportunities through a host of new programs that prioritized the demolition, shrinkage, and privatization of public housing developments. As HOPE I through HOPE VI reshaped public housing as we know it, tenant admissions and evictions were also structured by a transforming welfare state. From Techwood to Perry Homes, public housing developments were initially targeted for revitalization, which soon shifted into redevelopment.

Residents were encouraged to participate in planning sessions over a number of years; eventually, tenants either left or were evicted under new punitive policies that seemed to prioritize the uplift populations from early public housing developments. This fractured, demobilized, and defeated tenant resistance was no match for a multi-interest Atlanta regime organized around the disposability and displacement of public housing residents for in-city land redevelopment. Tenant association leaders, some of whom were rumored to directly benefit from privatization through new units or letters of support to return to revitalized developments, rubber-stamped housing authority plans that would ensure the most vulnerable and marginalized residents would not be served by this public housing transformation.

> We did a survey, we did a lot of surveys, of tenants who really did believe the Olympics were a good thing. . . . They thought the attention from the city and money would help revitalize public housing . . . but the slight majority of tenants wanted to stay . . . particularly at Grady Homes, the elderly and disabled liked being close to the hospital, and felt they had no real options [for comparable rental housing] using the housing vouchers.
>
> —Maxwell Creighton, Community Design Services[1]

> We tried to get some HUD money to strengthen the resident associations, so they [residents] could strengthen themselves . . . the money went to the NPUs. Some of them [NPUs] were fighting for tenants, but others were fighting for homeownership.
>
> —Larry Keating, professor emeritus of Georgia Tech, cofounder of Community Design Services[2]

The new public housing residents in redeveloped, mixed-income, mixeduse developments lack tenant associations. Homeowners are encouraged to form their own associations, but tenant associations, according to a developer, "were not needed because there aren't the same problems in these new developments."[3] The outright eviction of deviant perspectives, the demobilization and defunding of tenant associations and other modes of representation, and Atlanta's ongoing redevelopment regime have eradicated one of the only vehicles for working-class and working-poor political action. As a site of class, gender, and race politics, public housing developments have long served the residents of Atlanta and other cities to advocate for those classified as deviants. The loss of these spaces generates new questions about where these politics can take place in the twenty-first-century city.

The Changing Role and Constructions of Deviance

When the first public housing developments opened in Atlanta in 1936 and 1937, Black communities and residents had few avenues to make legitimate claims on the state. Without political representation or participation, Black people and spaces were demonized and cast aside as political and social deviants. Local and national uplift politics responded directly to these characterizations by focusing on assimilating Black behavior, political interests, and urban forms around white, middle-class, patriarchal, heteronormative capitalist norms.

Blackness and Black space as deviance is an important part of early public housing political history. These origins of tenant association politics forever shaped its ability to function as an inclusive resource mobilizer—programs and policies that worked to assimilate Blackness were thus prioritized. Gendered recreation options for children and political education forums for men and women were photographed, publicized, and circulated across the country. These images were important to uplifting the race but also for clearly establishing a new form of deviance that fell outside of these photographs.

The 1951 Plan of Improvement helped spatialize the uplift project, as Black homeowners were finally granted enough land and mobility to leave public housing for private homeownership or rentals. It also created space for a new Black ghetto, a marginalized space of land lacking basic public infrastructure and amenities in the northwest quadrant of the city. Thus, postwar spatial transformation both assimilated old forms of deviance while constructing new ones. The biracial urban regime accepted and incorporated these assimilated interests, as the newly constructed deviants worked to advocate for their own interests in the public housing political opportunity structure.

Postwar deviance was constructed around family composition and gendered leadership norms. Single Black mothers and othermothers worked against the housing authority and other parts of the state apparatus to counteract their non-normative construction and legitimate their political needs and interests. Women such as Mary Sanford and Ethel Mae Mathews used the spaces and resource mobilization of public housing developments and tenant associations in the 1960s to organize deviants and create a political agenda serving Black women and their families.

The assimilation and incorporation of these deviant interests were the result of a political transformation of public housing and Atlanta more broadly. With the 1974 election of Maynard Jackson and the formation of a Black urban regime, many tenant leaders saw new pathways for political opportunity through the tight control of tenant associations and their member interests. Black domestic workers and other members of the working poor were elevated into positions of leadership locally and nationwide, as a new form of deviant soon emerged: the truant youth and their younger, precariously employed mothers.

The Atlanta Child Murders destabilized the city and nation and constructed two new deviants in or around public housing. But the first major construction and condemnation was on the space of public housing developments and their wider communities. As local, state, and federal funding sharply dropped with Reagan's 1981 OBRA, the long-disinvested public housing communities that were once a source of spatial uplift soon became spaces of territorial stigmatization, or the marginalization of people who reside in disinvested spaces. Truant youth and their mothers, othermothers, and caregivers were blamed for their disinvested surroundings, prompting a top-down response to secure and contain public housing developments, often through partnership with the police.

The arrival of the police—who were at first welcomed by residents anxious for attention and resources from the state and who later were ordered into these communities by the mayor—marked a new determinant of deviance. Deviance was no longer under the construction of policymakers, housing managers, and tenant association presidents but was also expanded to the police who occupied these spaces. With authorization by new state nuisance laws to condemn properties for suspected drug activity, police officers had the ability to construct and evict deviance spatially. Territorial stigmatization assigned deviance to those who resided in these developments.

> *The thing that we run into, in terms of trying to organize in public housing communities, to the extent that they exist, is how do you [do it]. . . . There is a lot of apathy . . . and leadership of course . . . the brain trust, a lot of brain drain in communities . . . leaves behind those who have greater levels of apathy. . . . We don't see the leadership going into the community . . . it's just not seen as politically advantageous. . . . You could do the same sort of stuff, you go to the churches, but you don't go into those [communities with people] who are highly marginalized. . . . There's been no significant drives to get people to register to vote. . . . You need to have some concerted strategy behind their frustrations and redirect that energy.*
>
> —Lindsay Jones, former pro bono attorney for public housing residents, founder of legal clinic [4]

The final years of public housing policy are an exercise in eviction by deviance construction. The Olympics and HOPE VI provided a new spatial organizing logic that displaced, demolished, and demobilized deviant politics. Strict enforcement of leases, lack of federal support for public housing preservation, and top-down mandates for strict admission policies for redeveloped units steadily displaced the people and interests who resisted the normative construction of public housing residents set forth in its policies. Without these populations, tenant association politics failed to represent those who most needed representation. The absence of deviance resulted in the physical-political transformation of public housing developments, removing the need for tenant associations in its privatized form.

Diverging Space, Creating Black Participatory Geographies

Construction and control of space has direct influence on political legitimacy and power. Land use and planning decisions are political actions, and urban politics are shaped by land allocation and valuation. The evolution of public housing developments as political opportunity structures and the simultaneous construction and assimilation of deviant interests into this structure are both contingent on how the space of the development is diverged for and against deviants. The political opportunities structure the options for divergence, and deviants are constructed and assimilated according to these spatial reappropriations.

Although deviance is constructed around Blackness and Black spaces, it is critical to consider how gender and class are also coconstructed through public housing's early history. The early Du Bois survey of Beaver Slide pushed back against Black household and community formation as immoral and instead provided a sharp race-class analysis around the precarity of Black work and housing. The public housing program, however, secured its multi-interest coalition around a classist, patriarchal, heteronormative, and ableist frame of Progressivism that attempted to uplift a nation of homeowners out of the submerged post-Depression working class.

Class and gender are constructed through the definitions of "family," "household," and "need" created during the initial application process. In creating these categories, public housing policy cast aside the real housing precarity and needs of single-person, nonrelated households that experience the cyclical pay described in Du Bois's study. Advocates such as Florence Read and early housing managers such as Annie Ruth Hill helped administratively override some of these categories by admitting single women into vacant units and allowing "over-income" households to remain in public housing.

These administrative exceptions are an early means of expanding Black participatory geographies by giving those intentionally excluded (by policy) from public housing access to the public housing political opportunity structure. The initial construction of public housing allowed disenfranchised Atlantans a direct means of communicating with and accessing the state. The ongoing divergences from that initial project to uplift deviance out of the slum created new forms of participatory geographies for politically marginalized groups in New Deal Black Atlanta.

Spatial divergence moved from the realm of administrators and advisory committee members to tenants in the postwar public housing development. Black women tenants focused on expanding the opportunity structure and the participatory geographies into the neighborhoods, schools, and community spaces surrounding public housing developments. By funneling local, state, and federal resources into improving and sustaining community infrastructure, the reach of the participatory geographies went beyond those formally enrolled in the public housing program.

Although the formation of the ACPH should have expanded Black participatory geographies through its citywide representation for marginalized groups, the shrinking political opportunity structure of the public housing development actually had the opposite effect on deviant politics. The ACPH marked the beginning of the shift toward increasingly conservative tenant politics and the destabilization of the political opportunity structure. As the dual forces of urban disinvestment and social need created new forms of public housing deviance, ACPH's control over limited public housing funding did little to address these needs through the modernization program. Modernization prioritized the deserving poor—the elderly and disabled, who were then underrepresented populations in tenant politics.

The decline of Black participatory geographies mimicked the decline of the public housing program. New transformations in public housing policy continued to assimilate long-standing leaders while evicting and further marginalizing newly constructed deviants. As developments and tenant associations were removed from Atlanta's landscape, deviance was displaced or dispersed into new concentrated geographies of housing choice vouchers.

> *Tearing down public housing was a terrible thing. . . . Like I see it now, you go and visit those sites, there is nothing on them, nothing but beautiful land. . . . I think about it, I know why the white man wanted this land. It's a prime property actually! And I'm like wow. And ain't nothing on it. And those people who lived in public housing are homeless now. And I told them, I told them what would happen.*
>
> —Shirley Hightower, former president of Bowen Homes tenant association, former member of the resident advisory board[5]

Without the institutional support of tenant representation, the new form of public housing permanently displaced Black participatory geographies. Studies show that housing choice voucher users have lower traditional forms of political participation; other studies show these voucher users are "detached" from traditional social networks that long sustained these participatory geographies.[6]

The Limits and Futures of Public Housing Politics

The 2011 demolition of Bankhead Homes is what actually began this project. When I saw the article in the *New York Times*, I was fascinated that the city with the first public housing developments was the first to demolish virtually all of them. In unfolding this history of public housing in Atlanta, I was continually inspired by the solidarity, political acumen, challenges, wins, and transformation of tenant associations over time and space. The end of Atlanta's public housing program was just as torturous and prolonged as the Perry Homes redevelopment process described in chapter 6.

In thinking about what public housing tenant associations produced for Black women in Atlanta, for nontraditional family structures, for poor people's politics, for deviants broadly—I am stuck with a question that I've had since I first saw that article in the *New York Times*: How can a city function without caring for its most vulnerable? It brings up core tensions in a capitalist society that prioritizes economic production over social reproduction. I hope this book demonstrates how necessary the work of public housing and its tenants, planners, policymakers, and administrators was in making the "mecca" of Atlanta a place for a thriving and sustained Black middle and working class.

Since the demolition of public housing in Atlanta, a series of deviant issues has surfaced in Atlanta's politics. From the controversial condemnation and closure of the last all-male homeless shelter in downtown Atlanta to the struggles against gentrification and displacement in the Summerhill and Vine City neighborhoods, the absence of public housing has created a vacuum as both a shelter for working-poor residents and a political opportunity structure to advance their interests. We know that public housing reduces the negative impacts of gentrification and can provide interventions of housing and social services that directly address the causes of those experiencing homelessness. Yet instead of providing this social safety net, the program's current transformation and ongoing privatization barely makes a dent in serving these populations in need.

There were many flaws in tenant associations, public housing policies, and the political mobilizations of these residents over time. The spatial uplift project permanently displaced impoverished households, and heteronormative nuclear families benefited from political opportunity intentionally denied to nonnormative households. Respectability politics weakened the ability to advocate for all Black Atlantans, limiting the expanse of Black participatory geographies. And the conservative turn that was produced by and helped facilitate neoliberal public housing policies fractured tenant alliances that would have provided a united front of resistance against public housing demolition and privatization.

> *No, that's [housing choice voucher] a joke, because every year you got to get that renewed . . . and then you have to pay the light bill, Sister, and water, that's a joke. . . . That's why I stay where I'm at . . . because I know . . . yeah you have your privacy, but you wind up spending more than your check, and then you get in a rut. . . . Just like those people say 'oh I want to get Section 8' . . . you wanna go all the way out into boondocks-land, no bus, no transportation, why would you do that?! But you can't tell them . . . they don't believe that! . . . Because the landlord, they don't have to take you back next year if they don't want to!*

> —Sister Elaine Osby, former president of Cosby-Spear tenant association, current resident[7]

What does the future of deviant politics and Black participatory geographies look like in a post–public housing city? Grassroots organizations and national tenant associations still provide political opportunity for well-organized and high-capacity residents. Revived democratic socialist, Black cooperative, and the working families' political parties have gained a foothold in the political structure of major U.S. cities. As of this writing, progressive elected officials are once again advocating for a return to investing in public housing, Medicare for all, and rent control. The destabilization from Trump's election has created this political opportunity, but the capacity to mobilize resources in response has suffered with the loss of public housing. However, the possibility of bringing new Black participatory geographies into cities without public housing is an exciting and mobilizing vision for the future.

Notes

Introduction

1. Faye Goolrick, "Who Wants Techwood? Businessmen Want the Land, the City Wants Improvements, the Tenants Want a Home. For the Nation's Oldest Public Housing Project, the Time for Fixing Up—or Tearing Down—Has Come," *Atlanta Constitution*, March 15, 1981, G18.

2. Techwood and Clark Howell Tenant Association Modernization Position Statement, Techwood Homes and Centennial Place Records.

3. See Mike Davis, *City of Quartz: Excavating the Future of Los Angeles* (New York: Verso, 1990), especially chapter 5, for the rise in defensible space in urban planning as a response to increasing crime and expanding police budgets.

4. Goolrick, "Who Wants Techwood?"

5. Larry Keating and Carol A. Flores, "Sixty and Out: Techwood Homes Transformed by Enemies and Friends," *Journal of Urban History* 26, no. 3 (2000): 275–311.

6. Charles F. Palmer, *Adventures of a Slum Fighter* (Atlanta: Tupper, 1955).

7. Allison Dorsey, *To Build Our Lives Together: Community Formation in Black Atlanta, 1875–1906* (Athens: University of Georgia Press, 2004), 154.

8. David Fort Godshalk, *Veiled Visions: The 1906 Atlanta Race Riot and the Reshaping of American Race Relations* (Chapel Hill: University of North Carolina Press, 2005).

9. See Christopher Silver, "The Racial Origins of Zoning: Southern Cities from 1910–1940," *Planning Perspectives* 6 (1991): 189–205, for a good discussion of how racial segregation ordinances shaped zoning codes. For more contemporary examples, see Larry Keating, *Atlanta: Race, Class, and Expansion* (Philadelphia: Temple University Press, 2000), and Ronald H. Bayor, *Race and the Shaping of Twentieth-Century Atlanta* (Chapel Hill: University of North Carolina Press, 1996) for an examination of the role of race and class in shaping the distribution of public goods and services (including public schools, housing, and interstates) in Atlanta from 1906 to 1990. See also Christopher Silver, *The Separate City: Black Communities in the Urban South, 1940–1968* (Lexington: University Press of Kentucky, 1995) for a wider scope of how Atlanta's planning approach differed from that of other southern cities, particularly through the contentious (and racist) urban struggles around desegregation.

10. LeeAnn Bishop Lands, "A Reprehensible and Unfriendly Act: Homeowners, Renters, and the Bid for Residential Segregation in Atlanta, 1900–1917," *Journal of Planning History* 3, no. 2 (2004): 107.

11. Godshalk, *Veiled Visions*, 111.

12. Neil Kraus and Todd Swanstrom, "Minority Mayors and the Hollow-Prize Problem," *PS: Political Science and Politics* 34, no. 1 (2001): 99.

13. Anne L. Schneider and Helen Ingram, "Social Constructions of Target Populations: Implications for Politics and Policy," *American Political Science Review* 87, no. 2 (1993): 334.

14. Ibid.

15. See Karen Ferguson, *Black Politics in New Deal Atlanta* (Chapel Hill: University of North Carolina Press, 2002), and LeeAnn Lands, *The Culture of Property: Race, Class and Housing Landscapes in Atlanta, 1880–1950* (Athens: University of Georgia Press, 2002). Black populations were usually forced into slum areas, or adjacent to slum areas, due to fears of residential integration that could suggest that Black and white residents were socially equal. Residential segregation was a standard practice in industrializing U.S. cities to limit Black political power and representation and preserve the property values and political power of white communities.

16. For language on the dark recesses of the slums, see "Charities Doing Much to Assist Negro Families," *Atlanta Constitution*, February 19, 1922, 5; for language on slums as safe harbors for criminals, see "Lynching and Negroes Discussed by Roosevelt," *Atlanta Constitution*, December 5, 1906, 1.

17. J. Phillip Thompson III, *Double Trouble: Black Mayors, Black Communities, and the Call for Deep Democracy* (New York: Oxford University Press, 2005), 87.

18. Katherine McKittrick, *Demonic Grounds: Black Women and the Cartographies of Struggle* (Minneapolis: University of Minnesota Press, 2009).

19. Margaret Kohn, *Radical Space: Building the House of the People* (Ithaca: Cornell University Press, 2003), 7.

20. *Williams v. Housing Authority*, 223 Ga. 407 (1967).

21. Ibid.

22. Carol Mueller, "Ella Baker and the Origins of 'Participatory Democracy,'" in *The Black Studies Reader*, ed. Jacqueline Bobo, Cynthia Hudley, and Claudine Michel (New York: Routledge, 2004).

23. Epifania Akosua Amoo-Adare, "Critical Spatial Literacy: A Womanist Positionality and the Spatio-Temporal Construction of Black Family Life," in *The Womanist Reader*, ed. Layli Phillips (New York: Routledge, 2006).

24. Henri Lefebvre, *The Production of Space* (New York: Blackwell, 1991).

25. Alexandra Moffett-Bateau, "The Development of a Black Feminist Methodological Theory," in *Feminist Erasures*, ed. Kumarini Silva and Kaitlynn Mendes (London: Palgrave Macmillan, 2015).

26. N. D. B. Connolly, *A World More Concrete: Real Estate and the Remaking of Jim Crow South Florida* (Chicago: University of Chicago Press, 2014).

27. Fayola Jacobs, "Black Feminism and Radical Planning: New Directions for Disaster Planning Research," *Planning Theory* 18, no. 1 (2019): 24.

28. Terrion L. Williamson, *Scandalize My Name: Black Feminist Practice and the Making of Black Social Life* (New York: Fordham University Press, 2017), 112.

Chapter 1. A New Deal to Plan the New South

The epigraph is drawn from "Atlanta University Housing Project Launched by Interior Secretary Ickes," *Philadelphia Tribune*, October 4, 1934, 20.

1. United States Census Bureau, *United State Census Population Figures by County,*

1900–1930. Categorization of a Black Belt county derived from Ronald C. Wimberley, Libby V. Morris, and Donald P. Woolley, *The Black Belt Databook* (Lexington: TVA Rural Studies, University of Kentucky, College of Agriculture, 2001).

2. See Tera Hunter, *To 'Joy My Freedom: Southern Black Women's Lives and Labors after the Civil War* (Cambridge, Mass.: Harvard University Press, 1998); and Allison Dorsey, *To Build Our Lives Together: Community Formation in Black Atlanta, 1875–1906* (Athens: University of Georgia Press, 2004), for detailed histories of the rural-to-urban migration of Black Georgians at the turn of the twentieth century.

3. Don Parson, *Making a Better World: Public Housing, the Red Scare, and the Direction of Modern Los Angeles* (Minneapolis: University of Minnesota Press, 2005).

4. David A. Chang, "'An Equal Interest in the Soil': Creek Small-Scale Farming and the Work of Nationhood, 1866–1889." *American Indian Quarterly* 33, no. 1 (2009): 98.

5. Ibid.

6. Edward L. Ayers, *The Promise of the New South: Life after Reconstruction* (New York: Oxford University Press, 1992).

7. Don H. Doyle, *New Men, New Cities, New South: Atlanta, Nashville, Charleston, Mobile, 1860–1910* (Chapel Hill: University of North Carolina Press,1990).

8. P. B. Haney, W. J. Lewis, and W. R. Lambert, "Cotton Production and the Boll Weevil in Georgia: History, Cost of Control, and Benefits of Eradication," *Georgia Agricultural Experiment Stations Research Bulletin*, no. 428 (Athens: University of Georgia, 2005).

9. Ayers, *Promise of the New South*, 5–8.

10. "Calls the Demagogue an Enemy to Business," *Atlanta Constitution (1881–1945)*, January 1, 1908, 5.

11. Lawrence H. Larsen, *The Rise of the Urban South* (Lexington: University Press of Kentucky, 2015).

12. Reiko Hillyer, *Designing Dixie: Tourism, Memory, and Urban Space in the New South* (Charlottesville: University of Virginia Press, 2014).

13. David Fort Godshalk, *Veiled Visions: The 1906 Atlanta Race Riot and the Shaping of American Race Relations* (Chapel Hill: University of North Carolina Press, 2005).

14. Christopher Silver and John Moeser, *The Separate City: Black Communities and the Urban South, 1940–1968* (Lexington: University Press of Kentucky, 1995)

15. Christopher Silver, "The Racial Origins of Zoning in American Cities," in *Urban Planning in the African American Community: In the Shadows*, ed. June Manning Thomas and Marsha Ritzdorf (Thousand Oaks, Calif.: Sage, 1997).

16. "Carey v. City of Atlanta," *Michigan Law Review* 13 (1914).

17. Ibid.

18. *Buchanan v. Warley*, 245 U.S. 60 (U.S. Supreme Court, 1917).

19. "Civil Engineers and Realty Men Favor Zone Plan," *Atlanta Constitution (1881–1945)*, February 22, 1922, 1.

20. "Big Losses Charged to Lack of Planning," *Atlanta Constitution (1881–1945)*, July 22, 1921, 3.

21. "City Planning Expert Urges Zoning System," *Atlanta Constitution (1881–1945)*, November 15, 1921, 7.

22. "Opposition Planned to City Zoning Plan," *Atlanta Constitution (1881–1945)*, February 23, 1922, 5.

23. Terron McGrew, "The History of Residential Segregation in the United States and Title VIII," *Black Scholar* 27, no. 2 (1997): 23.

24. Bartow Elmore, "Hydrology and Residential Segregation in the Postwar South: An Environmental History of Atlanta, 1865–1895," *Georgia Historical Quarterly* 94, no. 1 (2000): 32.

25. Ibid.

26. "Charles Wickersham, Rail Executive" *Atlanta Constitution (1881–1945)*. September 28, 1920, 7.

27. "Service Bureau for Community Highly Favored," *Atlanta Constitution (1881–1945)*, February 26, 1920, 1.

28. "Civil Engineers and Realty Men Favor Zone Plan," *Atlanta Constitution (1881–1945)*, February 22, 1922, 1.

29. Ibid., 16.

30. Robert Whitten, "The Atlanta Zoning Plan," *Survey*, April 1922.

31. Gail Radford, *Modern Housing for America: Policy Struggles in the New Deal Era* (Chicago: University of Chicago Press, 1997).

32. Stephen W. Grable, "From Private Realtor to Public Slum Fighter: The Transformation of the Career Identity of Charles F. Palmer" (PhD diss., Emory University, 1983).

33. Palmer, *Slum Fighter*, 13.

34. "Coca-Cola Buys $500,000 Scrip: Absorption of Amount by Company Will Assure Employees December Pay," *Atlanta Constitution (1881–1945)*, December 10, 1933, 1A.

35. Floyd Hunter, *Community Power Structure: A Study of Decision Makers* (Garden City: Anchor Books, 1963 [1953]).

36. Hunter, *Community Power Structure*; and Clarence Stone, *Regime Politics: Governing Atlanta, 1946–1988* (Lawrence: University Press of Kansas, 1989).

37. Stone, *Regime Politics*.

38. Letter from Charles F. Palmer to Dr. M. L. Brittain, August 1936, Charles F. Palmer papers, Stuart A. Rose Manuscript, Archives, and Rare Book Library, Emory University.

39. "Proceedings of the Conference on Low Cost Housing," *Georgia Tech Bulletin* 32, no. 4 (July 1935).

40. "Bauer Speaks Her Mind," *Architectural Forum*, March 1946, 119.

41. Although Techwood Homes gets the accolades for being the first public housing development in Atlanta when it opened on August 15, 1936, it is University Homes that was the first to receive federal approval for assembling its land ahead of Techwood Homes. On May 19, 1934, the federal district court judge granted the title to the 134 parcels of land that were assembled for University Homes. On April 29, 1934, the attorney general of the United States started the condemnation of properties for University Homes. However, on December 20, 1934, bids for construction on Techwood Homes were opened prior to those for University Homes. As a result, Techwood opened eight months ahead of University Homes. While this distinction seemed slightly trivial at the time, this lack of historic milestone contributed to the rejection of University Homes' historical preservation/National Landmark status application, which was approved for Techwood.

42. "A Negro Enterprise: The Georgia Real Estate, Loan, and Trust Company," *Atlanta Constitution (1881–1945)*, May 11, 1880, 24.

43. "Few Southern Land Owners," *Atlanta Constitution (1881–1945)*, May 19, 1888, 6 (from the *New Orleans Times-Democrat*).

44. "Will Build Negro Town: Two Hundred Acres of Land Near Decatur Secured," *Atlanta Constitution (1881–1945)*, May 21, 1901, 3.

45. "To Found a Negro City: Moses Bentley's Unique Scheme to Form a Negro Colony," *Atlanta Constitution (1881–1945)*, February 9, 1897, 3.

46. Ibid.

47. "Slums Disappear as John Hope Homes Project Starts," *Atlanta Daily World*, November 19, 1939.

48. John Lear, "Uncle Sam Uses Atlanta as His Housing Laboratory," *Atlanta Constitution*, August 28, 1938.

49. Ibid.

50. Parson, *Making a Better World*.

51. Ibid.

52. Karen Ferguson, *Black Politics in New Deal Atlanta* (Chapel Hill: University of North Carolina Press, 2002), 223.

53. "Negro Progress: Better Living for the Negro Race," *Atlanta Constitution (1881–1945)*, October 23, 1912, D2.

54. N. D. B. Connolly, *A World More Concrete: Real Estate and the Remaking of Jim Crow Florida* (Chicago: University of Chicago Press, 2014), 41.

55. Ibid., 90.

56. Ibid., 90.

57. Ibid., 88.

58. "Will Now Build a Reformatory: Negroes Working on a Movement of Great Importance," *Atlanta Constitution (1881–1945)*, June 14, 1903, B5.

59. Ibid.

60. C. A. Bacote, "The Negro in Atlanta Politics," *Phylon* 16, no 4 (1955): 333–50; and Alton Hornsby Jr., *Black Power in Dixie: A Political History of African Americans in Atlanta* (Gainesville: University Press of Florida, 2009).

61. *Williamson v. Housing Authority of Augusta, et al.*, 199 S. E. 43 (September 21, 1938).

62. Press release (no. 180) from U.S. Housing Authority administrator Nathan Strauss, September 28, 1938, Charles F. Palmer papers, Stuart A. Rose Manuscript, Archives, and Rare Book Library, Emory University.

63. Office of the Clerk of Board of Aldermen, City of Atlanta, Resolution by Special Housing Committee, May 27, 1938, Atlanta Housing Authority Archives.

64. Godshalk, *Veiled Visions*.

65. Research Atlanta, "Atlanta's Public Housing Policy," Research Atlanta Report (Atlanta: Research Atlanta, 1972).

66. "Supreme Court of Georgia 12519," *Fulton County Daily Report*, Thursday, September 22, 1938.

67. "10 Millions Slum Projects Mapped," *Heart's Sunday American* (Atlanta), Sunday, September 25, 1938.

68. Larry Keating, *Atlanta: Race, Class, and Expansion* (Philadelphia: Temple University Press, 2001).

69. Doug McAdam, *Political Process and the Development of Black Insurgency, 1930–1990* (Chicago: University of Chicago Press, 1982).

70. Peter Eisinger, *The Politics of Displacement: Racial and Ethnic Transition in Three American Cities* (New York: Academic Press, 1982).

71. McAdam, *Political Process.*

72. Peter Marcuse, "The Rise of Tenant Organizations," *The Nation,* July 1971; and Gail Radford, *Modern Housing for America: Policy Struggles in the New Deal Era* (Chicago: University of Chicago Press, 1996).

73. "Housing Act of 1937," http://www.gpo.gov/fdsys/pkg/USCODE-2009-title42/pdf /USCODE-2009-title42-chap8.pdf, accessed August 2015.

74. Edward Soja, *Seeking Spatial Justice* (Minneapolis: University of Minnesota Press, 2010).

75. Patricia Hill Collins, *Black Feminist Thought: Knowledge, Consciousness, and the Politics of Empowerment* (New York: Routledge, 2010 [2000]).

76. Floyd Hunter, *Community Power Structure: A Study of Decision Makers* (Garden City: Anchor Books, 1963 [1953]).

77. Parson, *Making a Better World.*

78. R. Allen Hays, *The Federal Government and Urban Housing: Ideology and Change in Public Policy* (Albany: State University of New York Press, 1995).

79. Parson, *Making a Better World.*

80. Wendell Pritchett, *Robert Clifton Weaver and the American City: The Life and Times of an Urban Reformer* (Chicago: University of Chicago Press, 2008).

81. Atlanta Housing Authority 4th Annual Report: "Democracy in Action," 1942, Organizational Records, Atlanta Housing Authority Archives.

82. Atlanta Housing Authority Annual Report, 1939–1941, Organizational Records, Atlanta Housing Authority Archives.

83. Rhonda Y. Williams, *The Politics of Public Housing: Black Women's Struggles against Urban Inequality* (New York: Oxford University Press, 2004); Connolly, *A World More Concrete*; John Arena, *Driven from New Orleans: How Nonprofits Betray Public Housing and Promote Privatization* (Minneapolis: University of Minnesota Press, 2012); D. Bradford Hunt, *Blueprint for Disaster: The Unraveling of Chicago Public Housing* (Chicago: University of Chicago Press, 2009); Arnold Hirsch, *Making the Second Ghetto: Race and Housing in Chicago 1940–1960* (Chicago: University of Chicago Press, 2009), Nicholas Dagan Bloom, *Public Housing That Worked: New York in the Twentieth Century* (Philadelphia: University of Pennsylvania Press, 2014); Lawrence Vale, *Purging the Poorest: Public Housing and the Design Politics of Twice-Cleared Communities* (Chicago: University of Chicago Press, 2013); Larry Keating, *Atlanta: Race, Class and Expansion* (Philadelphia: Temple University Press, 2010).

Chapter 2. University Homes

1. Adolph Reed Jr., *Stirrings in the Jug: Black Politics in the Post-Segregation Era* (Minneapolis: University of Minnesota Press, 1999), 19.

2. Charles Rutheiser, *Imagineering Atlanta: The Politics of Place and the City of Dreams* (New York: Verso, 1996).

3. See Reed, *Stirrings in the Jug*; and Robin D. G. Kelley, *Hammer and the Hoe: Alabama Communists during the Great Depression* (Chapel Hill: University of North Carolina Press, 2015).

4. Clarence Stone, *Regime Politics: Governing Atlanta, 1945–1988* (Lawrence: University of Kansas Press, 1989).

5. Clarence A. Bacote, "The Negro in Atlanta Politics," *Phylon* 16, no. 4 (1955): 333–50.

6. Ibid.

7. Ibid.

8. Ibid.

9. Kimberley Johnson, *Reforming Jim Crow: Southern Politics and State in the Age before* Brown (New York: Oxford University Press, 2010).

10. Iris Marion Young, *Justice and the Politics of Difference* (Princeton, N.J.: Princeton University Press. 2011 (1990)).

11. Editorial, author unknown, "A Negro's Protest," *Atlanta Constitution*, November 3, 1906.

12. Wendell Pritchett, *Robert Clifton Weaver and the American City: The Life and Times of an Urban Reformer* (Chicago: University of Chicago Press, 2008).

13. Ibid.

14. Pro Forma for Low Cost Housing Units, 1933, John Hope Presidential Papers, Box 173, Folder 6, Robert W. Woodruff Library Archives, Atlanta University Center Consortium. Subsequent materials cited in the Hope Presidential Papers are in this archive.

15. See Kevin Kruse, *White Flight: Atlanta and the Making of Modern Conservatism* (Princeton: Princeton University Press, 2005); and Matthew Lassiter, *The Silent Majority: Suburban Politics in the Sunbelt South* (Princeton: Princeton University Press, 2006).

16. Letter from P. C. McDuffie to Robert D. Kohn, February 1, 1934, John Hope Presidential Papers, Box 173, Folder 11.

17. Ibid.

18. The close proximity of Darktown to the CBD created a space of racial violence in the 1906 riots. During the riots, which began in Darktown, black citizens were attacked by white middle-class men for three nights in September. For a critical treatment of the political, social, and economic factors that shaped and produced this violent event, see David Fort Godshalk, *Veiled Visions: The 1906 Atlanta Race Riot and the Reshaping of American Race Relations* (Chapel Hill: University of North Carolina Press, 2005).

19. Letter from McDuffie to Kohn, February 1, 1934.

20. Ibid.

21. Ibid.

22. Letter from Charles E. Pychon to John Hope, February 6, 1934, John Hope Presidential Papers, Box 173, Folder 11.

23. See Don Parson, *Making a Better World: Public Housing, the Red Scare, and the Direction of Modern Los Angeles* (Minneapolis: University of Minnesota Press, 2005); and Karen Ferguson, *Black Politics in New Deal Atlanta* (Chapel Hill: University of North Carolina Press, 2002).

24. Letter from John Hope to Dr. Robert Kohn, February 6, 1934, John Hope Presidential Papers, Box 173, Folder 11.

25. Letter from Civic & Improvement League to John Hope, March 23, 1934, John Hope Presidential Papers, Box 173, Folder 9.

26. Letter from Florence M. Read to C. W. Lee, March 28, 1934, John Hope Presidential Papers, Box 173, Folder 9.

27. Biography of Florence M. Read, undated material, Florence M. Read Presidential Records, Robert Woodruff Library Archives, Atlanta University Center Consortium. Subsequent materials cited in the Read Presidential Records are in this archive.

28. Karen Ferguson, in her work *Black Politics in New Deal Atlanta*, conceives of the middle-person as a person with political legitimacy and influence between two disparate communities; for Read, it is Black and white elites, but for many Black elites, it was to broker relations between the Black working class and other Black elites in power. Select Black elites were middle-persons for Black and white elites.

29. Minutes of University Homes Advisory Committee Meeting, 1937, Florence M. Read Presidential Records.

30. Transcript, interview with Clark Foreman, November 16, 1974, interviewed by Jacquelyn Hall and William Finger, Southern Oral History Program Collection, University of North Carolina at Chapel Hill University Library, https://docsouth.unc.edu/sohp/B-0003/menu.html, accessed August 17, 2020.

31. W. E. B Du Bois, "A Study of the Atlanta University Federal Housing Area," Atlanta University, 1934, John Hope Presidential Papers, Box 173, Folder 5.

32. Ibid.

33. Ibid., 1.

34. Ibid., 1.

35. Ibid., 2.

36. "Open Atlanta University Housing Project Registration Monday; Moron Taking Charge," *Atlanta Daily World*, October 18, 1936, 1–8.

37. Ronald Bayor, *Race and the Shaping of Twentieth-Century Atlanta* (Chapel Hill: University of North Carolina Press, 1996).

38. March Minutes of University Homes Advisory Committee Meeting, March 23, 1936, Florence M. Read Presidential Records, Box 193, Folder 2.

39. Ibid.

40. Notes from John Hope personal correspondence, undated material, John Hope Presidential Records, Box 170, Folder 10.

41. March Minutes of University Homes Advisory Committee Meeting, March 23, 1936.

42. Ibid.

43. Ibid.

44. Ibid.

45. Note from Read's personal records, 1937, Florence M. Read Presidential Records, Box 193, Folder 20.

46. This conviction was overturned by the U.S. Supreme Court in 1937, which found the Georgia law of insurrection to be unconstitutional and in violation of the first amendment. The ruling helped redefine race in 1930s Georgia, creating new political organizing rights and protections for Black citizens.

47. Letter to Robert Weaver from Florence Read, 1936, Florence M. Read Presidential Records, Box 193, Folder 14.

48. January Minutes of University Homes Advisory Committee Meeting, January 12, 1937, Florence M. Read Presidential Records, Box 193, Folder 2.

49. Ibid.

50. Ibid.

51. Carol Stack, *All Our Kin: Strategies for Survival in a Black Community* (New York: Harper and Row, 1974).

52. January Minutes of University Homes Advisory Committee Meeting, January 12, 1937.

53. October 27, 1936, Resolution, Florence M. Read Presidential Records, Box 172, Folder 1.

54. January Minutes of University Homes Advisory Committee Meeting, January 12, 1937.

55. Letter to H. A. Gray from Alonzo Moron, July 8, 1937, University Homes Records, Atlanta Housing Authority Archives. Subsequent materials cited in the University Homes Records are in this archive.

56. Quarterly Report of Tenant Activities through June 30, 1937, University Homes Records.

57. 1939 Atlanta Housing Authority Annual Report, 1939, Organizational Records, Atlanta Housing Authority Archives.

58. Parson, *Making a Better World*.

59. David Andrew Harmon, *Beneath the Image of the Civil Rights Movement and Race Relations: Atlanta, Georgia, 1946–1981*. (New York: Garland, 1996).

60. Karen Ferguson, *Black Politics in New Deal Atlanta* (Chapel Hill: University of North Carolina Press, 2002).

61. Personal Notes and Other Materials from Alonzo G. Moron, 1936–1940, University Homes Records.

62. University Homes Tenant Bulletin, 1937, University Homes Records.

63. Letter to H. A. Gray from Alonzo Moron, July 8, 1937, University Homes Records.

64. Letters to Walton Oslo, June–August 1937, University Homes Records.

65. Bayor, *Race and the Shaping*.

66. Public Housing in Atlanta Survey, 1966, Box 2, Folder 4, Research Materials — Housing, Atlanta Community Relations Commission Collection, Robert Woodruff Library Archives, Atlanta University Center Consortium.

67. Letter to H. A. Gray from Alonzo Moron, July 8, 1937, University Homes Records.

68. Ibid.

69. Letter to Editors of *Tenant News* from Alonzo Moron, Summer 1937, University Homes Records.

70. Notes from Tenant Association Meeting, September 1937, University Homes Records.

71. Letter to Chief Hornsby and Captain Malcolm, September 1937, University Homes Records.

72. Letter to Captain Malcolm, September 1937, University Homes Records.

73. Letters to Chief Hornsby and Captain Malcolm, September 1937, University Homes Records.

74. Ibid.

75. Letter to H. A. Gray from Alonzo Moron, July 8, 1937, University Homes Records.

76. Bacote, "Negro in Atlanta Politics."

77. "First Time in 10 Years, Atlantans Vote for Mayor!," *Chicago Defender*, April 18, 1942.

78. Letter to Florence M. Read from Alonzo Moron, January 1938, University Homes Records.

79. Unsigned, handwritten letter from tenant, undated, University Homes Records.

Chapter 3. From Production of Place to Production of Space

1. Charles Levi Sanders, "The Study of the Relocation of Rear and Alley Tenants in Atlanta" (MSW thesis, Atlanta University School of Social Work, 1956).

2. June Manning Thomas, *Redevelopment and Race: Planning a Finer City in Postwar Detroit* (Baltimore: Johns Hopkins University Press, 1997).

3. Edward W. Soja, *Seeking Spatial Justice* (Minneapolis: University of Minnesota Press, 2010).

4. Donald Craig Parson, *Making a Better World: Public Housing, the Red Scare, and the Direction of Modern Los Angeles* (Minneapolis: University of Minnesota, 2005), 28.

5. Letter from A. T. Walden and J. W. Dobbs to Mayor William Hartsfield, August 20, 1949, William B. Hartsfield papers, Stuart A. Rose Manuscript, Archives, and Rare Book Library, Emory University. Subsequent materials cited in the Hartsfield papers are in this archive.

6. List of Influential Negroes, undated, William B. Hartsfield papers.

7. Memos from Charlie Brown campaign, 1949, William B. Hartsfield papers.

8. Newspaper clippings, 1949–50, William B. Hartsfield papers.

9. "Sees Peaceful Atlanta Mixing," *Chicago Defender*, April 16, 1951, 20, Proquest Historical Newspapers.

10. Winston A. Grady-Willis, *Challenging U.S. Apartheid: Atlanta and Black Struggles for Civil Rights, 1960–1977* (Durham: Duke University Press, 2006).

11. Ibid.

12. Letter from J. W. Dobbs and A. T. Walden to voters, September 2, 1949, William B. Hartsfield papers.

13. Tomiko Brown-Nagin, *Courage to Dissent: Atlanta and the Long History of the Civil Rights Movement* (New York: Oxford University Press, 2011).

14. Atlanta Housing Authority 21st Annual Report, 1961, Organizational Records, Atlanta Housing Authority Archives.

15. Ronald H. Bayor, *Race and the Shaping of Twentieth-Century Atlanta* (Lexington: University of Kentucky Press, 1996).

16. Letter from William B. Hartsfield, January 7, 1943, William B. Hartsfield papers.

17. Ibid.

18. Thomas, *Redevelopment and Race*, 80.

19. Harold Kaplan, *Urban Renewal Politics: Slum Clearance in Newark* (New York: Columbia University Press, 1963).

20. Ibid., 237–38.

21. Kaplan, *Urban Renewal Politics*.

22. Thomas, *Race and Redevelopment*.

23. Christopher Silver and John V. Moeser, *The Separate City: Black Communities and the Urban South, 1940–1968* (Lexington: University Press of Kentucky, 1995).

24. Atlanta Plan for Race Relations, 1956, Bureau of Planning Records, James G. Kenan Research Center at the Atlanta History Center. Subsequent materials cited in the Bureau of Planning Records are in this research center.

25. Ibid.

26. Silver and Moeser, *Separate City*.

27. Perry Homes Advisory Committee, 1953, Heman E. Perry Homes and West Highlands at Perry Boulevard Records, Atlanta Housing Authority Archives.

28. Report to the Housing Coordinator, 1960, Bureau of Planning Records.

29. Results of WSMDC Survey, 1954, West Side Mutual Development Committee papers, Bureau of Planning Records.

30. Silver and Moeser, *Separate City*, 140.

31. David A. Harmon, *Beneath the Image of the Civil Rights Movement and Race Relations: Atlanta, GA, 1946–1981* (New York: Routledge, 1996).

32. Bayor, *Race and the Shaping*.

33. Atlanta Housing Authority 16th Annual Report, 1956–1957, Organizational Records, Atlanta Housing Authority Archives.

34. See Arnold Hirsch, *Making the Second Ghetto: Race and Housing in Chicago, 1940–1960* (Chicago: University of Chicago Press, 1998); and Lawrence Vale, *Purging the Poorest: Public Housing and the Design Politics of Twice-Cleared Communities* (Chicago: University of Chicago Press, 2013).

35. Atlanta Housing Authority 18th Annual Report, 1958–1959, Organizational Records, Atlanta Housing Authority Archives.

36. Applications, move-in, and move-out figures from the Atlanta Housing Authority Annual Reports, 1938–1969, Organizational Records, Atlanta Housing Authority Archives.

37. Atlanta Housing Authority 16th Annual Report, 1953, Organizational Records, Atlanta Housing Authority Archives.

38. Memo from the departing housing coordinator, 1960, Metropolitan Planning Commission papers, James G. Kenan Research Center at the Atlanta History Center. Subsequent materials cited in the Metropolitan Planning Commission papers are in this research center.

39. Results of WSMDC Survey, 1954, West Side Mutual Development Committee papers, Bureau of Planning Records.

40. The Housing Problem in Atlanta, 1960, Metropolitan Planning Commission papers.

41. Ibid.

42. Report from the departing housing coordinator, 1960, Bureau of Planning Records.

43. 17th Atlanta Housing Authority Annual Report, 1955, Organizational Records, Atlanta Housing Authority Archives.

44. Michael B. Katz, *The Undeserving Poor: America's Enduring Confrontation with Poverty* (New York: Oxford University Press, 2013).

45. Bayor, *Race and the Shaping*.

46. Map of the city of Atlanta, 1954, Bureau of Planning Records.

47. Report on Meeting for the Northwest, 1967, Atlanta Commission on Community Relations Papers, James G. Kenan Research Center at the Atlanta History Center. Subsequent materials cited in the Atlanta Commission on Community Relations Papers are in this research center.

48. Perry Homes Tenant Association Notes, 1956, Heman E. Perry Homes and West Highlands at Perry Boulevard Records, Atlanta Housing Authority Archives. Subsequent

materials cited in the Heman E. Perry Homes and West Highlands at Perry Boulevard Records are in this archive.

49. Perry Homes Tenant Newspaper, 1957, Heman E. Perry Homes and West Highlands at Perry Boulevard Records.

50. Report on Meeting for the Northwest, 1967, Atlanta Commission on Community Relations Papers.

51. Kevin Kruse, *White Flight: Race and the Making of Modern Conservatism* (Princeton: Princeton University Press, 2005).

52. List of Atlanta parks, 1954, Bureau of Planning Records.

53. Report on Meeting for the Northwest, 1967, Atlanta Commission on Community Relations Papers.

54. Letter from Perry Homes Manager, 1958, Heman E. Perry Homes and West Highlands at Perry Boulevard Records.

55. Ibid.

56. Laura Pulido and Juan De Lara, "Reimagining 'Justice' in Environmental Justice: Radical Ecologies, Decolonial Thought, and the Black Radical Tradition," *Environment and Planning E: Nature and Space* 1, no.1–2 (2018): 76–98.

57. Tera Hunter, *To 'Joy My Freedom: Southern Black Women's Lives and Labors after the Civil War* (Cambridge, Mass.: Harvard University Press, 1998).

58. Jean Tyson, "Dorothy Bolden Speaks for Herself, Others," *Atlanta Journal and Constitution*, November 21, 1976, 14–G.

59. Ibid.

60. Lars Christiansen, "The Making of a Civil Rights Union: The National Domestic Workers Union of America" (PhD diss., Florida State University, 1999).

61. Council of Neighborhood Organizations Directory, 1961–1962, 1961, Andrew Young Papers, Auburn Avenue Research Library, Atlanta.

62. Perry Homes Tenant Newspaper, 1956, Heman E. Perry Homes and West Highlands at Perry Boulevard Records.

63. Floyd A. Hunter, *Community Power Structure: A Study of Decision Makers* (Chapel Hill: University of North Carolina Press, 1953).

64. Program for the Dedication of Perry Homes Community Center, 1958, Heman E. Perry Homes and West Highlands at Perry Boulevard Records.

65. Ibid.

66. Notes from the Perry Homes Tenant Association, undated, Heman E. Perry Homes and West Highlands at Perry Boulevard Records.

67. Atlanta Housing Authority Annual Report, 1961, Organizational Records, Atlanta Housing Authority Archives.

68. 20th Atlanta Housing Authority Annual Report, 1958, Organizational Records, Atlanta Housing Authority Archives.

69. Perry Homes Monthly Newsletter, 1957, Heman E. Perry Homes and West Highlands at Perry Boulevard Records.

70. 23rd Atlanta Housing Authority Annual Report, 1961, Organizational Records, Atlanta Housing Authority Archives.

71. Ibid.

72. 25th Atlanta Housing Authority Annual Report, 1963, Organizational Records, Atlanta Housing Authority Archives.

73. Report on Meeting for the Northwest, 1967, Atlanta Commission on Community Relations Papers.

74. Notes from the Perry Homes Tenant Association, undated, Heman E. Perry Homes and West Highlands at Perry Boulevard Records.

75. Atlanta did not experience the urban uprisings that were common in majority-Black cities in the years immediately following the passage of the Civil Rights Act (CRA). As Black working-class residents in U.S. cities resisted against decades of urban wage theft, residential and labor market discrimination, police brutality, and other forms of spatial marginalization, the structure of Black-white cooperation in Atlanta foreclosed direct action and protest as popular and accessible mechanisms of Black political expression. These urban rebellions differed from those at the start of the twentieth century, which were largely around the distribution and accessibility of public spaces and goods between white and Black residents during the Great Migration. The post-CRA conflicts were instead between Black residents and the police, or the state. Summerhill, a Black working-class neighborhood just southeast of downtown, was the site of the only major conflict between Black residents and police in this era of commodity uprisings. Police officers shot Harold Prather during pursuit over a car theft, and within hours a crowd gathered to protest. Mayor Ivan Allen and representatives from the Black clergy came to placate the crowd but were promptly outnumbered. Black and white elites condemned Black activists (including members of the Student National Coordinating Committee) for causing the riot. In reality, participants threw some rocks at police and officials and had dispersed within hours.

76. Garry Chuse, "Relations Commission Ousts Eliza Paschall; Underhanded Move to Sustain Racism," *Great Speckled Bird* 1, no. 1, March 15–28, 1968.

77. Interview with Ethel Mae Mathews, conducted by Jackie Shearer for Blackside, Inc. on February 23, 1989, for *Eyes on the Prize II*, Washington University Libraries, Film and Media Archive, Henry Hampton Collection.

78. Letter from Mrs. Irene Martin to Mr. Arthur F. Smith, May 23, 1969, Heman E. Perry Homes and West Highlands at Perry Boulevard Records.

79. Dennis Goldstein, "TUFF," *Great Speckled Bird* 2, no. 21, August 4, 1969.

80. Tenant Bill of Rights, 1969, Atlanta Urban League Papers, Auburn Avenue Research Library Archives.

81. Memo from departing housing coordinator, 1960, Metropolitan Planning Commission Papers.

82. George A. Coleman, "NAACP Suit Seeks MARTA Line to Perry Homes Area," *Atlanta Daily World*, December 6, 1979, 1.

83. "MARTA Breaks Ground for Bankhead Station, Office, and Retail Center," *Atlanta Daily World*, December 7, 1988, 3.

Chapter 4. Grady Homes

1. "Grady Homes Poll to Be March 19th," *Atlanta Daily World*, March 15, 1942.

2. Ibid.

3. Ibid.

4. "League of Negro Women Voters Holds Interesting Panel on Everyday Life," *Atlanta Daily World (1932–2003)*, November 22, 1953.

5. "Two Party Rally at Bethel Monday Night," *Atlanta Daily World (1932–2003)*, November 4, 1962.

6. "Gimmick Pushes Grady Registration," *Atlanta Daily World* (1932–2003), August 20, 1961.

7. Atlanta Housing Authority Annual Reports, 1942–1952, Organizational Records; and *The Voice* (Grady Homes tenant newspaper), 1942–44, Grady Homes and Veranda at Auburn Pointe Records; both in Atlanta Housing Authority Archives. Subsequent materials cited in the Grady Homes and Veranda at Auburn Pointe Records are in this archive.

8. *The Voice*, 1943, Grady Homes and Veranda at Auburn Pointe Records.

9. Karen Ferguson, *Black Politics in New Deal Atlanta* (Chapel Hill: University of North Carolina Press, 2002).

10. Clarence A. Bacote, "The Negro in Georgia Politics, 1880–1908" (PhD diss., University of Chicago, 1955).

11. Gary Pomerantz, *Where Peachtree Meets Sweet Auburn: A Saga of Race and Family* (New York: Penguin Books, 1997).

12. Notes from Grady Homes tenant meetings, undated, Grady Homes and Veranda at Auburn Pointe Records.

13. Larry Keating, *Atlanta: Race, Class and Urban Expansion* (Philadelphia: Temple University Press, 2001).

14. 17th Atlanta Housing Authority Annual Report, 1955, Organizational Records, Atlanta Housing Authority Archives.

15. Research Atlanta, *Which Way Atlanta?* (Atlanta: Research Atlanta, 1972).

16. Metro United Way de Tocqueville Award Program, 1987, Susie LaBord Papers, Atlanta Housing Authority Archives. Subsequent materials cited in the Susie LaBord Papers are in this archive.

17. Susie LaBord Day Dedication Program, 1989, Susie LaBord Papers.

18. Biography of Susie LaBord, 1991, Susie LaBord Papers.

19. Susie LaBord Day Dedication Program, 1989, Susie LaBord Papers.

20. Robert Dare, "Involvement of the Poor in Atlanta," *Phylon* 31, no. 2 (1970): 114.

21. Keating, *Atlanta*.

22. 34th Atlanta Housing Authority Annual Report, 1972, Organizational Records, Atlanta Housing Authority Archives.

23. Research Atlanta, *Which Way Atlanta?*

24. News clipping from *Tuscaloosa News*, 1977, Susie LaBord Papers.

25. Ibid.

26. Susie LaBord, letter to *Resident Viewpoint Newsletter*, 1974, Susie LaBord Papers.

27. Contract for Public Information and a Public Relations Program, March 1, 1939, Helen Bullard papers, MSS 58, Box 2, Folder 4, James G. Kenan Research Center at the Atlanta History Center. Subsequent materials cited in the Helen Bullard Papers are in this research center.

28. Ibid.

29. June Manning Thomas, *Race and Redevelopment: Planning a Finer City in Postwar Detroit* (Baltimore: Johns Hopkins University Press, 1997).

30. Amendment to the Housing Authorities Law, Additional Housing Commissioners Provided in Certain Cities, Etc. 1972, General Assembly of Georgia, http://neptune3.galib .uga.edu/ssp/cgi-bin/legis-idx.pl?sessionid=7f000001&type=law&byte=333023620.

31. Ibid.

32. Results from Employee Survey, 1976, Atlanta Housing Authority Ephemera, 1974–79, Helen Bullard Papers, MSS 58.

33. Recommendations for Lease and Eviction Procedures, undated, Atlanta Housing Authority Ephemera, 1974–79, Helen Bullard Papers, MSS 58.

34. Results from Tenant Survey, 1972, Atlanta Housing Authority Ephemera, 1974–79, Helen Bullard Papers, MSS 58.

35. Research Atlanta, *Atlanta's Public Housing Policy* (Atlanta: Research Atlanta, 1983).

36. Ibid.

37. 40th Atlanta Housing Authority Annual Report, 1978, Organizational Records, Atlanta Housing Authority Archives.

38. Letter to Ernest C. Jackson from Atlanta Branch of the NAACP, 1967, Desegregation of Public Housing, 1967–1968, National Association for the Advancement of Colored People Atlanta Branch records, Series 9, Auburn Avenue Research Library on African-American Culture and History.

39. Minutes from the ACPH meeting, 1971, Records of the Citywide Advisory Council on Public Housing, Atlanta Housing Authority Archives. Subsequent materials cited in the Records of the Citywide Advisory Council are in this archive.

40. Minutes from the November 1972 ACPH meeting, November 1972, Records of the Citywide Advisory Council on Public Housing.

41. Ibid.

42. Minutes from the February 1973 ACPH meeting, February 1973, Records of the Citywide Advisory Council on Public Housing.

43. Ibid.

44. Minutes from the March–June 1973 ACPH meetings, March–June 1973, Records of the Citywide Advisory Council on Public Housing.

45. Notes from ACPH meetings, 1971, Joint Committee for Selection of Public Housing Sites, 1971, Andrew J. Young Papers, Subseries 3A, Auburn Avenue Research Library on African-American Culture and History.

46. Minutes from the March–June 1973 ACPH meetings.

47. Minutes from the June 1973 ACPH meeting.

48. Minutes from the July 1973 ACPH meeting, Records of the Citywide Advisory Council on Public Housing.

49. Minutes from the June–August 1973 ACPH meetings, Records of the Citywide Advisory Council on Public Housing.

50. Ibid.

51. Minutes from the July 1973 ACPH meeting.

52. Memos from David E. Warner to Lester Persells on June–October 1973 ACPH meetings, June–October 1973, Records of the Citywide Advisory Council on Public Housing.

53. Memo from David E. Warner to Lester Persells on June 1973 ACPH meeting, June 1973, Records of the Citywide Advisory Council on Public Housing.

54. Memo from David E. Warner to Lester Persells on August 1973 ACPH meeting, August 1973, Records of the Citywide Advisory Council on Public Housing.

55. Minutes from the November 1973 ACPH meeting, Records of the Citywide Advisory Council on Public Housing.

56. Minutes from the January 1974 ACPH meeting, Records of the Citywide Advisory Council on Public Housing.

57. Ibid.

58. Maynard Jackson Papers, Mayoral Series, Internal Office Memoranda, Robert Woodruff Library, Atlanta University Center Consortium. Subsequent materials cited in the Maynard Jackson Papers are in this archive.

59. Jessica Ann Levy, "Selling Atlanta: Black Mayoral Politics from Protest to Entrepreneurism, 1973 to 1990," *Journal of Urban History* 41, no. 3 (2015): 420–43.

60. Leon S. Eplan, "The Genesis of Citizen Participation in Atlanta," in *Planning Atlanta*, ed. Harley Etienne and Barbara Faga (New York: Routledge, 2017).

61. John D. Hutcheson Jr., "Citizen Representation in Neighborhood Planning," *Journal of the American Planning Association* 50, no. 2 (1984): 183–93.

62. Poverty Action Plan, 1974, Maynard Jackson Papers, Mayoral Series, Poverty Policies.

63. David A. Harmon, *Beneath the Image of the Civil Rights Movement and Race Relations: Atlanta, Georgia, 1946–1981* (New York: Garland, 1996).

64. Ibid., 248.

65. Letter from Marvin Arrington to Lester Persells, July 30, 1970, Maynard Jackson Papers, Vice Mayoral Series, Box 8, Folder 2.

66. Ibid.

67. Peter Eisinger, *The Politics of Displacement: Racial and Ethnic Transition in Three American Cities* (New York: Academic Press, 1980).

68. Minutes from the November 1974 ACPH meeting, November 1974, Records of the Citywide Advisory Council on Public Housing.

69. Austin Scott, "Sanitation Workers' Strike in Atlanta Full of Ironies," *Washington Post*, April 17, 1977.

70. Ibid.

71. Joseph A. McCartin, "'Fire the Hell Out of Them': Sanitation Workers' Struggles and the Normalization of Striker Replacement Strategy in the 1970s," *Labor: Studies in Working-Class History of the Americas* 2, no. 3 (2005): 67–92.

72. "New Communications Committee Denies Council's Support for Mayor," *Tenants News* 6, vol. 4, May 1977, Organizational Records, Atlanta Housing Authority Archives.

73. Ibid.

74. Rebecca English, qtd. in "Advisory Council Reverses Its Action on Mayor, Garbage Strike," *Tenants News* 6, vol. 5, June 1977, Organizational Records, Atlanta Housing Authority Archives.

75. Martin Luther King Sr., qtd. in "Atlanta Baptist Ministers Support Mayor," *Atlanta Constitution*, April 5, 1977.

76. "Advisory Council Reverses Its Action."

77. Ibid.

78. Ibid.

79. Article Two: Purposes of the United Tenants Council, Inc. By-Laws, 1979 Records of the Citywide Advisory Council on Public Housing.

80. Ernie Suggs, "The Rev. John H. Cross, Jr.: 1925–2007: Birmingham Church Was Bombed," *Atlanta Journal-Constitution*, November 17, 2007.

81. United Tenants Council, Inc. File, 1979–1981, Records of the Citywide Advisory Council on Public Housing.

82. Pomerantz, *Where Peachtree Meets Sweet Auburn*.

83. Frances Fox Piven and Richard Cloward, *Poor People's Movements: Why They Succeed, How They Fail* (New York: Vintage, 1978).

84. George Lefcoe, "HUD's Authority to Mandate Tenant's Rights in Public Housing," *Yale Law Journal* 80, no. 3 (1971): 463–514.

Chapter 5. "What Are We Doing to Help Ourselves?"

1. Maurice J. Hobson, *The Legend of the Black Mecca: Politics and Class in the Making of Modern Atlanta* (Chapel Hill: University of North Carolina Press, 2017).

2. See Jason Hackworth and Neil Smith, "The Changing State of Gentrification," *Journal of Economic and Social Geography* 92, no. 4 (2002): 464–77; and Larry Keating, *Atlanta: Race, Class, and Expansion* (Philadelphia: Temple University Press, 2010).

3. Research Atlanta, *Public Housing* (Atlanta: Research Atlanta, 1983).

4. Anne Schneider and Helen Ingram, "The Social Construction of Target Populations: Implications for Politics and Policy," *American Political Science Review* 87, no. 2 (1993): 334–47.

5. Atlanta Housing Authority, "Activities Report: Atlanta Housing Authority, 1979–1980" [atlpp0296], Planning Atlanta Planning Publications Collection, Georgia State University.

6. Irene V. Holliman, "From Crackertown to Model City? Urban Renewal and Community Building in Atlanta, 1963–1966," *Journal of Urban History* 35, no. 3 (2009: 369–86.

7. Ibid., 370.

8. Katie Marages Schank, "What's in a Name? East Lake Meadows and 'Little Vietnam,'" *Atlanta Studies*, March 16, 2017, https://www.atlantastudies.org/2017/03/16/whats-in-a-name-east-lake-meadows-and-little-vietnam/.

9. Ibid.

10. Federal Bureau of Investigation, "Atlanta Child Murders," Investigative Report, 1982, FBI Vault, https://vault.fbi.gov/Atlanta%20Child%20Murders.

11. Art Harris, "Profiles of Atlanta Child Murder Victims," *Washington Post*, May 3, 1981.

12. Hobson, *Legend of the Black Mecca*.

13. Joyce Leviton, "A Grieving Mother Spurs the Hunt for the Child-Killer Who Is Terrorizing Atlanta," *People Magazine*, November 10, 1980.

14. Toni Cade Bambara, *Those Bones Are Not My Child* (New York: Pantheon Books, 1999), 16.

15. Leviton, "Grieving Mother Spurs the Hunt."

16. Reclaiming family members from deviance after death endures as a Black feminist practice even today as articulated by the Mothers of the Movement organization. The mothers of Trayvon Martin (Sybrina Fulton), Sandra Bland (Geneva Reed-Veal), Michael Brown (Lezley McSpadden), Jordan Davis (Lucy McBath), Hadiya Pendleton (Cleopatra Pendleton-Crowley), Dontre Hamilton (Maria Hamilton), and Eric Garner (Gwen Carr), and the activists and other mothers who support them, spend an exhausting amount of time ensuring these victims of state violence are viewed as children, and not—as the media and the state would suggest—as a "monster" or "threat."

17. Robert M. Press, "Atlanta 'Coming Together' to Quell Violence against Black Children," *Christian Science Monitor*, November 17, 1980.

18. Eugene Robinson, "City 'Too Busy to Hate' May Be Set to Crack," *Washington Post*, March 23, 1981, A1.

19. E. R. Shipp, "3 Atlanta Mothers to Visit Harlem Group," *New York Times*, March 15, 1981.

20. Milton Williams, "Fearful Atlanta Residents Get Involved," *AFRO*, April 18, 1981.

21. Ibid.

22. See Donna Jean Murch, *Living for the City: Migration, Education, and the Rise of the Black Panther Party in Oakland, California* (Chapel Hill: University of North Carolina Press, 2010); Keeanga-Yamahtta Taylor, *From #BlackLivesMatter to Black Liberation* (Chicago: Haymarket Books, 2016); Cedric Johnson, *Revolutionaries to Race Leaders: Black Power and the Making of African American Politics* (Minneapolis: University of Minnesota Press, 2007); Robyn Spencer, *The Revolution Has Come: Black Power, Gender, and the Black Panther Party in Oakland* (Durham: Duke University Press, 2016).

23. Williams, "Fearful Atlanta Residents."

24. Robinson, "City Too Busy to Hate."

25. Ibid.

26. Ibid.

27. Cade Bambara, *Those Bones Are Not My Child*; and James Baldwin, *The Evidence of Things Not Seen* (New York: Henry Holt, 1985).

28. Eugene Robinson, "Atlanta Police Arrest Two in Citizens' Patrol: 'We Are Not Vigilantes,' Says One," *Washington Post*, March 21, 1981.

29. Robinson, "Atlanta Police Arrest Two."

30. Elie McGrath, "Exploiting Atlanta's Grief," *Time Magazine*, April 6, 1981, 18.

31. James A. Tyner, "'Defend the Ghetto': Space and the Urban Politics of the Black Panther Party," *Annals of the Association of American Geographers* 96, no. 1 (March 2006): 105–18.

32. Judith Butler, *Notes toward a Performative Theory of Assembly* (Cambridge, Mass.: Harvard University Press, 2015), 67.

33. Eric Gary Anderson, "Black Atlanta: An Ecosocial Approach to Narratives of the Atlanta Child Murders," *PMLA* 122, no. 1 (2007): 194–209, 203.

34. Robert M. Press, "Atlanta 'Coming Together' to Quell Violence against Black Children," *Christian Science Monitor*, November 17, 1980.

35. 2010 Georgia Code, Title 16: CRIMES AND OFFENSES, chapter 9: FORGERY AND FRAUDULENT PRACTICES, article 4: Fraud and Related Offenses, §16-9-55, Fraudulently obtaining or attempting to obtain public housing or reduction in public housing rent,

approved April 13, 1989, https://law.justia.com/codes/georgia/2010/title-16/chapter-9/article-4/16-9-55/.

36. 2010 Georgia Code, Title 41: NUISANCES, chapter 2: ABATEMENT OF NUISANCES GENERALLY, §41-2-7: Power of counties and municipalities to repair, close, or demolish buildings or structures; health hazards on private property; properties affected, approved April 10, 1989, https://law.justia.com/codes/georgia/2010/title-41/chapter-2/41-2-7/.

37. Ibid.

38. Robert Vargas and Philip McHarris, "Race and State in City Police Spending Growth: 1980 to 2010," *Sociology of Race and Ethnicity* 3, no. 1 (2016): 96–112.

39. 2010 Georgia Code, Title 8: BUILDINGS AND HOUSING, chapter 3: HOUSING GENERALLY, article 1: HOUSING AUTHORITIES, part 3: HOUSING AUTHORITY COMMISSIONERS, §8-3-50: Appointment, qualifications, and tenure of commissioners; reimbursement for expenses, approved April 13, 1989, https://law.justia.com/codes/georgia/2010/title-8/chapter-3/article-1/part-3/8-3-50/.

40. Art Harris, "Atlanta's Mayor a Trooper: Young Looks Overseas to Boost Jobs at Home," *Washington Post*, January 3, 1983.

41. Ibid.

42. Ibid.

43. Ibid.

44. Donna Williams Lewis, "More Whites Needed Downtown, Mayor Says," *Atlanta Constitution*, February 10, 1987.

45. Ibid.

46. Tyrone Hinton, "Presentation to Resurgens," Speech given on Tuesday, August 14, 1974, Organizational Records, Promotional Materials, Atlanta Housing Authority Archives.

47. "Public Private Partnerships: An Idea Whose Time Has Come," *Atlanta Housing Authority Employee Newsletter*, Winter 1987, Organizational Records, Atlanta Housing Authority Archives.

48. Facts on the Atlanta Housing Authority, 1989, Organizational Records, Atlanta Housing Authority Archives.

49. Bunnie Jackson-Ransom, "The Reverend Dr. Gerald L. Durley," *Atlanta Business Journal*, April 15, 2016.

50. Meeting minutes, University/John Hope Homes Interagency Council, April 26, 1989, University Homes Records, Atlanta Housing Authority Archives, Housing Authority of the City of Atlanta. Subsequent materials cited in the University Homes Records are in this archive.

51. Ibid., 4.

52. Ibid., 4.

53. Meeting minutes, University/John Hope Homes Interagency Council, July 26, 1989, University Homes Records, 2.

54. Ibid., 3.

55. Meeting minutes, University/John Hope Homes Interagency Council, February 28, 1990, University Homes Records.

56. Meeting minutes, University/John Hope Homes Interagency Council, September 27, 1989, University Homes Records, Atlanta Housing Authority Archives, 2.

57. Notes for September meeting minutes, University/John Hope Homes Interagency Council, September 30, 1989, University Homes Records, 1.

58. Meeting minutes, University/John Hope Homes Interagency Council, September 27, 1989, 1.

59. Meeting minutes, University/John Hope Homes Interagency Council, November 15, 1989, University Homes Records, 1.

60. "The Denuding of Cleveland, One Scrap at a Time," *Here and Now*, NPR, November 13, 2013, https://www.wbur.org/hereandnow/2013/11/13/scrappers-of-cleveland, accessed August 19, 2020.

61. Meeting minutes, University/John Hope Homes Interagency Council, March 26, 1990, University Homes Records, 1.

62. Ibid.

63. Meeting minutes, University/John Hope Homes Interagency Council, April 25, 1990, University Homes Records, 1.

64. Ibid., 2.

65. Meeting minutes, University/John Hope Homes Interagency Council, May 23, 1990, University Homes Records, 1.

66. Associated Press, "Violent Crimes Increased by 5.5% for 1988, Establishing a Record," *New York Times*, August 13, 1989.

67. Peter Applebome, "Drugs in Atlanta: A Lost Generation," *New York Times*, December 13, 1989.

68. Ibid.

69. "Police Presence in AHA Must Continue," *House Notes* 4, no. 3 (March/April 1990): 5.

70. "Possibility of Police Abuse Is the Key Issue," *Atlanta Constitution*, May 22, 1991.

71. Ibid.

Chapter 6. Deviancy, Demolition, and Demobilization

1. William Peterman, "The Meaning of Resident Empowerment: Why Just About Everybody Thinks It's a Good Idea and What It Has to Do with Resident Management," *Housing Policy Debate* 7, no. 3 (1996): 473–90.

2. Ibid.

3. Carl F Horowitz, "Jack Kemp's 'Perestroika': A Choice Plan for Public Housing Tenants," Heritage Foundation, Policy Brief, March 26, 1992.

4. Interestingly, in the same session, Alice L. Brown of the NAACP Legal Defense and Educational Fund of New York presented a historical argument that made a case for reparations for Black public housing families. "From the 1940's, when within the congressional record you can read that there was to be Negro housing and then there was to be public housing. Given this historical circumstance, given the continuation of this racial segregation in public housing and in distressed public housing, I think there needs to be at least two responses of remedies and solutions. One being obviously the equalization or an attempt to equalize facilities and developments" (ibid., 25).

5. Newspapers at the time also put the word "activist" in quotes. See, for example, David Treadwell, "'Activist' Kemp Tours Atlanta to Examine Housing Problems Faced by Inner Cities," *Los Angeles Times*, February 15, 1989.

6. Tenant association meeting minutes from Grady and Perry Homes also include discussions about resident management and the appeal following contentious relations during the devolution and mismanagement periods of AHA.

7. Daphne Spain, "Direct and Default Policies in the Transformation of Public Housing," *Journal of Urban Affairs* 17, no. 4 (1995): 357–76, 371.

8. Letter to Earl Phillips from Verna Mobley, May 21, 1992, RMC Correspondence 1992–1998, University Homes Records, Atlanta Housing Authority Archives, Housing Authority of the City of Atlanta. Subsequent materials cited in the University Homes Records are in this archive.

9. Letter to Earl Phillips from Verna Mobley, March 22, 1993, RMC Correspondence 1992–1998, University Homes Records.

10. 42 USC 1437r—Public Housing Management, (d): Waiver of Federal Requirements, https://www.law.cornell.edu/uscode/text/42/1437r.

11. Ibid.

12. Community Profile Questionnaire (Multiple Developments), 1991, Community, Government, and External Affairs Records, Atlanta Housing Authority Archives. Subsequent materials cited in the Community, Government, and External Affairs Records are in this archive.

13. Model Resident Management Contract Guide for RMC/HA Management Contracts, July 1993, RMC Correspondence 1992–1998, University Homes Records.

14. Letter from Cecily M. Banks to William Allison, July 2, 1993, RMC Correspondence 1992–1998, University Homes Records.

15. U.S. Congress, Senate Committee on Banking, Housing, and Urban Affairs, 1990, National Affordable Housing Act, Congressional Report.

16. Community Empowerment Strategic Plan, 1994, RMC Correspondence 1992–1998, University Homes Records.

17. Kathe Newman and Robert W. Lake, "Democracy, Bureaucracy, and Difference in U.S. Community Development Politics since 1968," *Progress in Human Geography* 30, 1 (2006): 1–18, 5.

18. Daniel J. Monti, "The Organizational Strengths and Weaknesses of Resident-Managed Public Housing Sites in the United States," *Journal of Urban Affairs* 11, no. 1 (1989): 39–52.

19. Preston H. Smith, "'Self-Help,' Black Conservatives, and the Reemergence of Black Privatism," in *Without Justice for All*, ed. Adolph Reed Jr. (New York: Routledge, 1999). See also John Arena's description of the role of nonprofits in "selling privatization" in chapter 3 of Arena, *Driven from New Orleans: How Nonprofits Betray Public Housing and Promote Privatization* (Minneapolis: University of Minnesota Press, 2012).

20. Arena, *Driven from New Orleans*, 54.

21. Ibid., 62–64. Arena discusses the use of the People's Institute for Undoing Racism as a "key intellectual" to instilling neoliberal ideas about public housing (privatization, poverty dispersal, people's capitalism, or tenant ownership) as common sense during the trainings that were mandatory for organizations that wanted to work within the post-Katrina redevelopment regime. The white neighborhood organization, however, did not undergo this training. In Atlanta, particularly during the Olympic Legacy program, this reorientation toward neoliberalism as common sense trickled down from the developer-led Corporation for Olympic Development in Atlanta and PATH.

22. In-person interview with William "Bill" Allison, former head of Economic Opportunity Atlanta, August 18, 2017, Midtown Atlanta.

23. Cynthia Durcanin, "Politicking and the Poor: Public Housing Groups Flex New Muscle," *Atlanta Journal-Constitution*, February 8, 1990.

24. Letter from Verna Mobley to Newt Gingrich, undated, RMC Correspondence 1992–1998, University Homes Records.

25. Smith, "'Self-Help,'" 274.

26. Keeanga-Yamahtta Taylor, *From #BlackLivesMatter to Black Liberation"* (Chicago: Haymarket Books, 2016). See chapter 3, "Black Faces in High Places," for a critical treatment of black electoral responses to the needs of the Black working poor and working classes.

27. Patricia Hill Collins, "Gender, Black Feminism, and Black Political Economy," *Annals of the American Academy of Political and Social Science* 568 (2016): 41–53, 48.

28. Larry Bennett, Janet L. Smith, and Patricia A. Wright, eds., *Where Are Poor People to Live? Transforming Public Housing Communities* (New York: Routledge, 2006).

29. Community Empowerment Strategic Plan, 1994, RMC Correspondence 1992–1998, University Homes Records.

30. One of the signatures was Leon Mobley, who resided with Verna Mobley.

31. Letter from George H. Freisem III (Freisem, Swann, and Malone, Attorneys at Law) to Nina Hickson-Perry (AHA general counsel), August 8, 1994, Community Activities series, University Homes Records.

32. Barbara Cruikshank, "The Will to Empower: Technologies of Citizenship and the War on Poverty," *Socialist Review* 23, no. 4 (1994): 29–56.

33. Kim McKee, "Community Ownership in Glasgow: The Devolution of Ownership and Control, or a Centralizing Process?," *European Journal of Housing Policy* 7, no. 3 (2007): 319–36, 334.

34. Lawrence Vale, *From the Puritans to the Projects: Public Housing and Public Neighbors* (Cambridge, Mass.: Harvard University Press, 2000).

35. U.S. Congress, Hearing before the Subcommittee on Housing and Urban Affairs of the Committee on Banking, Housing, and Urban Affairs, U.S. Senate, 102nd Congress, 2nd Session, on To Explore Both the Origins of Distressed Public Housing and Ways to End Its Destructive Impact on Families, Communities, and Affordable Housing Agenda, March 25, 1992 (Washington, D.C.: U.S. Government Printing Office), 12.

36. Ibid., 13.

37. Ibid.

38. Ibid., 29.

39. Ibid.

40. "About HOPE VI," Overview, HUD, https://www.hud.gov/program_offices/public_indian_housing/programs/ph/hope6/about.

41. Ibid.

42. See James Curtis Fraser, Ashley Brown Burns, Joshua Theodore Bazuin, and Deirdre Áine Oakley, "HOPE VI, Colonization, and the Production of Difference," *Urban Affairs Review* 49, no. 4 (2013): 525–56; and Brigitte U. Neary, "Black Women Coping with HOPE VI in Spartanburg, South Carolina," *Journal of African American Studies* 15, no. 4 (2011): 524–40.

43. Matthew J. Burbank, Charles H. Heying, and Greg Andranovich, "Antigrowth Poli-

tics or Piecemeal Resistance? Citizen Opposition to Olympic-Related Economic Growth," *Urban Affairs Review* 35, no. 3 (2000): 334–57, 336.

44. Neal R. Peirce, "Atlanta Olympiad Raises Tough Questions about Housing the City's Poor Population," *Washington Post*, June 22, 1991.

45. Steven P. French and Mike E. Disher, "Atlanta and the Olympics: A One-Year Retrospective," *Journal of the American Planning Association* 63, no. 3 (1997): 379–92.

46. Frank W. Johnson, "Let the Games Begin: Relocation and Redevelopment of Public Housing in Atlanta, Georgia" (PhD diss., Temple University, 2013), 70–71; and Lee May, "Olympic Plan Could Erase Eyesore," *Los Angeles Times*, October 22, 1991.

47. Chandra D. Ward, "Atlanta and Other Olympic Losers," *Contexts* 12, no. 3 (2013): 46–51.

48. Larry Keating and Carol A. Flores, "Sixty and Out: Techwood Homes Transformed by Enemies and Friends," *Journal of Urban History* 26, no. 3 (2000): 275–311, 288.

49. Ibid.; see also Lawrence Vale, *Purging the Poorest: Public Housing and the Design Politics of Twice-Cleared Communities* (Chicago: University of Chicago Press, 2013).

50. Johnson, "Let the Games Begin."

51. Vale, *Purging the Poorest*.

52. Sallye Salter, "Teams Compete to Map Future of Techwood," *Atlanta Journal-Constitution*, July 6, 1991.

53. Vale, *Purging the Poorest*, 101.

54. Flores and Keating, "Sixty and Out."

55. Carrie Teegardin, "BROKEN HOMES Millions in Public Funds Should Have Turned Kings Ridge into a Place Low-Income Atlantans Could Call Home," *Atlanta Journal-Constitution*, October 26, 1997.

56. Initial press releases for Phillips's "middle of the night" departure were favorable as the Housing Authority scrambled to deal with both Phillips's ambitious plans for redevelopment and HUD's recent PHMAP score. During Renee Glover's initial year at AHA, the press accused Phillips of abandoning the authority, of leaving it a mess for Glover to fix. Phillips immediately went to work for the Seattle Housing Authority, suggesting that he knew for some time he was leaving.

57. Matthew J. Burbank, Charles H. Heying, and Greg Andranovich, "Antigrowth Politics or Piecemeal Resistance? Citizen Opposition to Olympic-Related Economic Growth," *Urban Affairs Review* 35, no. 3 (2000): 334–57.

58. Sonya Ross, "Atlanta's Poor Demand Share of Games," *Las Vegas Review-Journal*, June 28, 1991.

59. Kevin M. Kruse, *White Flight: Atlanta and the Making of Modern Conservatism* (Princeton: Princeton University Press, 2005).

60. Seth Gustafson, "Displacement and the Racial State in Olympic Atlanta: 1990–1996," *Southeaster Geographer* 53, no. 2 (2013): 198–213, 199.

61. See Adolph Reed Jr., *Stirrings in the Jug: Black Politics in the Post-Segregation Era* (Minneapolis: University of Minnesota Press, 1999; Michael Leo Owens, Akira Drake Rodriguez, and Robert A. Brown, "'Let's Get Ready to Crumble': Black Municipal Leadership and Public Housing Transformation in the United States," *Urban Affairs Review*, January 29, 2020; and Lester Spence, *Knocking the Hustle: Against the Neoliberal Turn in Black Politics* (New York: Punctum Books, 2015), for quantitative and qualitative descriptions of the Black urban regime's neoliberal policymaking.

62. See Arena, *Driven from New Orleans*, for an in-depth investigation of the centaur neoliberal state in post-Katrina New Orleans.

63. For excellent descriptions of intersectional approaches to understanding Black feminist politics and decision-making, see Ange-Marie Hancock, "Intersectionality as a Normative and Empirical Paradigm," *Politics & Gender* 3, no. 2 (2007): 248–54; Kimberlé Crenshaw, "Demarginalizing the Intersection of Race and Sex: A Black Feminist Critique of Antidiscrimination Doctrine, Feminist Theory and Antiracist Politics," *University of Chicago Legal Forum* 1, no. 8 (1989): 139–67; Patricia Hill Collins, *Fighting Words: Black Women and the Search for Justice* (Minneapolis: University of Minnesota Press, 1998); Nadia A. Brown, *Sisters in the Statehouse: Black Women and Legislative Decision Making* (New York: Oxford University Press, 2014).

64. Center for American Women and Politics for Higher Heights Leadership Fund, "The Status of Black Women in American Politics," 2015.

65. Ibid.

66. Ibid.

67. Duchess Harris, *Black Feminist Politics from Kennedy to Obama* (New York: Palgrave MacMillan, 2012), part 3; Brown, *Sisters in the Statehouse*, 179.

68. Center for American Women and Politics for Higher Heights Leadership Fund. "Voices. Votes. Leadership. The Status of Black Women in American Politics," (Brooklyn: Higher Heights).

69. Letter from Beverly Hall, EdD, to Renee Lewis Glover, July 6, 2005, Redevelopment Series, Grady Homes and Veranda at Auburn Pointe records, Atlanta Housing Authority Archives.

70. Dave Hill, "Globalisation and Its Educational Discontents: Neoliberalisation and Its Impacts on Education Worker's Rights, Pay and Conditions," *International Studies in Sociology of Education* 15, no. 3 (2005): 257–88.

71. Letter from Hall to Glover, July 6, 2005.

72. Erika Gubrium, Sabina Dhakal, Laura Sylvester, and Aline Gubrium, "Sisyphean Struggles: Encounters and Interactions within Two U.S. Public Housing Programs," *International Journal of Social Quality* 6, no. 2 (2016): 89–108.

73. Zenzele Isoke, *Urban Black Women and the Politics of Resistance* (New York: Palgrave Macmillan, 2013).

74. Michele Wallace, *Black Macho and the Myth of the Superwoman* (New York: Random House, 1979).

75. Kathy A. Scruggs and S. A. Reid, "Baby Girl Laid to Rest," *Atlanta Journal-Constitution*, May 29, 1996, 1.

76. Ibid.

77. S. A. Reid, "'Clean Sweeps': New Effort Follows Death of Young Resident Who Choked on a Cockroach," *Atlanta Journal-Constitution*, June 1, 1996, D1.

78. Scruggs and Reid, "Baby Girl Laid to Rest."

79. Ibid., 2.

80. Support letter from Chief Beverly Harvard to Renee Glover for Drug Elimination Plan grant, July 31, 1997, Community, Government, and External Affairs Records.

81. Determination of Baseline Law Enforcement Services, in Drug Elimination Plan Grant Application, August 1, 1997, Community, Government, and External Affairs Records.

82. Ibid.

83. In 1996, President Clinton signed legislation that would end welfare as we know it (the Personal Responsibility and Work Opportunity Reconciliation Act, or PRWORA) the same year that HOPE VI was authorized as a national program available to all public housing authorities. The systemic dismantling of the welfare state, after long acting as a vehicle for socioeconomic mobility and political advocacy, is another factor in the weakening and demobilization of the public housing development as political opportunity structure.

84. DEP grant signatory page, August 1, 1997, Community, Government, and External Affairs Records.

85. Letter from Christopher W. Waring (deputy assistant secretary for public housing investments) to Renee Lewis Glover, October 10, 1996, Redevelopment Series, Heman E. Perry Homes and West Highlands at Perry Boulevard Records, Atlanta Housing Archives. Subsequent materials cited in the Perry Homes and West Highlands Records are in this archive.

86. Letter from Elinor R. Bacon (deputy assistant secretary, Office of Public Housing Investments) to Renee Glover, April 13, 2000, Redevelopment Series, Heman E. Perry Homes and West Highlands at Perry Boulevard Records.

87. Neighborhood Market Analysis of the Perry Homes Development, August 27, 1996, Land Interest Group, 2, Redevelopment Series, Heman E. Perry Homes and West Highlands at Perry Boulevard Records.

88. Ibid., 1.

89. Letter from Bacon to Glover, April 13, 2000.

90. Interview with Eric Pickney and Hope Bolden, Integral Group LLC, August 16, 2017.

91. Atlanta Housing Authority Relocation Cost Models: Perry Homes, Attachment to memo from Douglas S. Faust to Comprehensive Grant Review Process Task Force, May 21, 1997, Redevelopment Series, Heman E. Perry Homes and West Highlands at Perry Boulevard Records.

92. Perry Homes Master Planning Session, Memo from Lauren Segal to Trish O'Connell, August 24, 2001, Redevelopment Series, Heman E. Perry Homes and West Highlands at Perry Boulevard Records.

93. Ibid.

94. Ibid.

95. Ibid.

96. Ibid.

97. Revitalization Plan Requirements (for Perry Homes) attachment in an interoffice memorandum from Dwan Packett to Lynn Cassell, Doug Faust, and John Watson, September 15, 1997, Redevelopment Series, Heman E. Perry Homes and West Highlands at Perry Boulevard Records.

98. Ibid., F-4.

99. See Deirdre Oakley and George Greenidge Jr., "The Contradictory Logics of Public-Private Place-Making and Spatial Justice: The Case of Atlanta's Beltline," *City & Community* 16, no. 4 (December 2017): 355–58; and Dan Immergluck, "Large Redevelopment Initiatives, Housing Values and Gentrification: The Case of the Atlanta Beltline," *Urban Studies* 46, no. 8 (2009): 1723–45.

Conclusion

1. Interview with Maxwell Creighton, Community Design Services, May 3, 2017.

2. Interview with Larry Keating, professor emeritus, Georgia Tech, November 25, 2016.

3. Interview with Noel Khalil, Columbia Residential, July 31, 2017.

4. Interview with Lindsay Jones, attorney and judge, June 29, 2017.

5. Interview with Shirley Hightower, former president of Bowen Homes tenant association, June 28, 2017.

6. For decreased voter turnout among voucher holders, see Claudine Gay, "Moving to Opportunity: The Political Effects of a Housing Mobility Experiment," *Urban Affairs Review* 48, no. 2 (2012): 147–79. For detached social networks in HOPE VI housing see Brigitte U. Neary, "Black Women Coping with HOPE VI in Spartanburg, South Carolina," *Journal of African American Studies* 15, no. 4 (2011): 524–40.

7. Interview with Sister Elaine Osby, former president of Cosby-Spear tenant association, August 17, 2017.

Index